LOST
DEVON

LOST DEVON

CREATION, CHANGE AND DESTRUCTION OVER 500 YEARS

TODD GRAY

THE MINT PRESS

First published in Great Britain by The Mint Press, 2003

Hardback edition ISBN 1-903356-31-8
Softback edition ISBN 1-903356-32-6

Cataloguing in Publication Data
CIP record for this title is available from the British Library

Cover illustration: Dartmouth by Willem Schellinks, 1662.

The Mint Press
18 The Mint
Exeter, Devon
England EX4 3BL

Page design by Topics – The Creative Partnership
Typeset in Frutiger 57 Condensed
Cover design by Delphine Jones

Printed and bound in Great Britain by Short Run Press Ltd, Exeter

Contents

For Marjorie Bird

They plucked down the rood from the screen,
And flung to the moles and the bats,
Then capered like goats on the green,
And tossed up their greasy old hats –
Too-ral-loo

HARRY HEMS,
LATE NINETEENTH CENTURY[1]

Acknowledgements

I am extremely grateful to the staff of the Devon Record Office, Plymouth Local Studies Library, the Torquay Reference Library, the Westcountry Studies Library, in particular Tony Rouse and Katharine Dunhill, the University of Exeter Main Library, the University of Plymouth Library (Exeter), the Newton Abbot Museum, the Sidmouth Museum, Allhallows Museum, and the Devon & Exeter Institution for their time and patience. John Allan, Stuart Blaylock, Peter Child, Clare Greener, Richard Parker, Margery Rowe and Professor Malcolm Todd have read part or all of the book in draft and I am extremely grateful to them for their many useful comments. The book has also been considerably improved through the advice and assistance of a great number of other people and I would like to particularly thank Michael Addington-Hall, Kim Auston, Shirley Blaylock, Roger Brien, Nigel Canham, Christine Caldwell, Philip Carter, Jill Cave, Barry Chandler, Rebecca Child, Peter Christie, Brian Clark, Paul Cleave, Humphrey Clemens, Felicity Cole, Tony Collings, David Colwill, Jo Cox, Malcolm Crook, Lady De Vere, Judith Farmer, Dr Tom Greeves, Cecily Greenhill, Bill Horner, Francis Kelly, Sam Lawrence, Bob Letcher, Fiona Mackay, Hugh Meller, Philip Newman, Margaret Parkinson, Dick Passmore, Mike Pidgley, Margaret Reed, Michael Rhodes, Matthew Saunders, Jean Sharmin, John Smith, Keith Stevens, Sir Harry Studholme, Amanda Sutherland, Geoffrey Sworder, Pru Williams and Robert Wilson-North. Any and all mistakes are of course my own. Finally, I would like to thank Devon County Council for the support given to the research of this book.

Introduction

Over the last five centuries Devon's history has largely mirrored that of the country but it has had particular experiences that have shaped a distinct character of heritage. In the early 1500s its social and economic framework was shaken, like the rest of the country, by the religious changes introduced from London. The near immediate response from Devon was the Prayer Book Rebellion and the prospect of civil war, but calm prevailed and the following generation produced men who symbolise the nation's new Protestant identity: Raleigh, Drake, Hawkins and Grenville remain some of the most illustrious figures of the sixteenth century. In the 1530s local churches began to be emptied of centuries of religious objects and many were destroyed: previous generations had venerated them as being sacred but the new regimes of Henry VIII and his heirs Edward and Elizabeth denounced them as superstitious. This

destruction, which lasted a generation, coincided with great creative efforts being made in other directions. Men from Devon took their first steps across the Atlantic and helped create an empire which over the following 400 years replaced the cultural landscape of medieval Catholic Devon with riches, and the subsequent heritage, previously undreamed of. At the same time as rood screens, holy statues and relics were being burned on bonfires Devonians were establishing economic ties with the New World. Religious differences with the Spanish, Portuguese and French helped redefine the English overseas, and provided them with a convenient moral justification, as they extended their efforts in the Americas, Africa and Asia. It is with the latter end of the sixteenth century, during the reign of Elizabeth, that Devon helped define the national character through trade, fishing and privateering. Creation and destruction came together as these men carved out livelihoods partly at the expense of continental Catholics and the indigenous peoples of the Americas and Africa.

A Dawlish eating house, by George Townsend, nineteenth century, typical of the many buildings erected to serve the needs of tourists and which were later either renovated or demolished.

As Devon grew wealthier in the seventeenth century its villages, towns and cities increased in size and opulence even in unexpected places along the fringes of Dartmoor which were still extracting wealth from tin-mining. However, the driving force of the economy was the woollen cloth trade and in the late sixteenth and seventeenth centuries it had what was considered state-of-the-art technology. Exeter was at its height, not only as the religious and legal capital of the county, but also as the centre of the cloth trade. All parts of Devon and segments of society were involved to some degree in cloth-making and the industry's decline in the middle of the eighteenth century was followed by a more localised industrialism; the Teign valley had its Stover Canal ship granite from Dartmoor and clay from Bovey, various minerals were extracted along the Tamar valley, and the railway town of Newton Abbot, once hailed as the 'Swindon' of Devon, was the envy of many small market towns throughout the county. The greatest industrialised centre was created at Plymouth by the navy: in the late eighteenth and through into the twentieth centuries that town was dominated by the development of the Dockyard and it easily eclipsed Exeter as the economic centre of the county. However, the lack of general industrialisation helped Devon to reinvent itself as a major holiday destination. Coastal fishing villages, such as Sidmouth, Exmouth, Dawlish, Teignmouth and Torquay, were transformed in the late eighteenth and early nineteenth century into seaside resorts. This left an infrastructure of roads, hotels, gardens and promenades and all the other amenities that visitors expected and created another level of cultural legacy. This was expressed by a visitor in 1854 who wrote of one seaside resort:

> It has a kind of winning way, that grows on you, you hardly know why, for it is best described by negatives. It is not fashionable, nor showy, nor cheap, nor has it good shops, except for cakes and pastry, nor does it seem to be peopled by scarcely any but females. But still it is a place that most people like.[2]

Of the many that could have been described, he was writing of Paignton.

Ilfracombe in 1824, before the great building boom for tourists in the mid to late nineteenth century, when it was more recognisable as a port.

More than twenty years ago the Devon landscape was described as the result of the interaction of political, cultural, economic and technological forces.[3] The county's wider cultural legacy is the result of many generations of diverse growth and change: the hundreds of thousands of Devonian Elizabethans, Georgians and Victorians have added, amended and altered to their county. Over the last five centuries the increased wealth of the county has left behind a rich heritage partly because since the Reformation there has been little war in Devon, as in the rest of the country, except during the 1640s and 1940s: while many parts of continental Europe have had to endure war, Devon has been lucky to continue to build, enhance and develop.

Even so, an astonishing portion of its cultural landscape has vanished. A sense of romanticism surrounds the concept of loss whether with lost gardens or buildings. Possibly it lies with the human desire to strive for the unreachable but too often there is little or no explanation of the causes. The nature of change is more complex: loss is not just about sudden destruction but also encompasses gradual change, adaptation and creation. The Reformation is often portrayed as England's greatest source of destruction and yet many objects were merely reused in other ways. Along with their transformation from sacred to superstitious many items were subsequently treated as inconsequential building materials before being rescued and reappraised as works of art. But there have been other forces responsible for more widespread destruction and the interplay of creation and destruction needs to be considered. Without understanding the nature of change it is impossible to effectively preserve and sustain our cultural and natural heritage.

Lost Devon focuses on elements of the county's heritage but the definition of what that constitutes is not easily made. One recent study of Devon's heritage examined buildings, gardens and settlements[4] whereas this book extends to manuscripts and some discussion of more unusual topics including varieties of plants. It is beyond the scope of this study to fully assess the natural environment but some themes are considered. This book seeks to explain the reasons for loss through a number of different processes of change over the last five hundred years. There are obvious limits to what any book of only 192 pages can cover and this study can hope only to introduce themes and show some examples. In some instances an example of a building is given where others could just as easily have been made. Of the many thousands of Saxon buildings, only some churches could claim to be survivals and even then, not one appears at all similar as it did before 1066. Norman buildings have also radically changed: Exeter's St Nicholas Priory and Rougemont Castle are the earliest survivors but the majority of the structures of this period have not survived and many Elizabethan, Georgian and Victorian buildings, numbering in their hundreds of thousands, have likewise been lost. This book is then, by necessity, a personal choice and no doubt the emphasis or selection of individual examples could vary tremendously given the number to choose from.

The means by which Devon's cultural heritage has been changed include theft and disappearance, loss of function and or of the necessary financing, commercial redevelopment, a sense of improvement, changing fashion and taste, the incidence of natural disasters, the role of religion and the impact of war. Devon in the sixteenth to early eighteenth centuries was at the economic forefront of England but by the middle of the eighteenth century it fell behind as other parts of the country experienced the Industrial Revolution. The nineteenth century saw an economic decline in many parts of Devon and the lack of rebuilding on the scale elsewhere preserved many parts of the county's heritage. In 1882 one writer noted this comparative lack of change ('no extensive network of railways so far covers it; no collieries or furnaces seam its fair surface. Such mining and other industries as are carried on have so far done little to mar its beauty')[5] with

the result that Devon was seen as a particularly beautiful part of the country. Part of its attraction to visitors in the nineteenth century was this lack of industry with which they were familiar in London, the Midlands and further north. Lack of money can sometimes aid preservation, if dereliction does not set in. In 1882 it was appreciated that heritage can easily be lost through zealous improvers: the writer noted:

How much has been lost even in recent times? What a tale the restoration of churches tells; how many parochial registers have been lost; how many volumes of churchwardens' accounts destroyed; how much stained glass treated as rubbish; how many cromlechs thrown down, circles obliterated, kistvaens demolished. This kind of thing goes merrily on, and by-and-by those who come after us will have nothing left to gaze upon, and books alone will be available to them for information as to the memorials which once existed of their forefathers. Efforts are made, but with little effect. How difficult it is to stay the rising tide of restoration.[6]

He also noted the following year *'Oh restoration, what crimes are committed in thy name!'*[7]

Many parts of Devon's heritage have been lost including, for instance, country houses. These have had a mixed history and those that remain in family ownership, such as Great Fulford, Powderham and Castle Hill, are exceptional. Instead, the majority have either been lost, such as Lindridge and Dunsland through fires and Silverton Park from demolition, or have had to adapt to modern use such as Bicton, Harefield, Stover and Tawstock Court (now schools), Haccombe, Oxton and Peamore (converted into flats), Bishopstowe, Borringdon, Combe House, Kitley and Langdon Court (hotels), Duryard (student accommodation), Bystock (sheltered accommodation), A La Ronde, Arlington Court, Bradley, Castle Drogo, Killerton, Knightshayes, Overbecks, Saltram and Shute Barton (National Trust) and Oldway Mansion, Follaton, Knowle and Forde House (headquarters for local government). The history of country houses is seldom straightforward: certain buildings survive because they were originally built for other uses, such as Buckland Abbey, Torre Abbey and Hartland Abbey, and later adapted as private domestic residence. Others have tried various means to raise revenue, such as the attempt by the Courtenay family to establish a School of Domestic Science at Powderham Castle in the 1940s and 1950s.[8]

OPPOSITE PAGE
Two panoramic views of Plympton St Mary from the Castle, c.1835, which differ greatly from the same view today.

A view of the mouth of the river Dart, looking towards Dartmouth from near the Castle, drawn in 1662 by Willem Schellinks. Even this rural scene has many changes with today.

A great number are now open to the public on a fee-paying basis but many others have not survived.

The book concludes with a discussion of the issues concerning how one can define 'Lost Devon': the continual process of change can result in the removal of buildings but it often also brings about new ones. With other parts of heritage, for example manuscripts, the loss of one does not involve the generation of others and ancient monuments cannot be replaced.

Chapter One

Devon's Heritage: from identification to preservation

Devon has a cultural and natural heritage that is rich and varied. One of its most conspicuous components is the landscape, the result of a continual process of alteration with new elements being added as others disappear and the vast majority in a state of change or adjustment. Some of the changes are more noticeable than others. Devon's landscape is diverse with significant chunks of urban and suburban areas. The countryside ranges from coastline to moorland, woodland and river valleys: Start Point, Exmoor, Haldon Forest and the Taw valley are all rich but very different landscapes. Ornamental landscapes are also important although there are few exceptionally large country houses with vast estates as there are in other parts of the country. Natural history is a major part of Devon's heritage whether it is the land or those other living things we share it with. Even so, buildings, whether complete or in ruins, are probably first identified as examples of heritage: as man-made expressions of a particular use, and often heavily identified within a time period, they can be viewed on a distinct basis. As significant as they are as key elements in the county's heritage, there are many others as well. We must also consider art, written heritage in documents and printed works and where it survives, folklore, customs, dialect and songs.

Devon has a very different character from much of the rest of the country and its great geographical size, as one of the largest counties, has contributed to considerable variations in places from one end to another. In the past five hundred years each has been defined by industries that are no longer important. Fishing for herring is no longer the main employer of Clovelly just as it is many generations since the pursuit of Newfoundland cod was the principal focus of Dartmouth. Equally, lace-making is not practised in Honiton other than as a recreational activity, cloth-making has not been a major employer in Exeter since the Victorian period and tin mining has long gone from Tavistock. Other places are equally associated with activities which have gone or are nearly so: Staverton is no longer dominated by the making of cider, ship building is a distant memory in Topsham and in Plymouth the servicing of the navy is less important now than it has been for generations. Each of these industrial activities profoundly changed the way of life in each of those communities and redefined their characters.

As important as these industries were to these parts of Devon, over the years many of the associated buildings have gone. There are prominent survivals: Clovelly's great stone quay is the legacy of late sixteenth-century herring fishing, the Butterwalk in Dartmouth is just one of many rows of fishing merchants' homes of the early seventeenth century, in Exeter's Cathedral Close can be seen the Georgian home and shop of Mrs Treadwin, the county's leading dealer in East Devon lace, and a short walk away is the medieval hall of the Company of Weavers, Fullers and Shearmen. Across the length of Dartmoor are the scarred remains of medieval tin mining which are often unnoticed by those walking across the moor, there are still ancient orchards left in Staverton, out-buildings related to Georgian ship construction are to be found in Topsham and probably the entire built-environment of Plymouth can be associated to some degree with the royal navy. Likewise, countless domestic homes in each of these places were built, and are still lived in, on the profits of industries based around fish, cloth, lace, tin and cider. The surviving buildings should be seen as representing the many thousands of others which have not survived and which history has not recovered. For example, a series of ancient thatched sheds which once stood in the market place at Hatherleigh were used in selling woollen cloth but as the industry declined they became of little consequence. They were ultimately swept away by fire and a redevelopment of the site in the late 1830s.[9] They are typical of these buildings for which there is little or no memory.

These industries generated not only buildings but all the accruements that define ordinary life and give us our heritage. Nearly forty years ago an impassioned speech was made by the President of the Devonshire Association on 'Our Changing Heritage': he noted that the fast pace of life and the changes it was bringing were a threat to the county's heritage. Viscount Amory urged protection of the countryside, the built environment and oral traditions. He praised the restoration of Dartington Hall by Dorothy and Leonard Elmhirst as a worthy example to follow.[10] The realisation of that heritage is probably more widespread now and a greater understanding can be made of it. Certainly a broader analysis of what constitutes our heritage can be made but it has taken centuries for that knowledge to accumulate. In particular, it has taken many generations to define it, to distinguish between the ordinary and those things which are distinctive to Devon, and to assess how rare some survivals are. For example, in 1815 Francis Stevens chose a Seaton farmhouse as a representative Devon farmhouse. But would we, given the extent of information now available, have selected that particular building? Only a few years earlier the Reverend Richard Polwhele thought that thatching in Seaton was superior to that generally in Devon and houses there had an unusually 'finished air'.[11] An argument could be made for a Dartmoor longhouse being a more vernacular example or indeed of a cob building that is more associated with this part of England.

The accumulation of knowledge: local societies, libraries, museums and archives

When John Leland visited Devon as part of his great national tour in the early sixteenth century he expressed no interest in the heritage of the county: he assessed the economic strengths of villages, towns and the surrounding countryside and he was careful to note the wealth of individuals and of the church. When he wrote a place was 'pretty' he meant economically vibrant and expressed no interest in concepts of beauty or romantic individuality.[12] No writer was specifically concerned with the details of local history until the following generation when in the late 1500s John Hooker, the Chamberlain of the city of Exeter, sought to write a history of his native Devon. He gathered together the city's papers and one of his legacies is this civic collection, arguably the best series of civic documents outside London. Hooker never finished his history but gentlemen copied the incomplete manuscript and passed it from one to another. It fell to others to write and publish county histories but the influence of Hooker's work is easily seen in all subsequent work. Devon's earliest historians of the greatest consequence were Tristram Risdon, Thomas Westcote and William Pole in the seventeenth century, Richard Polwhele in the late eighteenth century and Daniel and Samuel Lysons in the early nineteenth century.[13] These men worked on their own and their publications, although greatly plagiarising by modern standards, made considerable contributions.

Each was interested in Devon's general history and parochial details: they described features in the landscape and the buildings and people they found there. Polwhele was particularly interested in churches, often providing the dimensions and extensive notes of the monuments, glass and furniture. For instance, when describing Kenton, a church he was well acquainted with, he proudly noted the pulpit, which was richly carved, had been the trunk of a single tree. Polwhele's descriptions are generally very detailed but occasionally he found little of interest such as Combpyne which he considered 'has nothing in it worth our observation'.[14]

Alongside their work can be seen a gradual process of the accumulation of knowledge. From 1747 to 1756 Dean Jeremiah Milles solicited information from every cleric in the county by sending out a questionnaire.[15]

Specimen of Honiton Lace by Mrs Treadwin, 1853. She wrote 'the lace trade has been carried on in Devonshire for more than two hundred years, for there is in the churchyard of Honiton a stone in memory of James Ridge, bone-lace dealer, who died in 1617, and left a sum of money for the benefit of the poor of Honiton... although the lace trade at that time was extensive, it must then and for a long time after have principally consisted in producing the net or Honiton ground (a net much like the present machine net), in which the sprigs first separately made were worked in on the pillow. the manufacture revived, until from employing only a scattered few it affords a good livelihood to the majority of the female labouring population in that part of Devon which may be enclosed by a line from Seaton to Exmouth, up the river Exe to Exeter, back the London road to Honiton, thence to Seaton, including many thousand hands. Within the last four years the demand has been enormous, and at one time so far exceeded the supply that the quality of the work for the time materially suffered. So careless and indifferent are the great majority of 'hands' as to the beauty of their work, that I am invariably obliged to have any piece of work that I cannot give out a fac-simile to copy from, made in my own house, where I can hourly superintend the manner in which it is worked; in fact, during the time I was employed about the flounce engraved I did not leave my work-room at all during the working hours. As to the character of the lace-workers, as a body they dislike regular work. I do not mean to say they are not industrious, but they have a great dislike to working anywhere where regular attendance at certain hours is required, preferring to work at home by the piece, so that they can begin or leave work as they please; and they are generally fond of dress, and careless of the future. For the last four years at least the earnings of an average lace-maker who worked a fair ten hours per day are above the wages of a farm-labourer, 7 shillings; really good hands get much more. As to their education, they can generally read and write; but, unfortunately, even in those villages which may be considered dependent on the lace-trade, no attempt is made to educate, or in any way promote, any taste useful in the manufacture. To avoid some of the evils, and implant a better taste among my own hands, I formed a school; but having completely failed in inducing the grown-up work people to improve, I was obliged to commence again about two years since with children from about twelve to fourteen years of age. Of course it will yet take some time to develop itself fully; but the progress they have made satisfies me that a little knowledge of drawing, and more regular habits of work being drilled into the workers, will very materially improve the kind of work they produce. There is not a professed lace-designer in Devonshire; my own I have procured until this last year from Paris, since then from Somerset House and Nottingham.'

John Hooker, the county's first archivist and historian.

Other gentlemen also sent enquiries to clerics. By the middle of the eighteenth century gentlemen were meeting in small groups in inns and public houses throughout Devon to discuss literary matters. One such group met at Exeter's Globe Inn in the late eighteenth century,[16] Barnstaple had similar groups meeting from 1752 and again in 1767,[17] there was a Book Club or Reading Society in Tiverton in 1775 and at this time Plymouth men met first, as the Otter Club, in bathing parties off the Hoe and then later at the Pope's Head Inn which is, curiously, now the Plymouth Arts Centre. Another group met at the Bunch of Grapes in Kinterbury Street and yet another got together in their own homes.[18] Facilities were also built to meet the needs of visitors. The most famous of these was The Shed at Sidmouth, a billiard room which developed into Wallis' Marine Library in 1809 (see page 96).[19]

Permanent centres followed and the list of them is impressive. At Exeter the Athenaeum opened in 1807 ('for the purpose of holding public lectures and demonstrations of science, literature and the arts')[20] and in 1813 the Devon & Exeter Institution began and moved into its current building two years later,[21] in Plymouth the Proprietary Library and the Athenaeum (part of the Plymouth Institution and Natural History Society) opened in 1812 and in Torbay the Torquay Natural History Society began in 1844. It took longer for Barnstaple to have a permanent centre: the North Devon Athenaeum was not

An etching by Francis Stevens of a 'typical' Devon farmhouse in Seaton, 1815. He noted 'on one side may be seen the open stalls for oxen, with the cow house attached thereto; on the other, the cart hovel and stables for horse, the pump, the well, the watering trough, with the irregular paving of the ground littered with straw, the crib and other expletives, comprising all that can be desired to form a picture of the domestic habits of the humble farm'.

established until 1888 although other ventures had been attempted to provide public lectures and act as centres of learning including the Barnstaple Philosophical Society in 1823, the Mechanics' Institute in 1830 (which had 148 books within four months), the Gentlemen's News Room in the 1830s and the Barnstaple Literary and Scientific Institution in 1844. Other parts of Devon formed discussion groups, many of which later grew into permanent centres including the Budleigh Salterton Literary Institute in about 1856, the Chudleigh Literary Society in 1848, the Crediton Mechanics' Institution in 1832, the Cullompton Mutual Improvement Society in about 1848, the Dawlish Literary and General Knowledge Society in 1850, the Exmouth Mutual Improvement Society by 1849, the Hatherleigh Literary Institution in 1852, the Honiton Literary Institution by 1849, the Kingsbridge and Dodbrooke Literary Institution in 1843, the Modbury Literary and Scientific Institution in 1840, in Ottery St Mary the Mutual Improvement Society in 1847,

in Newton Abbot the Society for the Attainment of Useful Knowledge in 1836, the Plymouth Mechanics' Institute in 1825, the Stonehouse Mechanics' Institute in about 1847, the Teignmouth Useful Knowledge Society in 1848, at Tiverton the Working Men's Institution in 1876 and the United Ready Society (later the Literary and Scientific Institution) by 1849, the Topsham Working Men's Club by 1878 and the Totnes Mechanics' Institute in 1844.[22] Interestingly, Tavistock had its library founded in 1799, far earlier and more advanced than virtually all of Devon.[23] These bodies had various intentions: it was hoped at Moretonhampstead that it would keep men out of public houses. One writer noted with some despondency 'I fear the intellect of Moreton is too shallow to make much progress for some time'.[24]

There were also many libraries that were connected with particular interests. In Victorian Plymouth there were libraries at an extraordinarily wide range of places including the Plymouth Mutual Cooperative and Industrial

Anonymous view of the gate to the Victualling Yard, Plymouth, mid nineteenth century, a symbol of the decline of local service industries to the navy.

Society, the Plymouth Medical Society, the Western College, the Marine Biological Association of the United Kingdom, the Young Men's Christian Association, the Plymouth and Western Counties Liberal Club, the Theological Library of the Roman Catholic Cathedral and the Devon & Cornwall Natural History Society.[25] In neighbouring Devonport there was understandably a different type of private library: the Royal Dockyard Lending Library started in 1791 and was followed by the Devonport Civil and Military Library, Royal Naval Engineering College, the Dockyard Professional Library and the three Royal Marines' Divisional Libraries. There was also the Parochial Gratuitous Lending Library.[26] Exeter had a similar range of small libraries[27] but its most famous one was the medieval library at the Cathedral founded in the eleventh century. It also was largely restricted to church use and would have had a bigger impact had Sir Thomas Bodley not acquired in 1602 several hundred books to start his new library in Oxford.[28] In Devon there were other religious libraries but on a significantly smaller scale: parochial libraries still survive for Barnstaple, Crediton, Ottery St Mary and Totnes, some of them dating back to the seventeenth century, deposited at the University of Exeter's Main Library between 1957 and 1978,[29] as well as John Newte's library at Tiverton.[30] Hatherleigh had its own religious library founded in 1808.[31]

Public libraries were established much later. Exeter had its Public Select Library in 1807, along with a number of small private libraries from which books could be borrowed for a fee, but the city's first publicly funded library did not open until 1870. Interestingly, it acquired the stock from the Public Select Library the following year.[32] A national report criticised the city authorities for under-funding the library: it was suggested in 1891 that it 'is evidently being starved in order to feed the museum sector'.[33] At Plymouth the Free Public Library began in 1876 and was housed in the Guildhall. Five years later the Devonport Public Library opened and it incorporated the books of the Devonport Mechanics' Institute.[34] Barnstaple had its large private library in the nineteenth

century but other small towns had to wait for new buildings until the early twentieth century when private individuals made it possible such as Sir Thomas Benjamin Bowring at Moretonhampstead in 1901, Passmore Edwards at Newton Abbot in 1904[35] and Andrew Carnegie at Bideford in 1905 and Torquay in 1907.[36] The collections of books at these libraries more easily disseminated knowledge of Devon's heritage.

The libraries also collected objects, from 1813 in the case of the Devon & Exeter Institution and the Prince Regent gave casts of the Elgin Marbles to the Plymouth Institution,[37] but the creation of purpose-built museums gradually supplanted them and eventually collections were given to professional museums. Barnstaple has an interesting history in this respect. The Barnstaple Literary and Scientific Institution had a collection of artefacts but this was taken over by the North Devon Athenaeum, with its library freely open to the public in 1888, and it was housed separately.[38] The Athenaeum still owns its resources (books, documents and artefacts) but during the course of the past century its activities are either run with or have been superseded by the rise of professional services: its books and documents are housed separately within the public library while its artefacts are curated by the museum. It is interesting that the Athenaeum, along with its counterpart in Plymouth and the Devon & Exeter Institution, remain many generations after being founded crucial to local studies within each area. The separation of artefacts, books and documents is a modern practice: another building with mixed use was the Kingsbridge town hall which when built in 1850 had a reading room, large hall for both judicial and social meetings, two club rooms, two cells, a policeman's residence and a museum.[39] Shortly afterwards large museums were built in Devon: in 1866 a museum was founded at Exeter, in 1874 at Torquay and in 1898 at Plymouth. There had been an attempt to build a museum in 1897, and the foundation stone still lies waiting, but Plymouth's new building was erected on another site and opened in 1910. The lack of a central county museum, unlike those in Cornwall, Dorset and Somerset, has fragmented the collections but also created distinct identities for them. The collecting of local objects by the 38 local registered museums over the last two hundred years has resulted in extremely rich collections.

Surprisingly, archives were the last to be established. It would be difficult to demonstrate much of a public interest in documents before the Victorian period. There was some private demand: as mentioned earlier, John Hooker's manuscript history was sought after by Devon's seventeenth and eighteenth century historians. By the early nineteenth century it appears to have been possible for some gentlemen at least to peruse Exeter's manuscripts: in the 1820s John Harris, an Exeter surgeon, gained access to the city's great map book. He must have gone to the Guildhall as he noted his drawing of the North Gate was copied 'from the archives of the chamber'.[40] These men were interested in history but the many thousands of ancient documents were scattered across the county, many in isolated country houses, which would have made original research nearly impossible. Record offices in the county were not formally established until after the second world war: an office was begun at Exeter in 1946 (building on documents collected by Exeter City Library since the early twentieth century – by 1939 some 70,000 documents had been acquired) and East Devon in 1974 but the two were joined together into the Devon County Record Office in 1977, a milestone to those interested in the history of the county. Other offices were in Plymouth, based on the archives department of Plymouth City Council soon after established in 1949, subsequently the Plymouth & West Devon Record Office, and in 1988 the North Devon Record Office opened in Barnstaple.[41] The archive network has brought together many of the county's documents held in private homes, business firms, churches and by local authorities.

The establishment in 1862 of the Devonshire Association was a landmark in the county's studies. For the first time an organisation looked at Devon in its entirety. Its stated aims were 'to give a stronger impulse and a more systematic direction to scientific inquiry, and to promote the intercourse of those who cultivate science, literature or art in different parts of Devonshire, with one another, and with others'. In 1876 it was decided papers had to be restricted to local topics and reports have been delivered annually on such diverse topics as geology, botany, entomology, mammals, archaeology, ancient monuments, industrial archaeology, history, folklore, dialect, climate and art and literature.[42]

At the start of the nineteenth century the accumulation of information was mainly the preserve of men of leisure, many of them clerics, including John Prince, Richard Polwhele, John Swete, John Pike Jones and George Oliver. In the middle of the nineteenth century this began to change although the learned societies and private libraries had been formed to serve the interests of Devon's elite. Many restricted membership: initially the Devonshire Association only welcomed women as guests and the North Devon Athenaeum refused to provide a separate room for women because the founder believed 'it would be at the best a mere place of female gossip'. Neither were women allowed to be full members of the Barnstaple Literary and Scientific Institution in 1845.[43] In Torbay the Torquay Natural History Society debated four issues regarding lady members: it was suggested women could be honorary members and borrow books but that they could not attend monthly meetings nor have any input into the management of the society. At that meeting, in their first year, they decided not to allow women in as members of any kind.[44] Likewise, the first members of the Exeter Diocesan Architectural Society, nearly half of whom were clerics, were all men.[45] Women began to be included on an equal basis in the late nineteenth century but there was at least one exception and there may have been more: women were welcomed at the Dock Literary and Philosophical Society from its beginning in 1806.[46] They were not the only group

First of a collection of watercolours presumably by a visiting gentleman, 'View of the west part of the Valley of Rocks'. The Valley of the Rocks was one of the most famous sites in north Devon at the time.

'A view of the Valley of Rocks, it contains in length 8 furlongs & 3 furlongs broad, it lies in the parish of Linton [Lynton] in North Devon in the view of Bristol Channel'.

'A view of Phily [Filleigh] House the residence of Earl Fortiscue [Fortescue]'. Filleigh, now better known as Castle Hill, was considerably improved in the eighteenth and early nineteenth centuries. It remains one of the most significant ornamental landscapes in the county.

'The view of Taustic [Tawstock] House the residence of Sir Bowcher [Bourchier] Wrey, knight & baronet'. Former home of the earls of Bath, the mansion was rebuilt on the same site after a late eighteenth-century fire and is now a school.

generally excluded: in Plymouth the Proprietary Library did not at first welcome those 'by the accidental circumstances of [their] birth and fortune': one man had not been elected because he had humble origins. This exclusion created a schism and the creation of a rival society, the Select Society. Shortly afterwards both groups dissolved and the library reformed its membership policy so that it was open to all.[47]

Another change came with the movement of professional men, and later women, into the county through the establishment of higher education centres. Hitherto local men ran the societies but higher education brought into the county a group of specialists: the establishment of the School of Art in 1855, later to become the University of Exeter, and Plymouth Technical and Art School in 1887,[48] later the University of Plymouth, accelerated the advancement of local knowledge through lectures, articles, books and conferences. One of the first undertakings in local studies was the History of Exeter Research Group in 1920.[49]

Many of the societies published learned articles on local subjects, notably the Devonshire Association and the Exeter Diocesan Architectural Society (later the Exeter Diocesan Architectural and Archaeological Society), and in 1900 they were joined by *Devon Notes & Queries* (ten years later *Devon & Cornwall Notes & Queries*) and in 1904 by the Devon & Cornwall Record Society. By the end of the twentieth century even more specialised bodies were established: Devon Bird-watching and Preservation Society in 1928,[50] Devon Archaeological Exploration Society (1929, later the Devon Archaeological Society),[51] Devon Trust for Nature Conservation (1964, later Devon Wildlife Trust), the Devon History Society (1969), Devon Historic Churches Trust (1971), Devon Historic Buildings Trust (1973),[52] Devon Family History Society (1976), Devon Buildings Group (1986), Devon Gardens Trust (1989) and most recently of all, The Friends of Devon's Archives (1998). The creation of more localised societies was a feature of

the twentieth century but the first to be concerned with conservation was the Sid Vale Association which held its first committee meeting in 1846 but began in 1825 with a meeting to form The Sidmouth Improvement Committee.[53] Many others have followed.

Many of these Devon organisations were based on national institutions. The Devonshire Association, for example, was modelled on the British Association, the various Mechanics' Institutes followed that established in Glasgow in 1821, *Devon & Cornwall Notes & Queries* is a local version of the national *Notes & Queries* and the Devon and Exeter Horticultural Society was modelled in 1829 on what later became the Royal Horticultural Society.[54] Although Devon societies mainly followed national trends there was at least one notable exception: the first society to promote beekeeping in Britain was founded in Devon in 1797.[55]

The effect of these learned societies, libraries, museums and archives has been to transform the overall understanding of Devon's past and its heritage by providing unparalleled collections of information about the county. It is possible to be better informed than any other previous generation about the nature of the county's history and heritage and initiate, inform and guide public debate.

Recording and protection

In the past century hundreds of individuals can be identified who have diligently worked on aspects of Devon's heritage but not within modern definitions of that word. The earliest writers, John Hooker in the late 1500s and his successors in the following century, are known because their work was published and saved but there were others including Henry Davy of Upcott in the early seventeenth century who was 'a man commendable for his knowledge of antiquity'.[56] It would be difficult to prove that they were enthusiasts of what would now be considered heritage or even that they expressed interest in preservation. The loss of ancient things, whether buildings or monuments, was put to one single cause, time. There was no discussion of the natural world beyond its usefulness, manuscripts had yet to be of any wide consideration and ancient monuments were curiosities but there was not yet the framework or general understanding in which to place them. There were few buildings at that time of any consequence besides those erected for religious purposes and Elizabethan and Jacobean society was intent upon their utilitarian aspects and decidedly uninterested in discussion of their ornamentation. There were not many other ancient buildings of note: Devon had some ancient castles but many of the civic halls and country homes were recently rebuilt. The vast majority of the population lived in poor buildings which would have been considered architecturally undistinguished. The wealth of the sixteenth and seventeenth centuries, derived locally from cloth, tin-mining, overseas fishing, trade and privateering, produced the built environment over which later writers would enthuse. By 1630 Risdon, in his *Chorographical Description or Survey of the County of Devon*, was more concerned with contemporary Devon and wrote of the lineage of the local aristocracy and gentry and of their manorial and other landed wealth. He was less interested in what may be termed antiquarian interests; Risdon's descriptions of parishes included few references to ancient relics or remains. He detailed historical events but was less concerned with their by-products, in those elements which are now considered heritage. For instance, significant houses were noted in regard to their continued viability and the occasional reference to a building's 'decay' was not a lament for lost architecture but a comment on the owner's finances. Risdon's description of the great fires at Tiverton was concerned with the loss of wealth and not of losing buildings of architectural merit. There are few other interesting exceptions in which there are hints that Risdon is concerned with preservation: he praised Rougemont Castle in Exeter as 'famous for its antiquity',

Modbury was approvingly described as 'a place for multiplicity of ancient houses', he kept an early medieval coin found in the parish of Roseash 'for antiquity sake', he noted the 'antique beauty' and former 'magnificence' of Forde Abbey (historically within the county of Devon), and, finally, of particular interest, in his description of Tavistock Abbey he commented favourably that it 'by a laudable ordinance, had lectures read in the ancient Saxon tongue, and so continued to our grandsire's days, to preserve antiquities, laws and histories formerly written in that language, from oblivion; a thing almost now come to pass'.[57] But there is little concern expressed for the ruins of ancient Catholic buildings: perhaps it would have suggested continued adherence to the old faith.

A century and a half later there were considerable differences. The Reverend Richard Polwhele reflected national changes in the 1790s in being interested in trying to explain the past before the Romans and wrote much more about archaeological remains and church furnishings. He also wrote at length of the beauty of the landscape, a theme which did not concern Risdon who was interested in productivity. In one instance Polwhele referred to 'the English garden' as expressed at Mamhead and Powderham and noted particular gardens such as that of Mr Patch, which comprised the ditch of Rougemont Castle and is now known as Rougemont Gardens, and praised his efforts in highlighting the 'remains of antiquity' in the landscaping. There are more references to lost items such as ancient books he assumed were written by the Romans on their British occupation and referred to former religious buildings as having been sacrilegiously treated; in one instance, in a reference to a chapel in Whitestone near Exeter, he mentioned that the building was in ruins but enclosed in order to guard it from 'profanation'. Yet he made reference to the removal or destruction of various medieval bishops' memorial stones when new paving was inserted into Exeter Cathedral without adverse

'A view of Picwell House in North Devon with a distant view of the Island of Lundy'. Pickwell House, in Georgeham, was the home of the Harris family and later of the Newtons of Bridestowe who by 1822 had rented half to an estate farmer and left the rest vacant. It was rebuilt in the early twentieth century and a part of the old building remains.

'Watermouth House, Joseph Davy Esquire in Devon'. Now known as Watermouth Castle, the mansion was built in the early nineteenth century for Arthur Basset.

'Arlin[g]ton House, John Chichester Esquire' was built in the early nineteenth century near the site of earlier buildings and enlarged in 1865. It is now owned by the National Trust.

17. 'Ly[n]mouth House, John Lock Esquire'

comments. Polwhele also pointedly quoted a correspondent to the *Gentleman's Magazine* who wrote of the ruins of Buckfast Abbey:

a kind of wish may arise that we could have seen them in their pristine splendour, yet, on recollection, we feel a satisfaction in considering that it is for the advantage of ourselves and country that we see them in their present mutilated state, and that is now the most pleasing condition in which they can be viewed.[58]

Research completed only another century and a half later shows how society's attitudes had changed towards the past. W. G. Hoskins' *Devon* demonstrates the importance of the preservation of the natural and cultural legacy, understandable for a book written shortly after the second world war when the county's two largest urban areas, Exeter and Plymouth, were devastated by bombing. In the course of a few short hours centuries of history were destroyed and which was all too visible as Professor Hoskins researched and wrote.[59]

The character of research in Devon has been one of informal and individual effort. For instance, in the 1820s there was a group of men who made initial investigations into Dartmoor's reeves and discussed their findings in local newspapers.[60] In 1840 one local man attempted to record the findings of ancient coins in Exeter[61] and in 1861 the fore-mentioned James Davidson tried to list recent archaeological finds. His report shows an extraordinary effort by a man interested in the whole of Devon: he noted that at Ashburton several coarse urns of baked clay were found in the church's chancel during renovation work in about 1858, at Aylesbeare a man digging peat found a Roman silver coin in 1850, in Bishop's Orchard a labourer dug up Roman coins in 1813, in Bovey Tracey spear heads were found in 1851, at Christow a cromlech was destroyed by building work in 1817 and in Cornwood a prehistoric monumental stone had recently been used to build the railway. He listed

even more discoveries for parishes beginning with the remaining 21 letters of the alphabet.[62]

It was as late as 1882 that a call was made to preserve the county's heritage when J. Brooking Rowe gave his Presidential Address to the Devonshire Association. He highlighted the number of documents and monuments which had recently been destroyed, noted the rashness of restoration in parish churches and looked forward to the day when the county had a record office to deposit its documents. He cited John Ruskin to support him:

Of mere wanton or ignorant ravage it is vain to speak; my words will not reach those who commit them; and yet, be it heard or not, I must not leave the truth unstated, that it is again no question of expediency or feeling whether we shall preserve the buildings of past times or not. We have no right whatsoever to touch them. They are not ours. They belong partly to those who built them, and partly to all the generations of mankind who are to follow us. The dead have still their right in them. That which they laboured for, the praise of achievement, or the expression of religious feeling, or whatsoever else it might be, which they intended to be permanent, we have no right to obliterate. What we have ourselves built, we are at liberty to throw down; but what other men gave their strength and wealth and life to accomplish, their right over does not pass away with their death; still less is the right to the use of what they have left vested in us only. It belongs to all their successors.[63]

The Devon institutions were joined in the late nineteenth and twentieth centuries by an extraordinary number of other local and national bodies, some statutory and others volunteer-run, which have played roles, often confusing if not conflicting, in shaping Devon's heritage. One organisation which has acted as an umbrella group is the Devon Conservation Forum, a charity started in 1973. It acts as a pressure group and has sought not to preserve but limit the effects of change. In the one hundred years before it was formed a number of other groups were already operating on heritage issues. Four elements of Devon's heritage, antiquities, buildings, manuscripts and the natural world, can be identified that have fared in different ways.

Antiquities

Dr William Stukeley, a founder of the Society of Antiquaries, was one of the earliest, if not the first, outside investigator interested in Devon's antiquities. He visited in 1724 and was clearly fascinated by recently discovered artefacts as well as more familiar features in the landscape.[64] John Carter came to Exeter in the 1790s and his work on the cathedral was of an extraordinarily high standard. At the same time the Reverend Polwhele had the time and opportunity to adopt a more systematic approach. He was one of a number of men with similar interests including the Reverend John Swete who was the county's leading expert on the Picturesque movement.[65] Even then Devon did not have a man of the calibre of Stukeley and it took several generations before information was gathered and analysed. There was a lack of understanding in which to place these monuments and arguments raged over such matters as the importance of the Druids. It was one such dispute that caused a lasting rift between Swete and Polwhele. In the early nineteenth century objects were increasingly being discovered, described and sometimes listed. The pace intensified through the Victorian period.[66]

In 1881 William Crossing called for the preservation of Dartmoor's antiquities. This followed a debate in Parliament in the previous decade. Crossing cited the seventeenth-century writer Tristram Risdon who had regarded the moor as having only three remarkable things. In 1881 only Wistman's Wood still existed: the Stannary Parliament's table had been turned into a water trough at Dennabridge Farm and the stone which made up Childe's tomb was used in building at Foxtor Farm. Crossing noted damage elsewhere on the moor: stone from a cromlech at

Merrivale was split to build an outhouse, a kistaven at Hound Tor was used for road repairs and one ancient stone was reinserted 'upside down and inside out' when it was re-sited.[67] That same year the editor of The Western Antiquary called for a petition to Parliament for the preservation of antiquities in Devon and Cornwall. He warned that a useful superstition amongst the 'peasantry' was dying out: apparently it was believed that those who injured antiquities would be 'ill-wished'.[68] Two years later the Dartmoor Preservation Association was formed to protect and preserve ancient features. The moor had by then already attracted a great deal of sporadic investigation.[69] Locally information was spread through early reports of the Devonshire Association, particularly the reports on barrows, ancient monuments and Dartmoor, and then subsequently those of the Devon Archaeological Society (from 1928), Exeter Archaeology (from 1972) and North Devon Rescue Archaeology in the 1980s. Site work, particularly at Hembury, was pushed forward in the 1930s by Ralegh Radford, later Director of the British School at Rome, who linked Devon with the mainstream of English archaeology.[70]

The legal protection of Devon's monuments started in 1882 with the Ancient Monuments Act. The Devonshire Association did not form its Ancient Monuments Committee until thirty years later, by which time further acts were passed, but it was even later, after the first world war, that real work began. Ralegh Radford was appointed to prepare the first Devon list although Berry Pomeroy had already been scheduled in 1922. The Ministry of Works accepted fourteen additional sites. Inhabited houses, monuments, the property of the Crown or Government and any structure built after 1688 were excluded. Several dozen correspondents throughout the county assisted but it was noted that by 1922 a number of sites that were considered only a few years before had already disappeared.[71]

Since the late nineteenth century a mixture of statutory bodies, both local and national, have been involved in

View of Bishop taughton [Tawton] in Deavon.

View of The Cascades in the River of Lymouth.

Barnstable [sic] bridge, North Devon.

different degrees in protecting ancient monuments.[72] English Heritage is the successor to two national agencies: the Ministry of Public Buildings and Works operated from 1882 until 1970 when the Department of the Environment was formed. Its responsibilities in this respect were taken over by English Heritage in 1983. Protection in Devon has been managed through scheduling ancient monuments via national government. The number of these in the county is extraordinary: by 2003 there were 5,723 scheduled ancient monuments many of which are in Dartmoor. Devon County Council has the responsibility to curate the county's Sites & Monuments Record, which began in 1975,[73] and now has some 64,000 entries. It will shortly be reformed as a Historic Environment Record and include both archaeological sites and buildings.

The Royal Commission on the Historical Monuments of England began in 1908 and was given the task of creating a record of the country's ancient and historic monuments and to publish a county inventories.[74] That work was halted in 1979 when the focus on surveying and recording shifted to conservation. Unfortunately Devon research had not yet been fully published except separate reports.[75] The RCHME later absorbed the National Buildings Record which had begun in 1940 and its collection of photographs, many from the 1940s onwards, comprises several thousand images.[76] In 1998 the RCHME itself was merged with English Heritage.

As part of this process of protection, English Heritage holds in guardianship a considerable number of sites in Devon including Bayard's Cove Fort, Berry Pomeroy Castle, Blackbury Camp, Dartmouth Castle, Grimspound, Hound Tor deserted village, Kirkham House, Lydford Castle and town, Merrivale prehistoric settlement, Mount Batten Tower, Okehampton Castle, the walls of the Royal Citadel at Plymouth and Totnes Castle. Leigh Barton, a medieval house in Churchstow, was purchased in 1975 from Devon County Council which acquired the building in 1950. The lodging range was heavily restored, and the farmhouse extensively repaired, and returned to private ownership in 1999.[77] Initial work on Leigh Barton was in line with policy established by the Ministry of Works in which the site was cleared of materials later than the building's defining period. In 1976 the Department of Environment acquired Bowhill and the building's subsequent restoration included considerable work on cob. The Devonshire Association has subsequently leased the building.

Buildings

The protection of historic buildings came much later than that of ancient monuments In 1932 legislation was passed which permitted intervention to save historic buildings and in 1944 the first lists were made in a similar manner to those of ancient monuments. Three years later the law was extended to make the lists a statutory duty. In 1932 the first act only covered buildings erected before 1700, that of 1946 extended protection for buildings up to 1850 and finally, in 1963, virtually all restrictions were lifted. In contrast to ancient monuments, control of the alteration and demolition of listed buildings is carried out both through local and national government: this is overseen by English Heritage for listed buildings of Grade I or Grade II* but Grade II buildings, except in the case of demolition, are the responsibility of district councils. By 2003, 20,635 buildings are on the Devon lists and 51 gardens of historic importance on the register. The buildings comprise 421 Grade I buildings including Exeter Cathedral, the Palm House at Bicton, Smeaton's Tower and the Grotto at Endsleigh. Public understanding of the county's buildings heritage was sharpened by the appearance of Nikolaus Pevsner's two volume work on Devon in the Buildings of England series in 1952. The revised edition, published in 1989, made great use of the re-listing made in the 1980s.[78]

Local government has a patchy history of saving buildings for nearly a hundred years. Exeter City Council rescued St Nicholas Priory by purchase in 1913,

intervened to save the Chevalier House which was threatened with demolition in the 1930s, was given Bampfylde House in 1934[79] and purchased the 'Norman House' in Preston Street a few years before it was damaged in the city's bombing and subsequently demolished. It also acquired St Katharine's Priory in Polsloe in 1934 when neighbouring farmland was being overrun for housing (and after a period of further decline in 1982 converted it for use as a community centre). The saviour of the building was the formidable Miss Ethel Lega-Weekes who ran the 'Save the Priory' campaign in 1933. She worked with Arthur Everett, the archaeologist, and enlisted the support of the Exeter Diocesan Architectural and Archaeological Society. Another city venture was the 'House that Moved' and its much-acclaimed relocation in 1961. It also purchased Rougemont House in 1908.[80] Oddly enough, the city built the Custom House in the late seventeenth century and has had it so long that it is now, like the Guildhall, an ancient structure. Unfortunately, since HM Customs & Excise relinquished the lease in 1989 the Custom House has lost its sense of purpose. In Plymouth the Merchant's House was saved by the city council in 1969 because it was recognised as an unusual survival of the German bombing and of the commercial development along the Barbican.[81] The history of preservation in Plymouth differs radically than that at Exeter in that Plymouth has had active volunteer groups: the Plymouth Barbican Association, and Old Plymouth Society, have been more energetic than other civic societies in Devon. In 1929 the Old Plymouth Society restored the Elizabethan House, now a museum, and gave it to the City of Plymouth. The Barbican Association was formed in 1957 and has acquired 17 historic properties[82] which were under threat of demolition around Sutton Pool. It has made a tremendous difference. Torbay Council's involvement is different again: it reflects its history of tourism and providing amenities. Torre Abbey, with its park, was purchased in 1930 and then Cockington Court and 223 acres of land two years later. Its other great asset, Oldway Mansion and estate with 19 acres of grounds, was acquired in 1946 by Paignton Urban District Council for offices.[83] There has been a second movement following the purchase of individual properties. Councils have recognised the importance of the historic environment and been pursued conservation areas and regeneration schemes, often linked to the benefits of promoting tourism. Other local government involvement includes the use of historic buildings in part or wholly as headquarters such as East Devon at Knowle, South Hams at Follaton, West Devon at Kilworthy, Teignbridge at Forde House as well as Dartmoor National Park at Parke and Exmoor National Park at Exmoor House. Exeter City Council still meets at the Guildhall, a tradition of many hundreds of years but Mid Devon District Council is now selling its historic building headquarters, the Great House in Tiverton. On a more local level, Newton Abbot Town Council has owned St Leonard's church tower since 1971 after a long period of possible demolition.

Other bodies have been involved in recording and protecting local buildings. One of the earliest is the Society for the Protection of Ancient Buildings which was established in 1877 by William Morris. It sought simple repair and not intrusive rebuilding. The Society's first Devon agent resided in Mortehoe near Ilfracombe. In its early days it was interested in such places as Crediton,

Dartmouth, Denbury, Exeter, Parracombe, Peter Tavy, Plymouth and Throwleigh. Another of its cases was the home of the Fowel family in Ugborough. In 1911 the Society began to be interested in Fowelscombe, a sixteenth-century mansion in the parish of Ugborough on the edge of Dartmoor, which had been deserted for some time. Four years later a report was made by Basil Stallybrass who described a house in its death throes:

After a two mile walk from Wrangaton Station one approaches the house down a green glade which one crosses by an old two-arched bridge, the long manor with its four projecting wings unfolding itself from the trees on the left – a nearer view is disappointing. The stuccoed face, the deal window frames with their square labels of Roman Cement, the ill-proportioned entrance door and the sham battlementing all belong to the 'Strawberry Hill' period and decay has only made them look the more tawdry. Where the stucco has fallen away [in] some places and bits of old walling appear: the granite window of the hall with its four-centred head is undoubtedly original sixteenth-century work: so too is the window above the entrance; and the granite doorway on the right may possibly have been removed from the entrance when the present doorway was fabricated. But there is nothing else worthy of remark and the other sides of the house are featureless.

Fowelscombe in Ugborough, now a ruin.

Watercolour of Silverton Park, one of two unsuccessful houses built for George Wyndham, fourth earl of Egremont, 1879. It was built in the 1840s and demolished in 1901. He also built Blackborough House, which lies partly in ruins, and also Blackborough Church, which has recently been demolished.

The interior is for the most part roofless and is melancholy indeed. The century old decorations are peeling from the walls, the floors have fallen in, and the broken plaster partitions lie upon the ground. Nearly all the panelling has been removed – the two or three pieces which remain are painted deal, of classic type. The Hall is the only room worthy of notice. The 8 light window has already been noticed: of its mullions only the outer ones are of granite; the rest are replacements in wood.

Opposite the window is the fireplace, the most interesting thing which remains in the house, though its bears some signs of having been inserted in its present position. It is of granite with a hollow & round moulding to joints & head; on the latter the round mould with an added fillet enclosed a panel on either side, bearing the initials TF 15 37 MF (Thomas and Mary Fowell). The arcaded plaster panelling which covered the upper part of the walls has now for the most part fallen down, but it is mechanical wooden work of no value. Besides the fireplace a broad staircase formerly mounted between two walls – at the landing level is an original granite window 2 lights of which remain, looking into a central court. A passage under the stairs opens onto the court by an original granite doorway – the similar doorway on the opposite side I judge to be modern.

The building has been through many changes – three or four periods at least are distinguishable, but the sweeping character of the last renovation makes some of the history obscure. The hall is perhaps the nucleus to which at some time were added the porch, the room on the east marked Dining Room, a western wing with its staircase and finally the northern wing as far as the room marked Kitchen. The 'Strawberry Hill' period is accountable for the Drawing Room on the west; the Kitchen and offices which close the remaining sides of the central court; and the eastern wing; and the projecting 'towers'.

The accompanying plan illustrates this and gives some idea of the extent of the building. Even if repair was desirable its cost would probably be as great as that of erecting a new building of equal size: and is questionable if the few bits of old work are worth preserving in this way amidst so much that might well be left to perish. Given some wealthy man desirous of living in that spot, no doubt a more interesting house could be made out of these ruins than with a wholly new structure: the valley is sheltered, there is a southern aspect (though the situation looks damp) and the old bridge and bits of stone terraced garden could all be worked in. But failing such a one, I could not recommend more than the re-roofing of the hall and staircase behind the glazing of its windows, with perhaps some judicious demolition in other quarters. The cost of this would be approximately £100.

If this sum could not be obtained the fireplace should be preserved in some museum; while I should view with equanimity the granite windows and doors being embodied in some new building of appropriate character, though the Society could hardly make such a recommendation.[84]

Other work of the Society included a successful campaign to save the medieval tower of St Leonard's church in Newton Abbot and it was heavily involved in Exeter Guildhall in the early 1900s.[85]

Strong contributions have also been made by private individuals such as that of Sydney Simmons at Okehampton Castle. He initiated investigations and repairs from 1911 to 1913 and then in 1917 gave the castle to the Okehampton Castle Trust. Fifty years later it was given to the Ministry of Public Buildings and Works.[86]

The pace has increased in the last fifty years: for instance in 1961 the Country House Association acquired Flete House near Ermington on long lease and the building is now divided into nearly 40 separate apartments.[87] Just over ten years later, in 1973, the Devon Historic Buildings Trust was founded to rescue buildings at risk and then sell them. The first acquisition was a set of three cottages in South Molton. Since then it has been involved with more than twenty others including Larkbeare House in Exeter, the Victorian police station and borough gaol in Tiverton, Haldon Belvedere, Ireland House in Ashburton and rows of cottages in Ottery St Mary, Tavistock and Okehampton. Efforts are currently being made to rescue and renovate Cricklepit Mill in Exeter.[88] Since it began in 1965 the Landmark Trust has acquired Devon properties: it rescues distressed buildings, mostly in the United Kingdom, and then promotes their use generally as holiday accommodation. It is interesting

in part for collaborative ventures with the National Trust as well as for a range of unusual Devon properties including Sanders in North Bovey, Swiss and Pond Cottages at Endsleigh in Milton Abbot, Shute Gatehouse near Colyton, Wortham Manor in Lifton, Kingswear Castle, Crownhill Fort in Plymouth, Peter's Tower in Lympstone, the Library and Orangery at Stevenstone, and Margells in Branscombe. The island of Lundy is the largest single entity.[89] The role of the Devon Buildings Group has also been important since 1986.

Churches have had particular attention partly because they had a multitude of dedicated educated men with ample leisure time: much of what we know about them comes from clerics in the eighteenth and nineteenth centuries. James Davidson was particularly active. One of the most notable researchers was however a woman: in the early twentieth century Beatrix Cresswell recorded the county's churches.[90] There have been detailed studies of aspects such as monuments, bells, fonts and rood screens.[91] Continuing research has led to a study of monumental brasses,[92] and local branches of the National Decorative and Fine Arts Society have an ongoing programme of recording churches in the county. As the first class of ancient buildings to be investigated, much work had already been done when the Exeter Diocesan Architectural Society was created in 1842. It was formed to promote the study of ecclesiastical architecture but it did not intend to be involved in preservation. Instead it sought to influence the remodelling of existing buildings and the construction of new ones along prescribed ideas of good taste.[93] Their notions were influenced by the Oxford Movement, the high church group which was also known as the Tractarians, and the establishment in 1839 of the Cambridge Camden Society which was influenced by Pugin and his support of Gothic architecture. The EDAS was interested in ancient fabric in relation to certain principles including the removal of galleries and pews it considered intrusive: the society sought to restore buildings to a fourteenth-century ideal.[94] This was difficult in Devon because of the lack of these structures. The purpose of the EDAS was, naturally, appropriate to the 1840s. The Society agreed that they had to make:

all allowances on the one hand for those provincialisms in art which are analogous to the minor varieties of dialect and on the other for those real difficulties in the details of execution which display the original talent of the artist, we may still hope to attain throughout the kingdom a harmonious and consistent style of building, which is as far removed from an ignorant affection of vulgar originality as it is from a servile imitation of ancient models.[95]

One of the most curious histories of preservation is that of Frithelstock Priory near Great Torrington: five different groups were involved from 1887 to 1935. In 1887 it appeared as though the ruins were to be demolished. The neighbouring tenant had appealed to Lord Clinton, the owner, to make the building safe by removing it. A Devon cleric investigated it at the request of the Society for the Protection of Ancient Buildings and a scheme was offered in which the stone would be secured and ivy and various trees removed.[96] The EDAS visited five years later, in 1892, and reported the building was still in a ruinous state. Then in 1929 it was announced that the Devonshire Association was the custodian of the ruins through Lord Clinton. A management plan was agreed with the Office of Works and the Society for the Protection of Ancient Buildings. Six years later the Devon Archaeological Society were given custody of the site and finally in 1957 the Rolle estate sold the land to private owners.[97]

There have been other endeavours as well. The Friends of Friendless Churches, which began in 1957, acquired the medieval parish church of South Huish following redundancy in 1975 and the pre-Reformation chapel of the Ayshfords at Burlescombe in 2000. The Churches Conservation Trust (formerly the Redundant Churches Fund) was founded in 1969 and manages, by statutory

authority, ten Church of England buildings which are no longer needed for regular worship in Devon including St Martin in Exeter, North Huish, Torbryan, Satterleigh, Parracombe, Luffincott, West Ogwell and Bradstone. The Historic Chapels Trust owns Salem Chapel in East Budleigh. Finally, the Devon Historic Churches Trust has given financial assistance with repairs to places of worship since 1971.

Manuscripts

The first known sorting of Devon's documents happened in the late sixteenth century at Exeter when John Hooker placed the city's papers in 43 separate boxes. The papers were added to and sorted in 1624, 1656 and 1755 and in 1821 the Reverend George Oliver examined the papers and once again arranged them in separate sections. But it was not until the 1860s that the city authorities were 'awakened' to their sense of responsibility in having the papers properly looked after.[98] Stuart Moore, a barrister, was employed for two months in 1863, working he said from nine in the morning to ten at night, and not only gathered together the records but cleaned and catalogued them. Moore found the papers in what he described as a deplorable state. He collected together more than 8,000 individual documents, including 'two or three cartloads in the old receiver's office', and many other papers were found under the tiles of the Guildhall. It was reported that:

Up the narrow and rickety staircase leading to that dingy apartment may be seen traces of the joining of a part of a new building upon an old one... in the un-shapely apartments above are old chests full of dirty parchments in heterogeneous heaps, as if they had been emptied there as rubbish by a bricklayer's labours during the progress of the work 270 years ago. It must require a great deal of courage to plunge into these dense barrow loads of dirty, mouldy skins, to attempt to decipher them and to get them into form for intelligible reference. There are boxes full of records almost eaten up by worms; only a bit here and a bit there remains decipherable after cleaning, and the remainder crumbles to dust in the hand.

Moore reported that 'a great quantity of them I opine are useless and may surely be condemned to be burnt'. One onlooker suggested that the records should be moved to the museum where they would be more accessible but they were housed in a room above the cells, which was referred to as the 'City Record Room'.[99] A generation later, in 1910, there was concern that the papers were at risk from fire and there were moves to place the documents in more secure storage.[100]

In January 1881 the editor of *The Western Antiquary* called for an investigation into the state of Plymouth's civic documents and he requested they be edited and published. Three years later the Historical Manuscripts Commission investigated the records and expressed its disappointment that the earliest documents had not survived partly due to fire and also to neglect. A report was made and afterwards the documents continued to be arranged and catalogued.[101] It was not until 1949 that the city moved towards a record office: that year the City Librarian established a committee specifically to coordinate the town's manuscripts. There was concern at the destruction of papers during the second world war, notably those housed at the City Museum and those held in private hands, and within three years the collection had grown to some sixty-five boxes.[102]

But these were only the records of two cities: the rest of Devon's documents lay in private and public hands in many hundreds of locations across the county. When the Devon & Cornwall Record Society first met in 1904 the President argued that it was needed because of the deplorable state of Devon's manuscripts; they were under threat from damp and bonfires, being sold as waste paper and from the attention of rats and mice. He also looked forward to a bill then going through Parliament that would preserve local documents and envisioned the day when a record office would be built in Exeter and maintained at the public expense.[103] There had already been discussions about the state of the county's documents and the need for preservation: as early as 1882 there were calls to list and conserve Devon's archives and that year the Devonshire Association began compiling lists of documents. The Association was very much aware of the work of the Royal Commission for Historical Manuscripts which had begun in 1869.[104] The first authoritative listing of local documents was made of Exeter's papers but it took many years before smaller towns were looked at by professional archivists. The borough records of Tavistock, for instance, were discovered in an oak chest in 1886. A local man died and the papers, including the churchwardens' accounts, were found to have been in his possession.[105] By the end of the twentieth century some seven miles of local documents had been collected and housed in the three public record offices in Barnstaple, Exeter and Plymouth.

The natural world

The first individual to begin recording Devon's natural environment was John Hooker in the late sixteenth century.[106] But it was the Reverend Polwhele who collated more extensive material in the 1780s and relied upon ten main botanical recorders from across the county as well as a great many more for wildlife. His botanical work was followed in 1829 by *Flora Devoniensis,* the county's first major listing of plants.[107] Other more specialised studies of particular interest were made of Totnes and Sidmouth, an important work by Philip Gosse on marine life and several books on the fern craze of the mid to late nineteenth century.[108] Studies of other aspects followed through the nineteenth century.[109] Polwhele's notes on wildlife shows how rare birds were spotted but kept rare by being shot by locals: in this way a Topsham doctor had an osprey, a Modbury man a chough, a Dartmouth man a hoopoe, a Totnes man a grosbeak.[110] Persecution by man has lost Devon the white-tailed sea eagle, kite and goshawk while ospreys nested at Beer until the middle of the eighteenth century until they were disturbed. Birds are not the only species to be eliminated. Hunting had, long before 1500, exterminated the bear, beaver, wild boar and wolf. Polecats were thought to have disappeared about 1935 and the pine marten in the late nineteenth century but isolated reports have continued with pine martens being spotted at Denham Bridge on the river Tavy in 1973 and a polecat as recently as 1998.[111] According to one survey the red squirrel had disappeared in Devon by 1971 but isolated reports were made of subsequent sightings.[112] They were replaced by the American grey squirrel which has been resident in Devon for some time: they had spread to the environs of Plymouth by 1947 but in the mid 1950s there was only a small grey population in South West Devon.[113] Other introduced animals, which are more lost in Devon rather than lost to the county, are the mink, brown rat and Sika (or Japanese) deer. Wallabies have been spotted on Exmoor, Dartmoor, Haldon and near Teignmouth. One was discovered living near Totnes in 1989.[114] There was also a small family of Himalayan porcupines which escaped from a wildlife park near Okehampton and which established themselves from 1969 through into the 1990s in an area stretching from Great Torrington to Gidleigh.[115] At least two green parrots were naturalised along the Grand Western Canal in Halberton in about 2001.[116] Woolly monkeys escaped from their pens in Combe Martin in north Devon in the 1980s and for a short while naturalised in nearby woodland.[117] Muntjac deer, the small oriental deer, have also been breeding in the county since at least the 1970s: captive animals escaped from Dawlish and spread to Kingsteignton and Haldon Hill by 1976.[118] The Canada Goose was introduced as early as 1755 at Nutwell near Lympstone on the river Exe but they were removed from the garden because they were so destructive.[119] Presumably they did not have sufficient time or opportunity to escape into the wild. Other exotic birds include a Bald Eagle from the

Carolinas which was kept at Exmouth in the middle of the eighteenth century.[120] Finally, the most highly publicised escape has been that of the 'big cats' which have been reported throughout Devon, and if true, will have tremendous repercussions on native wildlife.

The introduction of exotic animals pales into significance compared to the number of foreign plants now in Devon. Over the last two hundred years tens of thousands of acres of rural countryside have been turned into suburban gardens and very few native plants have subsequently been planted. Instead hundreds of different plants from around the world have been purchased at garden nurseries with the consequence of the loss of a natural habitat for existing wildlife. While on the one hand undoubtedly enhancing the beauty of local gardens, it is nearly impossible to stand in most parts of Devon without seeing an introduced plant species.

Many ancient trees have been lost for a great variety of reasons. It was only in 1932 that trees could be protected.[121] Some, like those pulled down in the 1990s for the rebuilding of the A30 in East Devon, were recognised as such but were still destroyed. Many others were cut down before they could be recorded or appreciated: in 1795 one observer noted of the lower Exe estuary:

there is more fine timber than is perhaps to be met with in any other part of the county, Devon though well wooded in general has of late lost immense quantities of its noblest trees. An iron forge was introduced into America to thin its wide forests, but such a destroyer is not wanted in Devon, for we have a Dock Yard![122]

If a Georgian wanted to see Devon's ancient timber he or she needed to look at ships in harbours across the world.

The Council for the Protection of Rural England, now known as the Campaign to Protect Rural England, began its Devon branch in the late 1920s. In 1932 it published its study into the Devon landscape and among its objections then was the disfigurement of the countryside by petrol stations and scorned its establishment of 'hideous little structures by the roadside for the purveyance of indifferent refreshments'. Its principal concern was ribbon development, in preventing undesirable buildings between towns and villages. Among the villages singled out which suffered from 'rebuilding with incongruous materials and in attempts to be fashionable or up-to-date' was Lustleigh.[123] Its main work now lies in overseeing planning applications, advising on structure plans and regional plans, and in lobbying local planners.

The National Trust has played a considerable role in the Devon landscape. As a charity it is distinguished from bodies like English Heritage. It owns and manages property mainly according to direct management. The first acquisition of land was Prickly Pear Blossom Park, 22 acres of heath and woodland near Ottery St Mary, in 1904.[124] By 1932 it owned more than 1,000 acres[125] and in 1933 it was given its first property, at Widecombe-in-the-Moor, and since then the Devon properties comprise large houses (A La Ronde, Arlington Court, Bradley, Buckland Abbey – jointly managed with Plymouth City Council, Castle Drogo, Colleton Fishacre, Compton Castle, Killerton, Knightshayes, Overbecks, Saltram, Shute Barton and Watersmeet House), the mill at Wembury Beach, and the Baptist meeting house at Dalwood. The coastal path now extends to 91 miles and Lydford Gorge and the island of Lundy are two other properties.

Dartmoor National Park was established in 1951 and Exmoor National Park only three years later. The idea of setting Dartmoor aside for the public had been made some time before: as early as 1894 one local man suggested the county council should buy the moor in the same manner as Epping Forest had been purchased by the London authorities.[126] As mentioned earlier, by that date the Dartmoor Preservation Society had been formed and in 1890 it was strongly campaigning for rights of access to the moor.[127] The comparative lack of people living on Dartmoor has made it easier to record that landscape[128] and there is no other part of the county which has had so much written about it.[129] But unusually, the county's only World Heritage Site is in East Devon, now known as the Jurassic Coast.

Chapter Two

The manner of loss

Among the great number of reasons for the loss of items are some particular to Devon at the start of the twenty-first century. Although there are areas of great poverty, the county is fairly prosperous. Recently, the eighteenth-century organ at St Mary Arches was removed and the reason given was that it was worn out. Had this been a small town in the American Mid-West the organ would have been preserved as a historic treasure. If the organ was in many third world countries there would have been efforts to maintain it as a working musical instrument.

But the current state of society, with a wealth of treasures and ability to easily make new purchases, has led to the destruction of items that could otherwise have been kept.

Unconsidered changes

A number of topics cannot be covered in this book. For example, the boundaries of Devon have altered its boundaries: in 1844 Thorncombe became part of Dorset when Maker, on the west side of the Tamar, went to Cornwall. Everything within these parishes has been lost to Devon including two of its most well-known gardens, those at Forde Abbey and Mount Edgcumbe. A light-hearted argument could also be made regarding the loss of Wolford Chapel in Dunkeswell, it has been owned by the Ontario government since 1966.[130]

Also the lack of a detailed study of place names in Devon for more than seventy years[131] makes it impossible to make more than this reference to it. A cursory glance at any tithe map reveals a wealth of local place names that have, in many cases, not survived and it is in their nature to change. For instance, it was claimed of Axmouth that the orchard at the east end of its church

One unconsidered loss is the number of buildings which are planned but never built. These two Victorian views of Okehampton, probably by Edward Ashworth, show the Town Hall and the proposed replacement of it with a market. The plan was unsuccessful.

The unsuccessful Okehampton plan.

A second building which was not constructed: Ashworth designed a new market for South Molton in 1860 but the plan was rejected.

First of three paintings of inn signs at Hatherleigh painted in the early nineteenth century by John Smale Short. The artist wrote 'a young man named John Petherick who lived at the Royal Oak came outside his door with a loaded gun in his hand when a number of boys were at play opposite in the lower market house. The boys began to tease him by crying out 'shoot Jan shoot three red owls'. The man became so exasperated that he fired the contents of his gun at the boys when one of them named Westlake, who was sitting on the shambles, was shot dead on the spot and several others wounded. Petherick was apprehended and committed to gaol to take his trial at the assizes. He was acquitted of the murder in consequence of one of the witnesses pronouncing him to be insane at the time he committed the rash act. This John Petherick died in the year 1813, aged 69. The sign was painted similar to the drawing annexed. The house afterwards got into a dilapidated state and fell down which has since been rebuilt and made into three dwellings'.

Of the second sign the artist wrote 'about the commencement of the reign of George I (1714), the following curious occurrence took place at one of our fairs. A farmer sold some oxen to a cattle dealer on credit for which a note of hand was to be given and to be made payable at the next Hatherleigh Fair. During this dark age, when it was found difficult to obtain a person being able to write, a Mr Redstone was employed to write the intended security, for which purpose the parties repaired to the George & Dragon Inn. Mr Redstone enquired in what manner the note should be drawn. 'In what manner you please Sir' was the reply, 'as we are not able to write or read our selves'. Accordingly, the note was made and lodged in the hands of the landlord. At the time appointed for payment the cattle dealer was very punctual in performing his promise. The money paid and the note given up. The parties desired to have the note read over when the following lines was all it contained:
'The days of old when Sir Francis did flourish,
My breeches were tore, behind and before,
And my [blank] had nearly perished'.
The inn is still called the George and Dragon.

had been known as 'God's Acre' but was, by the early 1900s, known locally as 'Dog's Acre'.[132] Cecil Torr of Wreyland remembered in 1918 that a local man built a bungalow and named it *Chez-nous* but the locals thought it was Chestnuts. Another writer noted a fashion in Bishopsteignton in the late nineteenth century for renaming houses with each subsequent owner: he felt that later generations would find it difficult to trace the history of domestic buildings. But interestingly, he believed the positive aspect was that houses named after naval men were being renamed: there was 'a constant increase of western hero worship, the survival of fewer shrines may be all for the best'. Torr also noted the identification of houses with their owners: the Bovey Tracey home of a boy named Flood, who was christened with the name Noah, was known as the Ark. It is doubtful that it is still.[133] Another loss is signage for hotels and public houses.[134] One writer in 1894 reflected upon those in Teignmouth and thought the names for these 26 establishments could be separated into 13 groups: these included agricultural (Gardener's Arms), Astronomical (Half Moon), Artificial (Bee Hive, Locomotive, Ring of Bells), Geographical (London, Dawlish), Historical (Sebastopol, Royal Oak), Nautical (Anchor, Ship, Jolly Sailor, Life Boat), Proverbial (Bird in Hand), Regal (Royal), Titular (William IV, Queens,

Prince of Wales), Topographical (Market, Railway, Custom House, Old Quay, New Quay), Zoological (Black Horse, White Hart) and Miscellaneous (Commercial). In the following years the signs changed as well as the establishments.[135] Private signs evolve and disappear. That for William Ellis of Belstone in about 1902 was a curiosity then: his sign above the door to his thatched cottage announced he was a photographer, sold Dartmoor views, was a Dartmoor guide, repaired watches and clocks, sold chemical manure and seeds and was the port reeve of the manor.[136]

The definition of heritage could easily include local celebrations, festivities and observances. Plymouth no longer celebrates Armada Day nor Exeter either its day in honour of Queen Maude nor Jesus Day which marked the city's deliverance from the Prayer Book Rebellion.[137] The local manner of celebrating the christening of babies was also formerly very different. In the 1830s one unidentified writer related the experiences of a man of Stoke Gabriel who was then about 80 years old. He wrote:

On the day appointed for his christening, which in Devonshire is a time of great festivity, particularly in that part of it where the[se] circumstances happened, a

Signboard which was found in a panelled room at Ottery St Mary and given to a dental hospital in Leicester Square in about 1900.

Photograph of the Butterwalk in Dartmouth, early twentieth century, with a tobacconist sign advertising 'Let & Let Live'.

number of guests had assembled at the house of his parents, near Widecombe, on the borders of Dartmoor. The custom was, on those occasions, for the guests to assemble, to be regaled with plenty of good cheer; more especially, a cheese, commonly called 'groaning cheese' was introduced, which used to be cut as soon as the little stranger made its appearance and was generally chosen of that size as to last as long as the good woman sat up to receive the congratulations of her neighbours, & a portion of it used to be reserved by the nurse, from superstitious motives, to be given to the first child they met with on their proceeding to the church.

It so happened that the house from which the party set out was some two or three miles from the church. The weather for some time previously had been wild and stormy. A considerable quantity of snow had fallen and still lay thick on the ground, bearing down by its weight the branches of the old pine trees, which grow here & there in that moor land district, & giving a gigantic appearance to the magnificent amphitheatre of dark hills which enclose the valley of Widecombe. They set out, however, a large party; the nurse with the infant in her lap, on a double horse; all went on merrily and arrived, all thought, in safety at the church, when they began to prepare themselves for the ceremony. The gentlemen in stroking down their hair or perhaps combing it. The ladies in unfolding and putting on their clean white aprons, which at those days were generally carried on visiting occasions folded up in a nice clean handkerchief & tied round the waist, nurse very patiently waited until this ceremony was over & was then helped off her horse, when dreadful to relate! The child was found wanting, & no one could give any account of him!

This of course, caused great consternation to the whole party & they immediately retraced their steps in search of the lost one, who was at last found dropped in safety on the turf, at about a mile distance. He was

raised from his cold bed, to the great joy of his parents at least & his honour, rejoicing that he was not to lose his fee, baptised him by the name of John.

The nurse seems to have let the child slip through the enormous bundle of clothes in which he had been enveloped & thus did not discover her loss until the arrival of the party at church.[138]

As interesting as this may be to those interested in social history, the observance of special days is one that continually evolves. There is no 'traditional' manner in which any one observance is observed be it a christening, Christmas or local feast days such as the one in North Tawton held on 29 June which was called 'Nanny Night's Revel' until about 1880.[139] Many such occasions are observed according to each generation or family's particular way. These are impossible to preserve in any meaningful way other than as records of how they were formerly observed.

Social institutions are continually created, reformed or ended. For instance the local establishment of Friendly Societies followed those in the rest of the country with Axminster and South Molton taking the lead in Devon at the end of the eighteenth century. That at Bratton Clovelly was known locally as the Bratton Death Club and was intended to provide funds to assist with funerals. It was dissolved in 1897, like many others throughout Devon, a victim of social change as they were superseded by government legislation. Even the memories of their Club Walks, once a feature of village life, have diminished and merged with walking the parish bounds.[140] All of the societies formed by Devonians who lived out of the county have disappeared: the London Devonian Association was founded in 1888 but no longer exists nor does the London Bidefordian Society, the Society of Devonians in Bristol, the Devonians in Liverpool and District, the Portsmouth and District Devonian Society or the Devonian Society of Montreal.

Equally at risk of complete disappearance are forms of

First of two pen and washes by George Wightwick, of 1828 but sketched in 1858, entitled 'Devonshire Interior, Number 2'. He wrote 'the principal object is Miss Damart, with her funny little 'puds' of feet, and the huge oval scuttle bonnet of the period, 1828. Facts should speak for themselves, and the observer, will observe that there is not one touch of imagination in the picture. I spoke of the 'youngest child', ie the youngest of the mother who was seen at the pasty in the last picture. The child in the cradle is her grandchild: ask no more. The little boy nursing it is also – equivocal: the Devonshire customs are speculative. The peasantry scorn regularity, as may be seen by the Ballad of the Negro, which is by no means 'square' with the horizontal of the joists above, or with the perpendicular of the chimney piece. The fire opening illustrates the fallacy of supposing that an arch can not exist without a key-stone…'

transport: public hire chairs had been common in Plymouth and Exeter in the eighteenth century but by the middle of the nineteenth century they were dying out. Sedan chairs were replaced by horse-drawn carriage but at least one Devon example has survived in the Royal Albert Memorial Museum in Exeter.[141]

It would be hard to argue that some foodstuffs should not also be considered. One Victorian's enthusiastic schoolboy memories of mutton pies made by a Kingsbridge baker make interesting reading: the 'crisp crust and juicy mutton' illustrates how society's food has changed and how much has been lost.[142] There are no longer the food hawkers formerly found in the streets: at Plymouth in the middle of the nineteenth century Mr Pash and Mr Norman called out 'Pies all hot, hot baked potatoes', another shouted 'Ginger breads 3d a packet and 1 over' and yet one more called 'sheep's trotters, $1\frac{1}{2}$d each, all hot'. In winter another man shouted 'Muffins and crumpets, all hot'. There are also no longer

the Victorian Basket Women who carried meat, butter and vegetables chosen in the markets by local ladies and brought it home for them.[143] Few recipe books survive which show the introduction of new foodstuffs and the changes in diet and cooking.

Few folk songs have survived for Devon and the main collection is one collected by the Reverend Baring Gould in the late nineteenth century but his recordings were not wholly accurate in respect to bawdy songs: the cleric censored words he thought improper.[144] Perhaps the county did not a great tradition of folk singing but we shall never know. Dialect and folklore have long been collected by the Devonshire Association but oral traditions in the county have become a minority interest perhaps because so little has been preserved.

No doubt the greatest loss to the county are the experiences of Devonians who pass away each year, each of whom has made an individual contribution to the history of the county and only a small portion of their

lives are remembered. Many people, particularly the poor, were also forced to emigrate; as early as 1637 four men were sent to Barbados.[145] This might not seem like punishment today but then it was a death sentence. Manuscripts relating to Devon are taken by these emigrants, or produced by them abroad, and most remain overseas. William Harding was one emigrant to Newfoundland: he was born in Bideford in 1793, worked as a blacksmith in Plymouth Dock and was there on the news of the victory at Waterloo. He recorded his memories ('what rejoicing there was! Poor mothers and sisters rejoiced to see their children and brothers come back safely and the main street that we had to pass through there was an arch erected across the street with *See the heroes come on it*'), commented on local people such as John Wood of Appledore who made iron work for ships ('a rank Methodist') and recalled Bideford's celebration in 1810 for the fiftieth anniversary of George III's reign. He remembered:

A dinner was cooked for hundreds of poor people in a large street where most of the gentry of the town lived called New Buildings. Tables were placed each side of the street from end to end, and the ladies and gentlemen served out plenty to eat and drink to the poor men, women and children. The band playing their instruments of music all the time of dinner, they played many pretty tunes and among the rest were God Save the King, Rule Brittania and the Roast Beef of Old England. Before and after dinner every trade and calling marched in succession with a specimen of their different trades and callings. Each trade had its Coats of Arms. Ours as blacksmiths, was a yellow silk flag with 3 crowns and under the crowns 3 hammers. It was sent down from the Board in London and cost ten pounds. That was paid for by ourselves. At night the town was illuminated & beautifully, thousands of people from neighbouring towns & villages were there to see the sights.[146]

Second view of the same cottage in the West Devon village of Marystow, picturesque in a nostalgic fashion but few today would want to swap places. Wightwick wrote 'my dear friend William Jacobson [later Bishop of Chester] said he would meet Mr Wightwick and Miss Damant at Maristow, on a certain day, to picnic it. I will come, said he, if it rains cats and dogs. Mr W. and Miss D. (all proper, they were engaged), went. It rained furiously. Mr Jacobson did not come. The young couple (they are an old one now) went for shelter into a cottage... Strictly speaking, the sketcher must be supposed to be in the fire, before he could take it; but he was not in the fire, and yet he took it. The woman is minding her pasty, which she is making for her husband's dinner tomorrow. The youngest child is minding its mother. The next youngest is sitting on the stairs, minding nothing in particular. The rest of the maidens are out at service'.

Thoughts and recollections of those who remained in Devon can also be lost. In the early nineteenth century one Hatherleigh man noted three comments placed in his parish register from the eighteenth century. The cleric had written:

James Boyd, Scots peddler, and Joanna Pengelley, spinster, both living in this parish married 23rd October 1755. This man, aged about 60, was six feet tall & proportioned accordingly, his spouse, aged about 40, and born in the parish of Belstone near Okehampton, was barely three feet and one inch in stature.

Bartholomew Vogwell, fellmonger, and Alice Bissett, spinster, married 22nd May 1757. This woman had five bastards by a married man, had done penance in the church and yet boasted herself to be no whore because as she said she kept to one only. For this her shame is registered.

Thomas Lillycrop, blacksmith, and Mary Abel, spinster, married 17 April 1763. This wench was without constraint from friends married on Sunday to a young lusty fond husband & without provocation from him ran away the next Wednesday with a soldier. She was assisted in her escape by Mary the daughter of James Angel, senior, which latter wench knew her to be going to her adulterer.[147]

The three episodes in the lives of these twelve people show the continuing interest in the unusual and even the joy of shared gossip irrespective of whether individuals are living or dead. Few of the many millions of such tales are recorded and so are lost to time.

One other recorded example is a book of notes written by a Tavistock schoolboy from the late seventeenth century: while practicing his Greek and Latin he copied popular sayings of the time, some of which are still said and others have been forgotten, including 'to strive against the stream', 'a great cry but little wool', 'brag is a good dog but hold fast is a better', 'every dog will eat dirty pudding', 'near is my shirt but nearer is my skin', 'I talk of chalk and you of cheese, 'save a thief from hanging and he'll cut your throat', 'give a man luck and show him into the sea', 'the more haste the worse the speed', 'to teach one's granddame to suck', 'as cunning as a dead pig', 'the farthest way about is the nearest way home', 'if the sky fall we shall catch larks', 'many talk of Robin Hood that never shot in his bow' and 'its better to play a small game than to stand out'.[148] Fortunately his notes were kept but many aspects of millions of other Devonians were not. In most regards the experiences of past Devonians were very much like those today but historical events and changes in society shaped the lives of people in ways which are now difficult to understand. The life of Thomas Roberts is a good example of this. He was born in the eighteenth century and while a young boy in the navy at Plymouth he had the unfortunate experience of his hands being shattered by an exploding grenade. Both hands were amputated and he had wooden replacements. Roberts subsequently went to Clovelly Court where he served as secretary to Mr Hamlyn and taught local boys to draw and write. In 1797 he moved to Hatherleigh and established a boarding school for boys. He taught navigation, among other things, and dug out a pond on the moor for his students

Engraving of the Logan or Rocking Stone in about 1800. It is difficult to know how easily it may have once rocked.

to sail their hand-made boats.[149] It would be difficult not to feel not only compassion but admiration for this man and his achievements.

Uncertain reasons for loss

Possibly the majority of losses have taken place for reasons which can no longer be ascertained. This is the case of the Nutcrackers, a Logan Stone which measured some eleven feet in diameter, in Widecombe-in-the-Moor, which in the 1790s was described as having been removed by its owner. Like all other similar stones it was so carefully balanced that a little movement made it rock back and forth: the 'common people' were said to frequent it during the autumn to crack their nuts. For some uncertain reason, possibly malice, the stone was deliberately taken to a new location where it ceased to operate.[150]

There are no known reasons for why so few household accounts have survived for Devon. Of the hundreds which were written between the Reformation and the Civil War, only four are known still to exist.[151] Few others survive before that date and it is surprising that there are not more for the eighteenth and nineteenth centuries. It could be assumed that subsequent generations saw little reason to save such papers and discarded them but fire, damp and even jam-making has claimed some accounts. Other original material has long been missing: in 1928 it was pointed out that a map of Barnstaple, allegedly dating to 1584, was then missing. It is uncertain what happened to it.[152]

Many villages and towns had prominent trees but the reasons for their not surviving have not often been recorded. For instance, Seven Trees, a nineteenth-century house in Plymouth, is now owned by the National Health Service but the collection of trees it is named after has long been forgotten. Many other local places are named after long-forgotten trees or will be once the trees have died: this includes Three Ash Cross near Membury, Three Elms Cross near Clyst St Lawrence, Three Firs in Clyst

Hydon, Three Limbed Oak near Thorverton, Three Sycamores Cross near Colyton and Three Tree Lane near Teignmouth. Increasingly places are also given names which bear no actual significance to them particularly those names with social aspirations such as bartons and manor houses. Other places are named after two, four, five, seven, eight, nine and twelve trees but curiously not one Devon place seems to be associated with six trees. House names are another example in which the associated tree, flower or shrub has long disappeared from memory. Other examples of prominent trees can be drawn from maps such as that of Cullompton of 1633 which shows a tree prominently placed in the High Street but no further information on it has been found at least by this author.[153] Many trees have had local significance such as Stumpy Oak at Hawson's Cross in Buckfastleigh,[154] the Great Oak of Umberleigh,[155] the Hankford Oak in Monkleigh,[156] Great Tree at Bretonside in Plymouth,[157] the Old White Elm in Beer,[158] the Paradise Tree in Bideford,[159] King John's Oak at Shute,[160] and the Wishing Tree at Berry Pomeroy.[161] The Sprite Tree, otherwise known as the Echo Tree, stood in Stowford parish until it was cut down in 1930 for some undetermined reason. Associated with this beech tree was the story it was haunted by the ghost of a page boy.[162] One writer recorded a number of notable trees in the late eighteenth century; Bidwell Tree stood in Dartington in the late eighteenth century and was renowned for its size, an impressive beech tree was in Rackenford churchyard, another beech in the parish of High Bickington was said to have been planted on the day that Charles I was executed and two trees that grew in Woolfardisworthy in North Devon on the St James Tree estate had a legend that two supporters of the Duke of Monmouth were executed on them. Their subsequent histories is less easy to trace than the yew trees which Polwhele recorded in churchyards at Kenn, Mamhead, Stoke Gabriel, Dartington and Staverton.[163] The natural long life of a yew tree has been enhanced by the prominence and security of their public locations often denied trees on private land. The reasons for the loss of other prominent trees are often not recorded. This is also true of the thousands of mulberry trees sent to Devon in 1609 by James I. He had hoped to start a silk industry in the country and among those who received trees was the Earl of Bath whose main residence was Tawstock in north Devon. There are no known reasons why his one thousand Devon trees, nor any of the others, have perished.[164]

Equally uncertain is the current location of the Norman font at Chagford. It was found buried in the parish church in about 1865, broken while being removed and then the fragments taken to the rectory for safekeeping where they were allegedly buried in the garden. Holsworthy's font, also thought to have been Norman, was likewise last used as a garden ornament.[165] A Royalist cleric travelled through Devon with the King's army during the Civil War and noted stained glass in churches such as at Spreyton, Lifton and Tavistock as well as at Exeter Cathedral: the reasons for the lack of this glass today could be ascribed to Puritan soldiers, Victorian renovators or many others.[166] Many buildings have an uncertain history of loss: one writer was puzzled if a curious small building at the entrance to Buckland Monachorum's churchyard had been lost through fire in 1832 or left to fall into a dilapidated state.[167]

It is rare to be able to chronicle changing uses of many items: one exception is a piece of carved granite used as a market cross that was placed against the market house in South Brent but when that building was demolished the cross was removed to a court behind the Anchor Hotel. Sometime afterwards it was broken and used to construct a building in nearby Diptford.[168] Some losses are more gradual: the Logan Stone on the Teign River, near Drewsteignton, was famous for its movement in the eighteenth century but a hundred years later it hardly moved.[169] But many buildings, probably the majority, are merely adapted to meet current needs rather than being demolished. Others change for a great number of reasons including changes in fashion, technology or for commercial reasons but these are seldom recorded.

Some elements of Devon's heritage have changed for reasons that do not easily fit in any of the sections that follow. For example, the reason given for Gabriel St Clere pulling down his medieval home in Budleigh is unusual: St Clere was said to have been remorseful over his lavish life of 'excessive hospitality' which he regarded as sinful. He sold the timber, stone and glass but another writer doubted him and thought he had merely feigned madness.[170] In the eighteenth century one local man lived at Hatherleigh in what was described as a wooden house drawn on wheels: he was a barber, with a sign which said 'I shave neat and clean, a new face for a halfpenny by me Humphry Toms', but although the reasons for the non-survival of his abode have not been recorded, they could be discussed in several sections below.[171]

Chapter Three

Neglect, vandalism and theft

A considerable portion of Devon's heritage has been lost through vandalism, theft and neglect. For others the causes are uncertain. Whole collections are missing such as the papers of the Veitch family. This firm, which sent plant hunters across the world in the nineteenth century, made an extraordinary impact on not just Devon's landscape but on Britain as a whole. Even though the firm's legacy lives on in gardens and parks across the county the loss of the papers is unfortunate because it deprives us of understanding it more fully.[172] An

interesting group of bronze Penates, found at Exeter in the 1770s, has since been lost. These Roman household gods were evidently owned by Sidmouth's Orlando Hutchinson but their subsequent history is a mystery. He intended to give them to the Royal Albert Memorial Museum in 1875.[173] Devon has had three collectors of Pacific artefacts in the eighteenth century, two of which were, confusingly, connected with captains with the surnames Cook and Cooke. Both have since been dispersed. The first was collected by Captain Joseph Cooke of Wortham Manor, including high status objects, and sold at The White Horne in Lifton in 1813. Some items have since been collected by the Royal Albert Memorial Museum. The second relates to the illustrious

Engraving of the Penates found at Exeter in 1778 at the corner of High Street with Broad Gate. They were discovered some three feet below the pavement during the digging of a cellar. A large quantity of oyster shells surrounded the figures.

Captain James Cook and his 3rd expedition to the Pacific in 1781. It was purchased for Richard Hall Clarke of Bridwell in 1806 and housed in a private museum in the grounds. The objects, including Hawaiian bowls, drums and temple images, were sold in 1967 with no understanding of their international significance. It is possible sale objects remain in Devon with owners who do not understand the significance of their purchases.[174]

Some losses are accidental: on a November night in 1937 'a motorised machine' was involved in an accident in which Marchant's Cross in Meavy was hit and broken into two parts. The cross was subsequently repaired and re-erected in the same place with the original stone stump placed at Meavy Church.[175] Likewise, in 1830 an accident with a cart broke the top of Alphington's cross.[176] A more serious case happened in 1957 when a timber lorry hit the Castle and Keys monument at Totnes: this early nineteenth-century monument was demolished shortly afterwards.[177] Many losses are due to neglect,

inaction, vandalism, theft or a combination of all four. In 1843 one writer, reflecting upon the church of Ottery St Mary, thought that 'time, wilful mutilations and theft have conspired to destroy many of the inscriptions and brasses which formerly existed in this church; and some there are, which are fast hastening to destruction'.[178] Forty years later another Devonian contemplated 'much which is worthy of careful preservation is very frequently lost or destroyed, either by the hand of the vandal or the person whose ignorance has prevented him from realising the irreparable injury of which his conduct has been the cause'.[179] There are some items of which very little is known and the reasons for their loss are equally uncertain. A map of part of Bideford in the 1690s has survived which was probably part of a larger collection. The owners, the Grenville family at Stowe, were lords of the manor of Bideford and had already commissioned the map-maker to survey their Cornish land. These maps, known as the Stowe Atlas, survive but the existence of

Photograph of the 'Taunton Monument' at Totnes, 1910. It was erected in 1825 by Mayor William Doidge Taunton on the New Walk, a place to promenade along the river. The folly was demolished in the 1950s.

Annery, in the North Devon parish of Monkleigh, in about 1850. It was demolished in the late 1950s after a long period of decline.

Devon maps has been conjectured because the single map has written on it the number twenty-eight and possible stitching suggests it was once bound.[180]

Neglect

Some items have been misplaced. For example, it is unknown what happened to three prehistoric urns found by the Reverend John Swete in the summer of 1773 at Haldon. He investigated these while workmen were appropriating building materials from a barrow known as Great Stoneheap. One urn stood some thirteen inches high and was at Oxton House in Kenton at the end of the eighteenth century but its current location is unknown.[181] It is probably disinterest that caused the loss of the citrus trees at Combe Royal near Kingsbridge. These trees were planted against a purpose-built stone wall which was probably built in the early nineteenth century. Its importance lies in that it may be unique in the country but the diligence needed in caring for these exotic trees

does not fit with its current use despite attempts by the Devon Gardens Trust and others in restoring the wall and reinstating the trees.[182]

Manuscripts have suffered particularly badly from disinterested neglect. In 1893 some of Exeter's documents were housed in paper boxes in a 'wooden lumber room' at the back of the Guildhall. Before they reached that room Stuart Moore, the barrister had been paid £1,000 to sort them, reported that the conditions, as discussed on pages 34–35, were in a deplorable state and recommended many were discarded.[183] At Torquay in 1839 local officials searched for parish records but only found a nearly empty box: they suspected that books, deeds and other papers had been spirited away. At about the same time parish documents were auctioned off, as part of the effects of a parish official, as waste paper.[184] In Barnstaple the town's documents were moved when the Guildhall was taken down in the early 1800s and then taken to an outbuilding where some were used for lighting fires. J. R. Chanter rescued the remainder a generation later.[185] Plymouth's documents also suffered through the same cause: in 1884 it was remembered that a significant portion of the town's papers were allowed to perish and others to fall into private hands when the collection was transferred from the old Guildhall to the Free Library.[186] It may have been a prevailing attitude: at about the same time it was said of Plymouth, and possibly of its records, that 'vandals have been running riot in the town for years, and it is almost hopeless now to preserve the relics of the past'.[187] At Bideford, as late as the 1940s, it was claimed that many of the ancient documents had been destroyed and of the remainder a great many had been laid aside or forgotten.[188]

Churches have also suffered, for instance it was claimed that the reason for the poor state of the church at Plympton Erle in 1835 was the parishioners' apathy.[189] This lack of interest or awareness can be seen across Devon. In about 1827 a clergyman convinced the parishioners of Lamerton to sell their ancient stained glass 'for a mere trifle' and a cartload of it left the village never to be seen again.[190] Many fonts have not had a

happy history. One unidentified rural parish replaced its ancient font and the vicar then used it as a flowerpot in his garden.[191] It also happened at Lympstone.[192] A Norman font at Sampford Peverell was also replaced by 1847 and used for catching rainwater at the schoolroom[193] while the font at Holcombe Rogus was discarded through lack of interest. In 1847 it was perceived as a curiosity: it was described as being 'a hexagonal cupboard, 2 foot 6 inches in diameter, upon a tall stem in diameter about 6 inches; two sides of the hexagonal served as a door to the cupboard, in the centre of which stood a small wooden pint bowl, nailed to the bottom, and strange to say, having an open water-drain.' The observer concluded 'It is well to be able to number it among things that were'.[194] By 1852 the church at Wembury had a new font because the ancient predecessor was taken home by a wealthy parishioner. The screen was destroyed because an 'ignorant churchwarden' pulled it down in spite of orders from the incumbent.[195] Even so, some fonts themselves have a curious lineage: that at Dolton was previously a decorated Saxon cross shaft.[196]

Was it because of indifference that the ancient carved

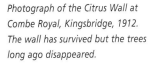

Photograph of the Citrus Wall at Combe Royal, Kingsbridge, 1912. The wall has survived but the trees long ago disappeared.

wooden bench ends at Chulmleigh were buried beneath the floor? In 1882 it was reported they had been rediscovered there and new ones carved based on the old designs; 'Harry Hems and his merrie men carved all these benches at Exeter'.[197] It is difficult to understand the treatment of two alabaster effigies removed during the rebuilding of the medieval church of St Mary Major in Exeter. The figures, described as nuns and presumably medieval stonework, were designated as rubbish and taken by a man as toys for his young children. After spending some time as playthings in a back garden the sculptures were eventually rescued by an Exeter merchant but their current whereabouts is unknown.[198]

Items of personal interest often become irrelevant once the owners are dead, for instance there are many thousands of photographs being taken in Devon each year and probably just as many destroyed because the memories have little subsequent value. Many trees are also planted for particular purposes but subsequently lose their designations and importance. Few villagers remember rows of trees planted to mark Royal occasions but nevertheless pass along Victorian avenues on a daily basis. Two hundred cherry trees given by Japanese diplomats in 1936 to the

University of Exeter were planted with due ceremony at the time but forgotten with some embarrassment during the second world war and the years that followed.[199] One of the last of these, nearly seventy years later, has recently been cut down along Prince of Wales Road and with it any memory has vanished like those of many thousands of other ceremonial trees before it.

Vandalism

Reckless acts of destruction has lost many parts of Devon's heritage. Was it greed or spitefulness that caused the theft of the commemorative coins placed in the foundation stone of Blackborough's new Victorian church[200] or the driving of hat pins into the ancient pews in North Bovey's church by 1853?[201] Most probably the east and west windows of Cornwood church needed replacing in the late nineteenth century but a later writer was surprised to find medieval tracery discarded in an adjacent hedge.[202] One of the most elaborate clocks made in Devon was destroyed through vandalism in the 1940s: Jacob Lovelace created The Exeter Clock, a highly ornamental piece of work, in 1739 (see following Illustration). It survived for just over two hundred years

Seventeenth-century grafitti in a Devon church.

Detail of lithograph of The Exeter Clock made by Jacob Lovelace in the early eighteenth century. It was destroyed by vandals in the 1940s.

and was at Liverpool Museum during the second world war when a bomb in 1941 caused damage. It met its final moments through a gang of boys who subsequently destroyed it.[203] Boys were also suggested as the reason why Crediton's ancient parish library was in a poor state in 1911: Beatrix Cresswell thought that Grammar School students mistreated the books.[204] Vandalism has been attributed to one of the county's leading aristocrats in the eighteenth century: Lawell House in Chudleigh was bought by Lord Clifford in 1768 but supposedly dismantled by him because the Princess of Wales, when travelling through the area, mistook it for Ugbrooke. He also obscured the view of the house with thick tree plantations.[205] The Otterton parish record book of ancient memorabilia was destroyed in about 1763 by what was later thought to have been 'mean and interested policy'. Possibly it was in the financial interests of a parishioner that legal papers were lost.[206] In 1900 William Crossing catalogued a number of acts he considered 'sheer wantoness'. He noted an apprentice had celebrated his freedom by wrecking havoc among ancient stones, two boys broke the shaft of Siward's Cross while searching for cattle and the clappers at Post Bridge and Bellaford were vandalised but the men later regretted their actions.[207] It could also be said that vandalism was the cause of the destruction of a Dartmoor cairn in 1892 by a group of Ordnance Map surveyors.[208]

Institutions have also been accused of vandalism. That was the reason given for the destruction of one ancient sycamore tree cut down in Plymouth's North Hill in the middle of the nineteenth century: one local man believed it was cut down to provide snuff boxes for the mayor and his fellow councillors. He felt the council were the great enemies of the local trees and that they actively cut down as many as possible.[209] One of the lasting, and more serious, accusations concerns Exeter City Council; it has been widely accused of acts of greater vandalism in the post world war two period when important buildings, such as Bedford Circus, were removed from choice rather than necessity.[210]

Other acts have been done in what could be described as, at best, an apparently unthinking manner. For example, a house painter at Plympton School painted over sketches on the walls by Sir Joshua Reynolds but was not thought to have been malicious. The sketches had been preserved but he was 'ignorant of their value and interest'.[211] Was it vandalism when labourers, who were renovating Prince Hall on Dartmoor, destroyed the granite tables and seats used for the Stannary Parliament at Crockern Tor? They used fragments for the new building but it seems improbable that other surface stone could not have been just as feasible.[212]

Public buildings have suffered particularly badly. Norman fonts were removed from many churches in the nineteenth century, in the spirit of improvement, and sent out to churchyards such as those at Luppit and Shaldon. These were later rescued and brought back into the churches but others have been lost altogether.[213] Another at Buckland-in-the-Moor was not destroyed but its base was so thickly covered with cement during its 'restoration' that it elicited the response:

it is almost incredible that anyone could be found with so little perception as to do this thing: to rob the font of its unique characteristic, and to degrade it in this particularly hideous way. Again, round the rim was a band of Norman stone ornament; this has been almost obliterated by the same offensive cement.[214]

Equally unexplainable were the Victorian restorations involving chiselling ornamentation from fonts: in about 1840 a chisel removed the decoration on the Norman font at Bickleigh near Tiverton.[215] In 1877 one study of Devon's effigies concluded that a main reason for the loss of so many of these ancient sculptures was the:

seemingly irresistible propensity for pure mischief, indulged in often by ordinary people visiting them or workmen engaged in the repair of the sacred edifice, and exhibited not only in carving wretched initials and dates everywhere, but also in defacing the salient parts of the figure, or cunningly worked ornaments of the tomb until what was once a beautifully harmonious composition, full of grace and symbolism, is reduced to an almost shapeless piece of mutilation.

The writer also blamed disinterest on the part of those responsible for their care.[216] Restorers at Trusham may have had good intentions but it is hard to justify their cutting the Norman font to accommodate a new pew.[217]

There has not been local incidents of civil unrest within Devon which has led to serious destruction of property other than the Prayer Book Rebellion and the Civil War. Throughout the dozens of local bread riots damage was limited and the closest Devon got to devastation of any consequence was in 1625 when crowds threatened to burn Exeter unless helped during an outbreak of plague.[218] But curiously, there was some damage done to Devon records in civil unrest outside the county: during the Gordon Riots at Bath in 1780 crowds burnt the Catholic archives for Devon housed there.[219]

Photograph of the figure of Venus, stolen at a press conference at Exeter.

Finally, there is one curious note of vandalism to a monument erected to mark other vandalism: in 1981 a tombstone earlier erected at Ide to mourn the loss of the tranquillity of the Ide Valley through road-building was itself destroyed by vandals.[220]

Theft

Unfortunately many items have been lost through theft. One of the most startling examples is of a Roman figure of Venus found in Exeter in the 1970s. It was stolen at a press conference on the Roman Baths.[221] Of course there are many thousands of examples of other thefts. For instance, in 1875 the removal of an Elizabethan portrait from Chudleigh was considered suspicious: until the middle of the nineteenth century the church had this painting on wood of a member of the Hunt family. It was of 'an elderly man in a kneeling posture, with a book open on a desk at his left hand and a high crowned hat on a table at his right. In the right hand corner of the tablet was painted '1601 *etat* 63 *Da Gloria Deu*'. The personage was dressed in a gown with long sleeves, guarded with velvet. Round his neck was a ruff, and descending from a ribbon was a golden badge, representing a small saw, chisel and mallet'. Enquiries were made as to how it left the church but the portrait was not found.[222] At Tavistock Abbey an ancient inscribed stone was discovered in the early nineteenth century but stolen shortly afterwards.[223] A fifteenth-century bell at Sheldon near Honiton was stolen in 1981 while at Gittisham a panel of stained glass, thought to be late medieval, was taken from the church in 1988.[224] Even more unusual disappearances, or thefts, can be identified: in about 1876 a pewter basin, which had been used as a font, was stolen from the church at Kentisbeare.[225]

The Chronicle of Barnstaple, one of the town's greatest treasures, and arguably its most important document, was lost as early as the end of the eighteenth century. It is unclear how it was taken from the town's collection of manuscripts. Possibly it was rescued from the heap of town documents destined for burning in the early nineteenth century but ownership, if it does exist, should rest with the town. This chronicle, written by Adam Wyatt, town clerk, from 1586 to 1611, had disappeared by 1810 and until recently the only copy was an incomplete one made sometime about 1770. Earlier extracts were recently discovered. This version appears to have been copied in the seventeenth century, possibly as early as the 1650s. The original chronicle, in which plague, grain shortages, extreme weather, privateering and the war with Spain are all detailed, may have existed as late as 1942 but it has disappeared.[226] The manuscripts of the eighteenth-century antiquarian William Chapple would be a significant find: they were last seen at Haldon House in the late nineteenth century.[227] Another important document which was stolen was Bickleigh's parish register: it was taken in 1574 and then recovered. Oddly enough, it was then lost again.[228] Other individual documents have been stolen and a great portion of parish records has been lost. Many parish registers written before the civil war have disappeared and it has been suggested that the office holders took them when ejected by Parliament. It is less likely that the successors would have thrown away the registers.[229]

Some unusual items have been lost not so much by theft as through an individual seizing upon private opportunity. The gibbet at Stoke Damerel, which was used to hang a notorious murderer in the early nineteenth century, is one good example. A local carpenter retrieved the wood after it collapsed and fell into the estuary. He used it to make commemorative ornamental snuffboxes. Few now would mourn the loss of the executioner's apparatus or of any of the others that also have not survived.[230] An unusual example of a heritage item which went missing is that of a white marble memorial to the Kelland family of Painsford. It had been erected in Ashprington church in the early eighteenth century but a portion of it somehow found its way out of that building and onto the antiquities market. The stonework is important in that it was the work of John Weston, a highly regarded mason who was working in Exeter at the beginning of the eighteenth century. His sculpture of the Last Judgement was said to have 'all the grace and movement of the Italian Renaissance'. Fortunately the most important part of it was saved through being purchased by the Royal Albert Memorial Museum in 1990.[231]

Thefts continue but not always in a traditional manner. The increasing interest in antiques and churches has led to burglaries aimed at heritage items.[232] For example, in

Sketch of a Millbridge execution, 1789, with a gibbet similar to that made into snuff boxes in the early nineteenth century.

The Last Judgement by John Weston, which has had a surprising exit from a Devon church but fortunately has been acquired by Royal Albert Memorial Museum, with a detail of the sculpture.

2003 three late fifteenth-century paintings were taken from the rood screen at Torbryan church near Torquay and an altar cross and two plates, possibly made in the eighteenth century, were stolen from Calverleigh church.[233] Many large country houses which are unoccupied, most aptly illustrated by Poltimore outside Exeter, have suffered the removal of great portions of decorative work. Finally, burglaries in more ordinary homes have the unfortunate effect of taking personal items; once stolen these objects lose the family and other associations they hold once in the hands of subsequent owners.

Chapter Four

Change of purpose and funding

Loss also occurs when there is a change in function or funding. One of the less commonly-thought of losses involves the selling of property. Important fittings are vulnerable to being sold separately from their historic contexts: one example of this was the sale of a series of English historical sculptures associated with Charles Smith for the sculpture gallery at Anthony Salvin's Mamhead. They were auctioned in London in 1987.[234] Also lost were some items of furniture built by William White for his Gothic revival Bishop's Court which was also sold separately from the building in the 1990s. Furniture is a continual concern given it can be sold independently. Endsleigh for example has pieces which are part of the original fabric of the house.

This type of change has often led to dilapidation: at least this was the reason given for the loss of the church-house at Cruwys Morchard which had its stones and timber reused to build a pound house to make cider in 1675.[235] It was also the stated cause for the rebuilding of the chapel of Combpyne Rousdon in 1872.[236] Chudleigh's workhouse was also reportedly ruined when it was taken down. It was rebuilt in 1818 and subsequently turned into the National School. Two years later the town's almshouse, a two-storey building of five rooms each with a wooden gallery, was sold by the parish and taken down presumably because it too was in a bad condition.[237] Another example is the ancient house of Netherton in Farway which in 1793 was described as 'a picture of ruin'. It could have been for any number of reasons why the building was allowed to reach this state, including loss of money, changing fashion, or dereliction through fire, damp or even death watch beetle, but no further information was given.[238] Many buildings have been

poorly built or reach a point where it is more feasible to rebuild than refurbish. This was the case with Blackborough's Victorian parish church which was demolished in 1994 because it was structurally unsound after only a century and a half.[239]

It is unusual to find, before 1800, the reasons given for rebuilding ordinary houses whereas public buildings are more likely to be recorded. One example is Widworthy's church which had its roof replaced in 1785 because the old one was 'decayed'.[240] On 6 March 1618 the Stannary Court at Chagford collapsed: a greater number than usual attended the court and the building, which stood on decayed pillars, collapsed under the weight and ten individuals lost their lives when the walls fell in. The attention paid to this event was partly derived from it being a public building.[241] Demolition of parsonages are likely to be recorded because permission was needed. Thus in 1837 a new vicarage was built at Abbotskerswell because it was in 'a very ruinous state and condition'.[242] Ashburton's ancient market house was pulled down in 1850 because it too was dilapidated. This medieval building, of some 120 feet in length and largely built of oak, was replaced by that now used as the town hall. In the middle of the nineteenth century the ground floor was used to sell vegetables and meat and the upper storey to sell grain.[243] It may be for the same reason that Okehampton's Shambles were pulled down in 1666.[244]

Many significant individual items considered worn out by their owners have found use elsewhere: the rector of Tiverton sent his rood screen to Holcombe Rogus in 1854 because he considered it beyond repair. It is still there.[245] Some items were regarded as too important and restored such as a stone image on Exeter Cathedral's West Front which fell in 1854 and broke. In other parts of the county the stonework might have been forgotten but the public prominence of the medieval stone screen gave it a happier future.[246] Other items have been lost because their owners had no interest. This may be the reason why Wembury House lost its once famous Elizabethan fish

The parish church of Blackborough in about 1840. It was demolished in 1994.

pool. It was situated on the shoreline where sluice gates allowed in tidal water but trapped the stray fish once the sea receded. The salt-water pond was probably unique in Devon although there was a Cornish counterpart. This marvel appears to have become disused as the fortunes of the house declined.[247]

Another unusual loss are the 'tomestones' or 'tombstones' on which business transactions took place. Barnstaple still has its stone in place at Queen Anne's Walk but that at Bideford was lost many years ago. It has been suggested that Hartland, Tiverton and Exeter, as well as Bristol, had similar stones.[248] Presumably the

increasing use of paper made deals using the public stones largely redundant.

One of Devon's more visible reminders of changing economics, with the loss of function and or funding, is mining. Tin became of less financial consequence as early as the seventeenth century and Dartmoor is littered with the remains of an industry which occupied locals for hundreds of years. Other mining operations with exhausted supplies, or no longer become financially viable, have often disappeared without leaving much physical evidence behind such as the Elizabethan silver mine at Combe Martin, the iron works on the edge of

Painting of Ashburton Market, by 1850 when the market was demolished.

Exmoor and the late Victorian iron mine at Newton Abbot. The latter mine, known as the Wolborough Iron Mine operated in the 1870s but when it closed the land was restored to agricultural use according to its lease.[249] Most commercial enterprises leave behind some physical reminders. One of the more surprising is the Sourton Tors Iceworks on north-west Dartmoor. Here from 1874 to 1886 an initiative was made to make ice using the natural elements. The tiers of ponds and remains of buildings can be seen today.[250] Attempts to mine lead and barites-bearing mineral veins in the Teign valley parish of Bridford were also financially unsuccessful but have left behind surface mineworks.[251] Commercial change led to the closure of the whetstone pits sited along the Blackdown Hills that were worked from the eighteenth to early twentieth centuries.[252] The evidence of quarrying, whether the few commercial ones or the hundreds of small private quarries used for personal use, is evident throughout Devon. Generally little can be done with

these excavated rock faces but in the late eighteenth century the Reverend Swete created a medieval hermitage out of his and on the Haine estate in Stowford the Harris family transformed a quarry into St Hubert's Hall, a small open-air arena with 17 stone seats as a meeting place for local huntsmen.[253]

Castles

Nearly every castle in Devon has lost its original purpose and lies in ruins. Berry Pomeroy was too far from London to be the significant country mansion that Lord Seymour anticipated in the sixteenth century. Devon's distance from the Court meant that neither Henry VIII nor any of his successors visited until Charles I came briefly in 1625.[254] The site of Torrington Castle had become a bowling green by 1822 and the chapel, which was converted into a schoolhouse, was demolished by 1780.[255] Exeter's Rougemont Castle is still, but not for much longer, the seat of county justice and has been since the

Norman Conquest. But it is no longer a defensive site. Inland castles such as Bampton, Lydford and Totnes are more likely to be in ruins given the little call for defence in those places. Only coastal defences were needed in the years following the Civil War. Dartmouth is still intact, and played its part in the second world war, but those at Teignmouth and Salcombe for instance have long gone. Plymouth's defences are the most impressive: with the citadel, St Nicholas's Island and the great string of Palmerston forts emphasising the town's national importance. The latter, a ring of inland fortifications, were built in the 1860s when there were public fears of a French invasion. But these quickly lost their purpose and other uses have been sought including a garden nursery and the Landmark Trust. The Ministry of Defence owns the remainder.[256] Other Devon forts have not fared as well. For instance, the late eighteenth-century fort at Sidmouth was abandoned after the Battle of Waterloo but brought back into service with the French invasion fears of 1859. However, it was never used, gradually fell into disrepair and absorbed into the town.[257] Temporary defences at Brixham, Torquay and Exmouth have also disappeared. The line of defence which is little noticed and will probably last long after many ancient castles have crumbled into dust are the second world war pillboxes, the indestructible mini-fortresses that stretch across Devon.

One reason for the loss of the defensive gates at Barnstaple, Exeter, Totnes and Plymouth was that they too no longer served a purpose. The last siege in Devon was more than three hundred years ago during the civil war and by the middle of the eighteenth century the gates were thought to be redundant and a hindrance (see pages 106–107). During the 1680s, when the Duke of Monmouth and then William of Orange disrupted the peace, there might have been doubts whether towns needed to be fortified but by the 1750s gates were being pulled down. No doubt some questioned this during the Napoleonic war but by then the deeds were done.

Country houses

A significant number of large country houses were no longer required by their owners and have found sad fates. Endsleigh, the Devon country house of the dukes of Bedford, is just one of many forced to find other uses. After being sold in 1962 after the death of the twelfth duke of Bedford, it was a hotel for a few years before being purchased by a fishing syndicate. It is on the market once again.[258] But others like Great Potheridge near Torrington were greatly reduced in size. It was damaged by fire and subsequently had some of its fixtures and fittings removed before being largely demolished in the eighteenth century. The building was home to General Monk and later his son Christopher who was a Member of Parliament at the age of 13 and later became Governor of Jamaica but after his widow's death in 1734 the house was reduced to a farmhouse. This portion remains[259] but many other large houses lie in complete ruins. There have been two large houses at Eggesford, or possibly three, in the last four centuries. The Chichester family's home was built in the early seventeenth century and possibly rebuilt in about 1718 in brick. It was taken down in the 1820s when a new building was erected for the Earl of Portsmouth. Yet only in 1913 was it offered for sale,[260] then used to house German prisoners of war and finally dismantled in 1917.[261] Haldon House, a grand early eighteenth-century mansion built for Sir George Chudleigh, was later expanded by Sir Robert Palk before being demolished in 1920. Baron Haldon, a Palk descendent, built and spent so extensively in Torquay that the family were bankrupt by 1893. The estate was sold and then a sale was attempted again from 1919 through to 1925 when finally a demolition sale was held. A small fragment of it survives now known as the Lord Haldon Hotel.[262] Upottery Manor in East Devon was an early Victorian home of Henry Addington, leading minister from 1801 to 1804 and later 1st Viscount Sidmouth. The house had 21 rooms, including six bedrooms, and following his death

Photographs of Eggesford, 1913.

Engraving of Haldon House, built in the early eighteenth century and demolished in 1920. Only a small portion survives.

in February 1844 it was rebuilt by his son William Leonard. Neither of the men used Upottery other than as an occasional residence. The second viscount asked the advice of Sir John Kennaway at Escott for an architect who suggested two men from Exeter. He mentioned John Hayward 'of whom many persons think highly' but recommended Samuel Alexis Greig who accepted the commission and signed a contract the following year. The foundation stone was laid on 25 June 1845 and the following March the roof was in place but Greig died suddenly in July of that year and the house was not completed until the following year.[263] The building was taken down in 1962 after the family sold the estate in 1954. The house had fallen into a dilapidated state and could no longer be financially maintained. A fine parkland still survives but without the grand house built for it.[264] Another stunning example is Silverton Park, home of George Wyndham, fourth Earl of Egremont, who also built Blackborough House and church. The mansion was known as Egremont Folly and called a white elephant because of its size and opulence. Silverton Park was not completed: it was said that the earl managed to

live in a portion of the building for four years before he died in 1845. It was estimated to have 187 rooms, fixtures included 230 marble fireplaces and the principal rooms had doorknobs made of amber. The estate began to be sold at the earl's death and in November 1901 the building was finally destroyed. Some 10,000 people came to see it and the demolition took several days. On the first day dynamite blew up the portion facing the railway. The stable block survived and was subsequently used as a farmhouse and then purchased by the Landmark Trust in 1987. Blackborough House, the earl's other home, had a similar fate. It was built in 1838 in two halves: part was for the rector and the other for the earl. But it was partly demolished during the first world war and remains half in ruins.[265] One of the most atmospheric ruins is Fowelscombe. This, as discussed on pages 31–33, was the home of the Fowel family near Ugborough from the sixteenth to eighteenth centuries. More than fifty years ago it was described as 'a romantic ruin' by W. G. Hoskins when it had already been deserted for several generations. Between 1890 and 1919, and probably earlier, the house was derelict. As

Upottery House was rebuilt for the second Viscount Sidmouth in the 1840s to a design by Samuel Greig. This drawing was made in 1846 by Edward Ashworth, clerk of the works, then thirty-one years old. Ashworth was based in Exeter and later worked on many churches in Devon including at Cullompton, Exeter and Tiverton. He had a room in Upottery while the house was being rebuilt.

View of the rebuilding of the impressive home of the Addington family also by Ashworth, 1846. Upottery was demolished in 1962.

Photographs by Edward Pocknell of Silverton Park, possibly shortly before it was destroyed.

discussed earlier, the surveyor for the Society for the Protection of Ancient Buildings felt it could not be rescued. Fowelscombe remains a ruin of walls.[266] Stevenstone in St Giles-in-the-Wood near Great Torrington is one of the largest houses in Devon to have fallen into ruin but even less remains than Fowelscombe and what there is has been covered with wild growth. The house was the main seat of the Rolles in the eighteenth and nineteenth centuries. It had been rebuilt from 1868 to 1872 for the Hon. Mark Rolle and after his death in 1907 the house was sold, reduced in size and a partial demolition sale held. During the second world war it was home to American soldiers and allowed in subsequent years to fall into further neglect. It was abandoned in 1945. Today it lies in utter ruins, covered with ivy with barely a stone visible. The grounds have been used in an imaginative way: several bungalows have been built in the kitchen garden, the laundry and two impressive ranges of outbuildings were converted to housing and the orangery and library are owned by the Landmark Trust.[267]

Public buildings

Public buildings have a similar relationship with loss of finances and function. One good example of this is Exeter's Public Baths. They were built in 1821 on the site of what is now the Southernhay United Reformed Church. The building was classical with Neptune grandly presiding over the entrance but it was demolished only 47 years later, in 1868, because the baths were not financially viable.[268] Changing social attitudes, or at least the introduction of new legislation, can also remove entire classes of buildings. The introduction of 'Care in the Community' in the 1980s made redundant a number of historic buildings. The Devon County Pauper Lunatic Asylum at Exminster opened in 1844 to a design of Charles Fowler.[269] After years of uncertainty it is now being converted into private flats. Another of Exeter's mental institutions, the Exeter Hospital for the Insane, later known as Exe Vale (Digby) Hospital, was built in the 1880s by R. Stark Wilkinson and converted to housing and the grounds used for an estate in the 1990s. The contrast in use is marked: previous generations were not

Engraving of the Public Baths at Exeter, built in 1821 but demolished only 47 years later. The current location of the statue of Neptune remains a mystery.

there by choice whereas today high prices have made them more exclusive. Another loss of an entire class of building are the 'homes for fallen women'. One useful example is the Devon House of Mercy in Bovey Tracey where the Clewer Sisterhood took in women perceived to be at risk of prostitution and other vices. It was built in Gothic Revival in about 1865. The number of 'penitents', described by one Victorian as 'maidens as hath gotten babies without ever goin' nigh a church' and another as 'hussies', declined in the 1930s and was one cause for closure of the building in 1940. The establishment also suffered a loss of funding with the deaths of benefactors and the financial climate of the depression. Its occupation by troops during the following war years did not make it any easier to reopen.[270] The building's conversion to flats ensured its survival but its closure reflected wider social changes in attitudes.

Health buildings are prone to constant modernisation and in Devon rebuilding on green field sites. For instance, Plymouth's hospitals have recently moved from Greenbank and Freedom Fields to Derriford while Exeter has had a similar migration to Heavitree and Wonford. Plymouth's homoeopathic hospital, which was started in 1870 near Derry's Clock, shows the string of buildings many institutions have had: it moved to Princess Square, then Flora Place and finally Lockyer Street before closing in 1977.[271] Redevelopment of existing sites at Plymouth has included conversion to housing and demolition. Exeter's hospital buildings have the marked difference between the continuing use of the Georgian hospital (Dean Clarke House) and the demolition of the modern hospital at Wonford because of concrete cancer.

The church at Revelstoke, situated on the cliff overlooking the sea, was made redundant when the Baring family at nearby Membland built a new church at Noss Mayo. It had fallen into decay partly because the population moved and in about 1869 part of the roof fell in. This medieval building, dedicated to St Peter, was largely abandoned in the 1880s and used as a mortuary chapel. It is now partly a ruin but has benefited by efforts to reclaim it in the 1960s.[272] The ancient parish church of Dartington was also made redundant when a new church was built some distance away in 1878. The tower was left but stone from the walls was used in the new foundations. Much of the internal fabric was reused in the new church.[273] The small medieval church of Broad Nymet near Bow was dilapidated and used as a storehouse in the 1830s. It remains derelict and disused through lack of any need for it.[274] The medieval church at South Huish near Salcombe has been ruined for generations and only relatively lately has it been rescued by the Friends of Friendless Churches. When a new church was built at Galmpton in 1867 the old church was dismantled with the ancient rood screen sold to Mr Ilbert of Bowringsleigh for a guinea, the bench ends went to Powderham, the south arcade to Dodbrooke and the font to Galmpton. The altar, altar rails, prayer desk, pulpit, roof bosses, window glass, doors and roof slates and lead were also sold and the pews became firewood. The church was demolished because Archdeacon Earle decided it no longer had a function although the parishioners disagreed. They were told if they could raise £300 the church would be saved but unfortunately the congregation was mostly comprised of poor fishermen and agricultural labourers and the building was demolished. Just before the first world war services were held on Sunday afternoons but these did not prove to be popular.[275]

Lazar houses survived the Reformation[276] but disappeared as leprosy declined in the seventeenth century. The hospital of St Mary Magdalen in Totnes was founded for eleven lazars at the end of the twelfth century but a lack of demand resulted in it being pulled down. In 1822 only the walls of the chapel were still standing.[277] The lazar house at Tavistock was demolished after 1761 and an almshouse built on the site.[278] That of St Mary Magdalene at Exeter, located in the parish of St Leonard's, survived until 1862 when it was demolished because the buildings were considered unfit. The hospital

South Huish Church
in course of demolition.

A.W.S.

South Huish Church
in course of demolition

Undated photographs of South Huish parish church, taken by A. Searley. He noted they were taken 'in the course of demolition'. The figure is one Dr Adams. The medieval screen from the church was purchased for Boweringsleigh.

Dartington church in 1842, it was pulled down a generation later but the tower still remains.

was then used for general purposes.[279] In the parish of Highweek near Newton Abbot an early sixteenth century lazar house was by the end of the eighteenth century occupied as an almshouse.[280] At Plympton the Maudlyn House became a workhouse in 1773 and then in 1841 became an asylum, school, police station and finally, in 1867, the buildings were sold, demolished and a new terrace of domestic dwellings erected.[281]

Early workhouses, also referred to as poorhouses, were the result of late Tudor legislation that required parishes to look after their poor and provide employment for those capable of work. The workhouses were for the 'impotent' poor, those deemed not able to work because they were infirm, old and physically or mentally ill. In Devon these buildings, paid through local rates, were the predecessors of modern sheltered housing, and, as discussed in pages 153–154, many were originally built as church-houses. The parish workhouse or poorhouse was a familiar sight but this began to change in the late seventeenth and early eighteenth centuries when fourteen corporations across the country pooled their resources and created larger institutions: the efforts of Exeter, Crediton and Tiverton in

Engraving of the Exeter Workhouse, 1744. This magnificent late seventeenth-century building was once the pride of Exeter and some two hundred and fifty years after being built was hit by Nazi bombs.

Two photographs taken at Kingsbridge by A. Searley, 1897, entitled 'The Three Graces' and 'Rev. William Watson, men and boys from the workhouse, Jubilee Day, June 22nd 1897'.

the 1690s were groundbreaking as were Plymouth's in 1707. That at Exeter impressed a visitor in 1700: he noted the building was built by the Presbyterians and made of brick fired on the spot. In the early nineteenth century these new institutions became the norm: a change in national legislation in 1834 closed parish institutions and some were then converted to domestic use. Parish buildings and even the money boxes used to raise money were redundant: at Hatherleigh the ancient box which stood at the south door, which had three locks and keys, was destroyed in the 1830s because it was 'of no use'.[282] The emphasis shifted in how to deal with poverty: larger

district establishments replaced parish buildings and they not only housed inmates but forced them to work. Twenty Union Workhouses were built in Devon at Axminster from 1836 to 1838, Barnstaple in 1837, Bideford in 1837, Crediton in 1698 and 1836–7, East Stonehouse in 1801, Exeter in 1699–1707, Holsworthy in 1853, Honiton in 1836, Kingsbridge in 1837, Newton Abbot in 1837, Okehampton in 1836–7, Plymouth in 1852–8, Plympton St Mary in 1836, St Thomas in 1836, South Molton in 1837–9, Stoke Damerel in 1850–4, Tavistock in 1837, Tiverton in 1698 and 1836–7, Torrington in 1837 and Totnes in 1837–9. These institutions dominated the

The Rotunda in Torquay, built to a design by Foulston in 1820.

treatment of the poor through the nineteenth century, in spite of scandals over abusive care, and continued until the first world war when many were emptied for use as hospitals or to house Belgian refugees or German prisoners of war. After the war many buildings were never reused for the poor. The redundancy of these buildings was gradually achieved as government policy in the 1920s shifted to providing assistance outside institutions.[283] Many Union Workhouses were redeveloped. Those at Kingsbridge, Newton Abbot and Tavistock for instance, now have health-care functions. Newton Abbot's building was in the first world war used as a military hospital and in the second world war as a hospital for the navy. It was later converted into a geriatric section of Newton Abbot Hospital.[284] Exeter's grand building of the late seventeenth century survived until converted for use as a hospital, was bombed during the second world war and a fragment of the original building may survive as part of the Royal Devon & Exeter Hospital.[285]

Finally, many individual buildings have been lost through changing funding. This was the fate of one of Torbay's most unusual buildings, the Rotunda. This market was designed by Foulston and erected in 1820 in what is now Torwood Street, then called Market Street. There were red sandstone columns and chestnut trees stood in the centre. The building initially housed traders from neighbouring parishes but became redundant through the great growth of Torquay and the needs for more larger premises. It was finally demolished in the name of traffic improvements but in 1930 some walls remained incorporated in the back of Allams & Sons.[286]

Graveyards

Some graveyards have become unused, particularly non-conformist ones, and their use has changed. A Quaker graveyard in Newton Tracey began in 1782 but by the 1950s its occupants were a flock of chickens and some vegetables.[287] Graveyards have been deconsecrated and used as open spaces or parks, such as the churchyard of All-Hallows-On-The-Walls in Exeter. The curious aspect of this Victorian church is that not only was it named after a church which had been demolished several generations before on a separate site, but the new church was built on an existing graveyard which had been in use for two hundred years. Individual monuments have been broken and many churchyards have been cleared of their memorials, particularly deconsecrated ones. Monuments in unusual places are often forgotten. One of the most curious was in Lustleigh's railway station which noted 'Beneath this slab, and stretched out flat, lies Jumbo, once our station cat'. It was claimed that the cat had had many lives in jumping between the wheels of trains before finally dying in its bed.[288] Other graveyards have been lost but not because they were forgotten. For instance, it was claimed in the early nineteenth century that several hillocks could still be identified on Hurlbridge Moor near Hatherleigh where the bodies of Civil War soldiers were buried. The ground had recently been ploughed and human bones and parts of swords had been found. The account was written about 180 years after the civil war, the same amount of time since the writer noted the event. Memories may have been kept well locally: he also recorded the robbery of an old man in the civil war at the nearby tenement of Prusland Down. This man:

in the time of the Civil Wars was afraid of being plundered, he therefore carried his money out in his garden and buried it. He had no sooner returned to his house and locked his door when he saw (thro' his

Engraving of the church of All-Hallows-On-The-Walls, Exeter, c.1850. The church was built in the late 1840s on the existing graveyard which had been consecrated in 1637. It was demolished in 1950.

window) a woman accompanied by a soldier enter the garden saying 'I saw the Old Roundhead hide away his money and we'll have it'. They accordingly went to work, dug up the money and carried it off to the great disappointment of the old man.[289]

The area may have had strong folk memories. The greater loss is that of the burials of suicides. That of Jane Pine of Sidmouth is a good example which was recorded by a local writer. Pine was a young unmarried woman who earned some money teaching children to read. She cut her throat, possibly with the knife with which she was employed to do weeding, and was taken to an isolated place one night in about 1810. Her body was placed on a bier by what was described as boisterous rabble carrying lanterns and torches and brought with 'great glee' through the lanes 'full of riot, blasphemy and profanity'. It was legally required that a stake was driven through the heart and in the centre of a crossroads above Knowle a pit was dug and the body interred. A pollarded oak tree nearby was cut with her initials to mark the spot.[290] It is

rare that these places are noted: one exception is *Henbury Forches,* presumably Hemborough Forks, on the border of Blackawton which in 1613 was noted as being the place 'where they are commonly buried that destroy themselves'.[291] It is not known how many others lie in isolated places throughout Devon because these individuals are also lost in a second sense: until 1837 records were of burials in consecrated ground and not suicides. The result is that these individuals disappear from history and the extent of such deaths is unknown. Victorian newspapers reported hundreds of suicides every year in Devon and it is likely in the earlier period there were nearly as many. Even less is known about the resting places of highwaymen who were buried, allegedly, in such places as Watching Place Cross three miles from Moretonhampstead, the crossing of the road from Moretonhampstead to Plymouth with that of one from Ashburton to Chagford.[292] Many family historians seeking ancestors have been stymied by what appears to be a lack of records and have not realised their actual history and resting places.

Chapter Five

Commercial redevelopment

Commercial redevelopment accounts, and rightly so, for an enormous number of changes and losses. Totnes bowling green, for example, was situated near St Peter's Quay and had been popular since the late seventeenth century but was swept away with the development of the riverside.[293] Others have been lost in smaller redevelopment schemes such as Deller's Café in Paignton.[294] An even more prominent case can be found in East Devon: the removal of the production of Axminster carpets to Wilton in 1836 caused the factory, built in 1828 to replace the eighteenth-century building, to be converted to domestic use.[295] Another example is the redevelopment of Kingsbridge's corn mills in 1798 which produced cloth for the East India Company, then blanket production for Newfoundland and finally in 1845 returned to grinding corn.[296] Buildings rise and fall with technological change: wind, water, steam and finally electrical power have created, and made redundant, many buildings. Economic forces shape industrial activity, whether with county's main industries such as fishing, mining, cloth-making and farming, or the ancillary ones including brewing, brick-making, engineering and rope-making. Many thousands of the buildings erected for these activities have been subsequently developed for other purposes. One aspect of this process is its unevenness, accelerated change during 'boom' years, such as the late 1980s, and stagnation, such as the early 1990s, during the economic downturns.[297]

Perhaps even the loss of Thomas Fowler's calculating machine of the 1840s could be attributed to competing commercial development. His invention was superseded by others and although this Torrington native built his machine, to considerable acclaim, it was not a financial success: the model, a wooden machine which stood five feet high, four broad and the same in width, had been exhibited in London. But at his death it was dismantled

Example of an Axminster carpet, 1851.

and returned to Devon in pieces in a case.[298] Its subsequent whereabouts is unknown. There was a second calculating machine: John Goss of Hatherleigh constructed an earlier machine which stood in a local bank until as late as 1909 albeit in a neglected state. The best known machine was that of Charles Babbage, son of a Totnes banker, but his machine, of about the same time, was never finished.[299] Another invention which should have been preserved is the Georgian diving machine of John Lethbridge of Wolborough near Newton Abbot. His experiments were made in his orchard during the great eclipse of 1715. The machine was wooden with iron hoops and holes for the arms. There was glass four inches in diameter that presumably was all he could see through. Five hundred pounds of lead was needed to sink it. Eventually Lethbridge dived at Porto Santo near Madeira, off the Cape of Good Hope and in the West Indies and over some twenty years he investigated Dutch, Spanish and English wrecks and salvaged some £100,000. It was last seen at Dartmouth in about 1800 although it has been recreated at the Charlestown Museum in Cornwall.[300] Other inventions, or at least attempted technological advances, seen in Devon include the flying apparatus of a man who crossed the river Exe from Exmouth to the Warren in 1845: he was 'singularly clad' and by 'a series of motions with his apparel' flew for some ten minutes.[301] Of even greater interest would be the flying apparatus used by another unknown man at East Budleigh: sometime before 1630 he is said to have attempted to have flown from the church tower using artificial wings. He plummeted to the ground, died and was buried in the churchyard. He was given the name *Noddy*, then indicating a fool or simpleton.[302] Other Devonians were given patents and some, such as John Heathcote and his lace machinery, are remembered but others, along with their ideas, are not such as John Williams and Sir Humphrey Marwood of Exeter who in 1692 had a patent for 'catching fish by means of a light burnt some fathoms under water', John Lewis of

Plymouth in 1734 for varnish, Christopher Gullet of Exeter in 1793 for a remedy for gout, George Bodley of Exeter in 1802 for a portable cooking stove, Edward Manly in 1810 for a writing apparatus and John Pearse in 1822 for a roasting jack.[303]

Water supplies are continually being redeveloped. Fresh water was a continual concern throughout the county, particularly in small towns. Kingsbridge had four conduits, one from 1611, which were moved in 1793 but then sixty years later made redundant when pipes brought water to houses.[304] In Totnes wooden pipes from the late seventeenth century brought fresh water through the town, as with other places such as Barnstaple and Exeter, and in 1882 trunks from elm trees, with circular holes some three inches in diameter, were discovered intact underground.[305] Exeter's water supplies have continually been upgraded since the Great Conduit, situated at the Carfax, the meeting point of High, Fore, South and North Streets, was demolished in the 1770s, its replacement moved only a few years later and its

Engraving of the Great Conduit, Exeter, demolished in the 1770s.

Knowle in the early nineteenth century, the county's first zoo.

successor taken down in 1834. The following generation made similar changes as efforts were made to reduce the threat of cholera, a concern of all small towns.[306] Two leats brought water from Dartmoor into Plymouth; one supplied the town of Plymouth and the other Plymouth Dock, later to become renamed Devonport. Plymouth's leat ran 17 miles from the river Meavy to Sutton Pool and is best known because of the involvement of Sir Francis Drake. Twenty-seven conduits throughout Plymouth provided water. The leat was open on Dartmoor but by the time the water reached Plymouth it was covered. That leat began in 1591 while Devonport's leat was not constructed until the late 1790s. It ran some thirty miles. The Plymouth leat was finally outmoded when Burrator Reservoir was built in the 1890s and Devonport's leat was gradually made redundant by other supplies. Sections of both can still be seen on Dartmoor although the appearance of Plymouth's leat was considerably changed by refurbishing in the nineteenth century and during the second world war. One length of the Plymouth leat, along with the conduit of 1598, is still visible on North Hill in Drake's Place Gardens near the museum.

There have been other leats on Dartmoor, at least four of which still flow.[307]

The redevelopment of Knowle at Sidmouth closed the county's first zoo. The *cottage orné* had been built by Lord Dispenser in 1810 but owned by T. L. Fish some twenty-five years later who brought rare birds and animals into the eleven acres of grounds. Among the animals were a gazelle, zebra, emus, kangaroos, Indian buffaloes, marmoset monkeys and two black swans. Fish died in 1861 and Knowle was turned into a hotel twenty years later. Curiously, it was probably one of Fish's kangaroos that escaped and made it nearly to Budleigh Salterton in November 1853. It seems ironic that at this time, when wayward Devonians were being sent to Australia against their wills, this kangaroo, which had been trapped and brought from Botany Bay, managed to escape his imprisonment. It hopped as far as South Farm, on the eastern side of the mouth of the Sid, where it surprised the locals. They shot it.[308] In contrast to Knowle's redevelopment, Plymouth's twentieth-century zoo, which was situated in Central Park, was closed in 1978 because of budget restraints.

Transport

Modes of transport quickly change through technical advances and have left behind a bewildering legacy. Even so, there are remarkably few examples of what could be argued as Devon's most traditional form of transport: there are only a handful of historical Devon ships. Perhaps the most famous was the *Golden Hind*, which curiously was one of the few to have had a concerted preservation effort: in 1581 Queen Elizabeth ordered that Drake's ship should be preserved for the nation and it was docked at Deptford until the timbers finally rotted in the middle of the seventeenth century. A plan was considered for building a brick wall to enclose the vessel but only some timbers were saved that were used to build a chair now in the Bodleian Library.[309] Very few of the many thousands of Devon's vessels survive and most examples are wrecks. One exception is a fourteenth-century vessel which was found by two clay-workers at Zitherixon Quarry near the river Teign at Kingsteignton near Newton Abbot in 1898. But unfortunately only a few timbers have survived from that discovery. A 'canoe' or logboat was also found.[310]

Some former coach inns from the late eighteenth and early nineteenth centuries survive in villages and small towns while those in the county's two cities have nearly all been swept aside in redevelopment. The same is true of their stables. Turnpike roads have survived, and are unknowingly daily used by many tens of thousands of people today, but nearly all toll gates have been lost. One exception is the set at Honiton. The end of those at Totnes was a cause of celebration: at midnight on 31 October 1881 the gates at Totnes Bridge were taken off their hinges and burnt in a great bonfire. One man commented he had waited twenty years but it was 'better late than never'.[311] The coming of the railway in the 1840s signalled the end of many coaching inns. The railways also had a significant, although unknown, effect on the countryside: no feasibility studies were made of the impact on the landscape and it is unknown what plant or animal life was lost. One loss was a group of

Red-cow Gate

The gates at the Red Cow toll house in Exeter, late nineteenth century. Nearly all tollgates in Devon have gone but many buildings have been adapted for modern use.

Photograph of the Dartmouth Coach, late nineteenth century. The long-distance coaches to London were swept aside by the railway in the mid nineteenth century but those using shorter distances within Devon continued through to the beginning of the twentieth century.

well-known elm trees near Barnstaple which were cleared to make way for the railway line in 1852. These elms, known as 'The Seven Brethren', were planted as a memorial to four brothers, John, Joseph, Richard and Thomas Ley, who were fishing on the river Taw in 1646 and caught an infectious disease from a bundle of discarded bedding they found floating in the water.[312] The construction of the railway through Newton Abbot eventually included converting the lecture and reading rooms of the Mechanics' Institute into the boiler and engine rooms of the stationary steam engines.[313] The chancel in Cullompton church was rebuilt in 1849 and excessively strengthened because one supporter, who happened to be an engineer responsible for the line, 'had an exaggerated notion of the vibration likely to be caused by the passing of the trains'.[314] There was demolition of various kinds during the laying of the lines: for instance Halfway House near Cowley Bridge at Exeter was taken down in the early 1840s, four prominent Scotch pine trees near Great Torrington, which were a local landmark, were cut down and at Plymouth the Royal Public Baths, a Regency building with classical

features, was demolished in spite of the discovery of a spa.[315] The amount of destruction caused to create parking for cars in the twentieth century would in itself fill a book. It seems surprising to us to discover that in 1911 Sidmouth officials were unsure how to process an application for a taxi cab licence and eventually gave only one because they felt there was not room for more in the town.[316]

It is difficult to appreciate today that Devon once had a great number of railways. The first rail line reached Exeter in 1844, to Teignmouth and Newton Abbot (1846), Totnes (1847), Plympton (1848–1959) and finally Plymouth in 1849. Other lines were opened to Tiverton and Torquay (1848), Crediton (1851), Barnstaple (1854 and 1871), Bideford (1855–1917), Paignton (1859), Tavistock (1865–1962 and 1890–1966), a second line to Exeter (1860), Exmouth (1861–), Kingswear (1864–), Lydford (1865 and 1874–1868), Moretonhampstead (1866–1964), Seaton (1868–1966), Brixham (1868–1963), Sidmouth (1874–1967), Ilfracombe (1874–1964), Okehampton (1871–1972 but reopened in 1997), Ashburton (1872–1971), Torrington (1872–1965),

Photograph entitled 'The first engine through'. Kingsbridge was connected by rail in 1893 and the line closed seventy years later.

Hemyock (1876–1975), Holsworthy (1879–1966), Princetown (1883–1956), Kingsbridge (1893–1963), Budleigh Salterton (1897–1967), Lynton (1898–1935), Yealmpton (1898–1947), Northam (1901–1917), Appledore (1908–1917) and Halwill (1925–1965). There were also a great number of branch lines within Greater Plymouth[317] and unusual lines included the Mamhead military railway which ran in the first and second world wars and used the labour of prisoners of war for cutting timber.[318]

The Teigngrace to Haytor line is generally thought of as Devon's first rail line. This tramway opened in 1820 to bring granite from Dartmoor to Teignmouth via the six and a half mile long Stover Canal. Horses pulled the trucks, which were modified road wagons, on the rails. It was intended to use metal rails but granite blocks, up to eight feet long, were quarried and utilised on the line closest to the moor and iron rails used at the Newton Abbot end. There were branches off to various quarries and the line was used for some forty years until it closed in the 1860s. A section near the road from Haytor to Bovey Tracey was used in 1898 for road-making but much of the line can still be seen imbedded in the moor and is still very much a part of the landscape. The granite is now part of other landscapes most notably that of the Arizona desert; after it was used to build London Bridge it was sold in the 1960s to be re-erected in the American West.[319] Other Dartmoor trams were connected to peat extraction in the 1840s: naptha, which can be extracted from peat, was carried on a tramway at Princetown and on the Zeal Tor tramway which used wooden rails and granite blocks. The latter was reopened for use with china clay extraction. In 1878 yet another line was opened: this was a five mile route from Bridestowe to peat works at Rattlebrook Head. It ran intermittently until the 1940s. The rails were finally removed in the 1930s and the line was later used as a vehicle track. A second china clay tramway was opened in 1858 and ran from Lee Moor to the quays at Cattewater in Plymouth alongside the main line to Exeter. There were branches to works at Wotter and from some brick works. The line used different types of rails and horse, gravity and steam power. These have long lost their original purpose but can also still be traced on the ground.[320] Possibly the best known of the lines was the Plymouth and Dartmoor Railway which ran some 25 miles from Sutton Pool to Princetown. Sir Thomas Tyrwhitt, the Dartmoor-based entrepreneur, opened the line in 1823 and hoped that profits from taking granite from the moor would make it feasible. It did last nearly sixty years but was not the hoped for financial success: it closed in 1880 but three years later was reconstructed and reopened to Horrabridge.[321]

There were, however, earlier rail lines than those on the moor. Rails were laid from 1756 to 1759 at Millbay in Plymouth to move quarry stone needed for building the Eddystone Lighthouse. Then, in 1812, rails were again used to transport stone at Pomphlett for the creation of the breakwater. Barges had rails fitted so stone could be ferried and placed on other rails on the breakwater.[322] Rails were also used on the canal which ran from Tavistock to Morwellham.[323]

Closures of Devon's railways continued to the 1970s, reflecting the wider history of private initiatives, but they remain a visible part of the landscape albeit being put to a number of different uses and some sleepers have been removed. For instance a miniature electric tramway has been built on the line from Seaton to Colyford, part of the Ashburton line was opened as a walkway in 1979 while much of the remainder was swallowed up by improvements to the A38 and the line round the north of Dartmoor from Exeter to Okehampton was reopened for a summer service in 1997. Viaducts have also been made redundant. One in the Walkham Valley was demolished in the 1960s but many others, like the Bannawell Street viaduct at Tavistock, are open to the public. The line from Ham Bridge to Clearbrook is now the Plym Valley Cycle Way, that from Barnstaple to Bideford was re-designated

Aquatint by Robert Havell after a painting by J. Cartwright, entitled 'An interior view of the Devon Haytor Granite Quarries', 1825.

Pen and wash by George Wightwick, no date given, of the Dartmoor railway. He wrote 'The theatrical form of this passage of the 'Iron way' is a reason for its selection. A little clearing away on the left hand, below the rail, would complete the regular horse-shoe of a dramatic auditorium. Such a natural formation near Rome would have afforded Marcellus a readymade shell for his playhouse. Imagination converts the rocks into a concentric series of seats above and below the curved corridor, and the trees become as the countless faces of assembled thousands witnessing a play performed by the Satyrs and the wood and water nymphs. The proscenium would then appear as a lovely part of the valley glittering with the ripplings and cascatelli, the weirs and the mirrors of the Plym; and a finer back scene than the woody bottom and sterile high lands of the moor could not be desired. Between the spot here represented and Plymouth, there is one view of such surpassing beauty, that the mention of it seems imperative, lest the spectator should deem the illustrations of this sketchbook adequate to the character of the railroad scenery. I allude to the grand amphitheatre of Can Quarry, to which picture could not do justice. From a most picturesque foreground the beholder looks down into a great basin, and as a hungry child would contemplate a huge China Bowl filled with a selection from all the rich delicacies of a Ball supper!'

the Tarka Trail in 1992 and part of the line from Okehampton to Tavistock is a cycle path now known as the Granite Way. Redundant buildings connected with the Rattlebrook peat works were blown up by the army in 1961[324] while former station houses have been put to a number of uses including restaurants such as Blackmoor Gate and Dartmouth, the Ottery St Mary station became a youth centre, the Braunton station a shop, Great Torrington a public house, and Bridestow a private home. Many other stations had their buildings demolished including St Budeaux and Ford in Plymouth. Two locomotives have been preserved, notably one now at Saltram and workers' cottages can be seen in Lee Moor and in other isolated spots across the county.[325]

New technology resulted in changing train systems and the legacy of the machinery left behind. For a short while in the 1840s all trains, both passenger and freight, from Exeter to Newton Abbot used atmospheric power and not steam. This system, which relied upon stationary engines pumping out air, was abandoned in 1848 but not before it was extended to Torquay and from Totnes

to Laira.[326] One passenger later remembered the train running out of power between Newton Abbot and Totnes and the passengers got out and sat in a hay-making field. One legacy is the engine house at Starcross, built by I. K. Brunel, and there is another at Torquay which, curiously, was not used for its original purpose, converted for use by Longpark Pottery and is still a commercial concern. They were known at the time as 'Brunel's Follies' and were used as stores, cellars or any other purpose.[327]

Both Plymouth and Exeter had tram services with Plymouth's service beginning in 1881. Trams were horse drawn and carried thousands of passengers a year. Three years later steam trams began but curiously they lasted only a few years and in 1889 were replaced by horse-drawn trams. The pace of technological change continued when, only ten years later in 1899, electric trams ran through the streets. By the start of the second world war the service was being replaced by buses and the war reduced the number of trams from 27 to 4.[328] The service lasted until 29 September 1945 when the

Pen and wash by George Wightwick, c.1830, entitled 'On the Dartmoor Railway'. He wrote 'here is a part of the 'most picturesque fore-ground' alluded to in the last description. Is it not Salvator-like? Is not the armed warrior on horseback capital? I did not 'do' him: Colonel Charles Hamilton Smith of Plymouth 'did' him; nor let the dear Colonel's power of drawing man, or horse, or both in conjunction, be judged by this sample, which is only good enough for the rest. How that same warrior (a bloody one I doubt not) can pass on, as he is passing, without turning his stupid bloody head to the left and reining up his horse to look at can Quarry, is to me – as the Devonshire people say – 'infinite'! The horse, indeed, does apparently see something worthy of his left eye, at least; but I have seen such men as well as such horses; nor shall I forget the ineffable disgust my feelings experienced, when, having brought out a London friend to be struck dumb on seeing the view commanded by this 'Devil's Bridge', he exclaimed, after a long silence, and with imperturbable sang froid, 'Is that a slate quarry? Who works it? I say, old fellow have you got a weed?' Oh dear!'

last tram ran.[329] At Exeter horse-drawn trams began in 1882 and electric trams ran from 1905 to 1931. Truncated tramline poles which made up the street railings below St David's church can still be seen.[330] It was reported recently that some visible reminders are left in Plymouth: a tram standard of 1898 survives as does some track work and the brick sheds at Devonport.[331]

Devon had eight commercial canals of considerable interest. The Exeter canal, the first to use the pound lock in England, was begun in 1563 and ran from the Quay to Topsham. It was extended in 1676 and again from 1825 to 1827. It is still in operation. The Grand Western Canal, originating with an Act of Parliament in 1796, ran between Tiverton and Taunton but failed to link the county with the national canal system as planned. By 1820 it stretched twelve miles between Tiverton and Burlescombe and only later was extended to Taunton. It was abandoned between Taunton and Holcombe Rogus after 1865 and from 1992 was opened as the Grand Western Canal Country Park. The Stover Canal was more financially successful. It began in the 1790s to bring clay from Bovey Tracey to Teignmouth. The prime mover was James Templer of nearby Stover. The canal ran nearly two miles to Kingsteignton and later, in 1843, a cut was made to Chudleigh. Granite was also shipped using the railway made in the 1820s. Most of the Stover Canal is now part of the Templer Way. A shorter competitor was the Hackney Canal which opened in 1843 and ran less than a mile from the river Teign to Kingsteington. It closed in 1928. Another venture was the canal from Tavistock to Morwellham Quay which ran from 1817 through to the end of the century. It brought coal and lime and exported mineral ores and slates. The upper

Photograph by A. W. Searley of Brunel's Atmospheric Tower, Torquay, as occupied by Longpark Pottery, early twentieth century. The building is still used for commercial purposes.

Photograph of South Brent station, late nineteenth century, now a disused station.

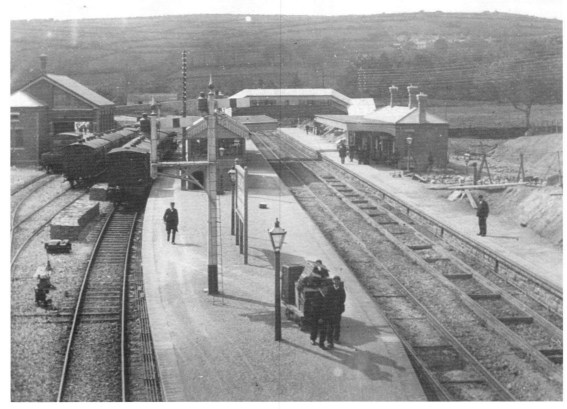

Aquatint of Oakford Bridge, 1824, by D. Havel after H. Hasseler. The bridge was reconstructed in 1994.

Tamar valley was the centre of a considerable mining industry, notably of copper, through to the 1890s. The main canal ran four miles and a branch a further two. Since the 1930s it has been used in generating electricity and part of it is open to the public.[332] A sixth canal was built from Marsh Mills outside Plymouth to Cann Quarry between 1827 and 1830. The intention was to bring stone nearly two miles to Plymouth but the canal seems to have operated for not more than a decade when it became a mill leat.[333] Another canal ran fifteen and a half miles from Holsworthy to Bude in Cornwall from 1823. It closed in about 1894 but reopened for a short while afterwards. Finally, the Clinton family built a six-mile canal at Great Torrington, to the river Torridge at Wear Giffard, from 1823. It closed in 1871 and the canal is now filled in.[334] Of these canals only that at Exeter is still in operation. There were many other proposed schemes which were not attempted. There are few references to the ecological impact that the creating of these canals

had. A rare example is a comment made in 1851 on the loss of marsh pimpernels, myrtles and sundews, as well as the wills o' the wisp, when the Stover canal drained some of the surrounding heathland.[335] Devon also had a number of ornamental canals in the grounds of private houses which are discussed on page 119.

New technology has resulted in continual changes to roads: in 1928 the oldest villager of Membury is reported to have commented on the village street being tarred for the first time by saying 'the place is getting more like London every day'. The postmaster responded 'yes, this tar is making a horrible mess, but I suppose it is necessary. Hardly a day passes but some motor or other comes to the village'.[336] In 1929 one local disapproved of motor-cycles at Sidmouth and of the 'fierce-looking leather-clad pilots incited by thoughtless companions out for a joy ride'.[337] Only rarely are comments made by previous generations on ecological damage. The protests in the early 1990s over the loss of ancient trees for the building of the A30 in East Devon did not save the oaks but it did raise the issue of conservation. The saving of the natural habitat was also the issue in the 1980s when the Okehampton bypass was eventually built. A few years before, while the A38 was being built, there was more destruction: Kenbury House, a small late eighteenth-century house in Exminster, was one loss. In the 1840s it had formal gardens, a long avenue of trees and a lake[338] but these were demolished in the road-building in the early 1970s and the site now lies under the wheels of thousands of cars each day. There is a similar story to be told concerning Ide: in the 1970s feelings ran high against the extension of the A30 between Pocombe and Peamore and a tombstone was erected to mourn the loss of the valley.[339] The building of the Okehampton bypass in the 1980s bisected the one thousand acre medieval deer park and overran a number of important sites including one with 'a spread of Neolithic pottery'.[340]

Bridges are also continually being revamped. At Exeter the medieval bridge, erected in the early thirteenth century, was replaced in the late eighteenth century. That bridge was demolished in the early twentieth century but its replacement only survived until the early 1970s. The common theme for the destruction of each was that they contributed to flooding but in each case the bridges were not able to handle the growing level of traffic.[341] Another apt example is the bridge between Sidmouth and Salcombe Regis. In the 1790s it was made from a single tree of some forty feet in length. But in 1855 the Alma Bridge replaced it. It was constructed in 1855 with the timbers of a wreck, the *Laurel,* and named after the Crimean battle fought the preceding year. Only 22 years later, in 1877, it was severely damaged by a storm and repaired but then replaced in 1900 because it was no longer suitable.[342] Another notable loss is that of the Floating Bridge over the Laira near Plymouth. This chain ferry was built in 1807 and lasted through to 1827 when it was abandoned because of the building of a permanent bridge nearby.[343] Others have continued such

as Dartmouth, first started in 1831, as does Torpoint.[344]

New modes of transport have been blamed for various changes including the desertion of the village of Staunton near Loddiswell. It was suggested that the introduction of the Kingsbridge Railway and subsequent closure of the coach service hastened the end of the village. Staunton had 26 houses in 1754 but declined to only 2 houses by 1878. However, there had been a steady decline to only 12 houses in 1841, more than fifty years before the railway came to Kingsbridge.[345]

Gardens

Walled kitchen gardens, always connected with large houses, have met various fates through commercial development: the National Trust has converted the walled garden at Killerton to a car park, those at Endsleigh and Flete are now commercial garden nurseries, Oldstone hosts a seasonal caravan park, those at Upottery and Stevenstone are used for housing while the University of Exeter's walled garden at Streatham Hall was demolished to build the new Islamic Centre. Commercial development has also taken the gardens of less wealthy people. In 1782 a Parliamentary Act was passed which provided four acres of waste land for workhouses and in 1819 parish churchwardens were given authority to use up to eight acres for local people. By then allotments were springing up, or being discussed, in such places as Bideford by 1844, Broadclyst by 1829, Buckfastleigh by 1849, Clyst St Lawrence by 1839, Great Torrington by 1853, Kenton by 1867, Heavitree by 1863, South Molton by 1834, Powderham by 1840, Tavistock by 1832, Tiverton by 1845 and Totnes by 1848.[346] Other parishes were just as early.[347] In 1887 local authorities were obliged to provide allotments on demand and yet they have continually been overrun by commercial development such as those along at Coxside in Plymouth which were moved in the 1990s to make way for land development. Many allotments are now on prized land: in the nineteenth century they were sited on land then considered remote but gradual development has encroached upon them and made the land valuable.

Many local fruit varieties have also been lost. In the late sixteenth century Exeter's John Hooker noted that varieties derived their names from a particular quality or the place they originated from. He wrote of the Cowick Quarenden (an apple) and the Sowton Pear. Other local old varieties which no longer exist include the Red Hill Crab also known as the Royal Wilding. This apple was discovered near Exeter in about 1711 on the road to Okehampton. The Meadyate was another popular apple that was discovered in Ermington near Plymouth. The cider was known as Hewbramble or Bramble cider because it was so rough: it caused a sensation as if a bramble had been thrust down the throat and then pulled back again. Devon had other varieties: the Backamore was named after Baccamoor Farm in Plympton St Mary and the Cowley Crab was associated with two trees found near Cowley Bridge on the road between Exeter and Crediton. All these varieties have been lost, as have many of the orchards. The popularity of cider accelerated until the eighteenth century when it became associated with 'Devonshire colic' and was increasingly less fashionable until largely replaced by beer and ale.[348] Orchards were planted across Devon, except in a few places such as Frithelstock and East and West Anstey, but in some parishes it was more important than others. South Devon produced the most cider for commercial purposes. Staverton near Totnes, for example, was said in the 1790s to have made some 8,000 hogsheads of cider a year. It had no less than 32 pounds and presses.[349] Apple orchards were a common sight and have helped define Devon's landscape but more than 6,000 acres of orchards were lost in the county from 1904 to 1979 and as of 1987 there were only 525 acres of commercial orchards and 190 acres of non-commercial orchards.[350] The two series of nineteenth-century maps of Devon, the tithe maps and the ordnance surveys, illustrate the great areas of the county which were once planted with orchards. The estate of Sir Courtenay Pole at Shute in East Devon was one such place. In the middle of the seventeenth century he planted an extraordinary range of fruit trees, not just apples but also pears, quinces, figs, nectarines, apricots, plums, cherries and melocotons. Pole may have been unusual even amongst Devon gentry for his fruit enthusiasm but his account shows a level of activity that is truly astounding. Plants were brought in from London as well as from a variety of places in Devon. Apple varieties included the French Longstay, Spanish Pippin, Old Wife, Golden Rennet, Apple Dainty, Codling and Gilliflower.[351] Few of these are still grown in Devon except possibly as curiosities.

Some other plant species were once thought been lost including the Plymouth Strawberry, *Fragaria fructo hispidia,* also known as the Prickly Strawberry. It was originally discovered on a heap of compost in 1627. The fruit was fleshy but with tubular leaves instead of pips. It has lately been rediscovered by plantsmen.[352] Another local plant which was nearly lost was the mazard, the dark cherry particular to North Devon at least from the late sixteenth century. There is also the continuing uncertainty as to whether Sir Francis Drake or Sir Walter Raleigh ever planted potatoes or tobacco in their native Devon. The early introduction of some individual plants have survived *in situ,* such as at Mamhead, but many others, including the *Magnolia grandiflora* 'Exmouth' brought to his home at Exmouth by Sir John Colleton in the eighteenth century, long ago disappeared.[353]

Hedges in Devon have made a tremendous contribution in defining the landscape. While in some parts of the county there are good examples of dry-stone walling, in the rest of Devon great earthen hedges, built with stone and covered with indigenous plants, act as boundaries and linear sanctuaries for wildlife. Changing farming practices has lost the county a tremendous number. For example in Woodbury miles of hedges were destroyed by Bicton College when it transformed one field into a 'prairie'.[354] But this is not necessarily new: as early as

1844 one writer, an Exeter surveyor, proposed hedges should be pulled down on economic grounds because they took up too much room.[355] That same year 'A Practical Man' urged his local newspaper to continue planting timber in hedges and thought the loss of hedges in favour of large fields would diminish the beauty of the Devon countryside. He warned it was easy to destroy but 'not so easy to get them back again'.[356] Some newly-erected hedges were pulled down as they were thought to infringe upon rights to common land such as happened in North Molton or Brixham in the late sixteenth century.[357] Replacing them according to the ancient way of construction is easy. In the early eighteenth century one man from Cruwys Morchard noted how to make a Devon hedge and wrote it should be some five feet high. Earth taken from either side created ditches and this was used as fill between the two stone sides of the hedge. The writer suggested willow or whitethorn to be planted in two rows in the earth and, curiously, if the hedge was for gardens he thought pyracantha or holly was best.[358]

Finally, rope was made throughout Devon and the walks, like that at Topsham, have gradually disappeared along with the growing of hemp as rope was cheaper from abroad and land was more valuable. Combe Martin was particularly known for its hemp gardens which were sometimes referred to as 'hemplands' as two in Higher Chapple Hay and Lower Chapple Hay were known in 1613.[359]

Buildings

Buildings are easily made redundant by changing commercial needs and pressures on land. It would be difficult to identify any one class of building not redeveloped for these reasons. Many market houses, for instance, have been lost. They have been destroyed by fire throughout Devon but at Ashburton the market house was taken down in 1850 because it was dilapidated while that at Thorncombe was demolished in about 1770 when the market was discontinued.[360] Rows of buildings and some streets have also disappeared but only a handful of entire villages in Devon have been lost in the last five hundred years. The one that is best-known, and to commercial development, is Hallsands in south Devon. Other villages have disappeared for less defined reasons including sixteen identified in one study[361] and another was

Hallsands in the nineteenth century, several generations before its destruction.

allegedly at Saunton Sands[362] but the greatest loss is this small fishing village of more than two dozen buildings which straddled the coastline near Slapton from the medieval period until the early 1900s. It had been protected from the sea by a bank of shingle when in 1897 there was dredging for gravel to extend the docks at Devonport. This removed the ancient safety barrier and shortly afterwards warnings appeared in local newspapers and in the *Transactions of the Devonshire Association* of the danger. It was not surprising that storms on 26–7 February, 22 September and 12 December 1903, and again on 5 March 1904, caused considerable damage: in spite of new retaining walls a number of cottages fell into the sea. In the following years storms did further damage and finally fourteen years later, on the night of 26 January 1917, one took the last of the village. The only remaining buildings were on the cliff top, built through a campaign in *The Western Morning News,* and a lifeguard station and chapel. However, this was the effective end of the village and the shells of the houses stand like gravestones along the cliffs. The dockyard, with its extracted gravel, survives. Commercial pressures provided the means by which nature destroyed the village.[363] That coast had another village, known as Under-cliff Lakes, which was reported as long ago as 1797 to have completely disappeared. Seven years previously the last houses, along with ten acres of arable land, were said to have been carried away. The village, also known as Under Cliff, Streate Sands and Streate Under Clift, was situated at the northeast edge of Slapton and had been inhabited from at least the middle of the seventeenth century, possibly as early as the beginning of the sixteenth. An unknown survey, possibly made in the mid 1700s, shows it comprised nineteen dwellings but nothing remains exist except records.[364]

Changing technology

The commercial need for keeping pace with new technology has continually altered local industry and all other facets of life in Devon. It has introduced and removed a great number of industries and buildings and this can be particularly seen in the maritime world. The building of large vessels is now restricted to Plymouth and Appledore, any other activity is concerned with smaller more specialised boats particularly yachts. But from early on vessels were built in a great number of places along both coasts. In 1619, for example, shipbuilding was along the South Devon coast at expected places such as Dartmouth and Plymouth but also surprisingly at Otterton as well as Plymstock, Ringmore, Malborough, Chivelstone, Stokenham, Blackawton, Stoke Fleming, Kingswear, Paignton, Teignmouth, Topsham, Colaton Raleigh and Withycombe Raleigh. In many places vessels were built on the gravelled foreshore.[365] Competition from other parts of the country and the introduction of steam, railways and motor transport contributed to the gradual decline of shipbuilding in Devon.

Tidemills, once an important source of power in such places as Bideford, Dartmouth, Instow, Kingsbridge, Plymouth, Stoke Gabriel, Topsham and Totnes, have left only a few visible reminders: for instance, the mill

A fireman at work in Kingsbridge, c.1900, an example in which change is also progress.

Anonymous view of the Upton Pyne mill, 1799. Few mills survive in Devon, the water treatment works was later built on this site.

Watercolour, attributed to F. J. Ellis, of a windmill near Churston Ferrers, c.1860.

building still exists at Topsham and the dam at Stoke Gabriel can be clearly seen. Windmills have left more traces behind although some can be confused with follies and day marks. There are several towers still to be seen in and around Torbay.[366]

Not one of Devon's lighthouses is manned, the last to have manual labour was Mortehoe in 1995.[367] Changing technology resulted in buildings operational but without the keepers.[368] An unusual survival of a successful building, which lost its function but managed to overcome it, is Smeaton's Tower. This lighthouse, the third on Plymouth's Eddystone (the first was destroyed by a storm in 1703 and the second by fire in 1755), was built in the 1750s and survived until it was replaced by a more modern building in 1882. Its rebuilding on the Hoe was a memorial to the work it did for more than two centuries.[369] Curiously, its redundancy has ensured its survival.

Land industries have a similar history. The hand-made lace industry of East Devon was seriously damaged by the introduction of machine-lace introduced in other parts of the country as well as in Tiverton. John Heathcoat, a manufacturer in Leicester who was forced out by 'the Luddite machine-breakers' there, took over a factory where he employed Devon men and women from 1816. They did not object to the machines nor curiously did the East Devon lace women travel en masse to Tiverton to burn his factory as their Midlands counterparts previously threatened.[370] Heathcoat's factory was a former woollen mill and in Devon these fell by the wayside as the Midlands and Yorkshire industrialised in the eighteenth century. But much of the county's cloth-making was a cottage industry made in homes throughout the countryside. The redundant factories which scarred other parts of the country in the twentieth century when manufacturing moved out of England was not a feature of the Devon landscape. Instead Devon's redundant buildings were mills, many of which were converted to other uses or to domestic use.

Housing

The pattern of housing development differs greatly between the county's two cities but both have encroached into surrounding rural areas. At Exeter the area west of the river, the parish of St Thomas, was used for garden nurseries through the late eighteenth into the early to mid nineteenth centuries but gradually these plots of open land were developed for lower and middle income housing. The north of the city centre became dominated by eighteenth and nineteenth century villas which in the middle of the twentieth century nearly all of which were swallowed up by Exeter University. The last of them, St Germans Lodge, a mid nineteenth-century villa, was also purchased for its land. It, like several others initially used for student accommodation, has been left derelict and within a few short years excuses will no doubt be made that it is a public danger, be pulled down and have new blocks erected on the land. This is a practice not unknown in the history of property redevelopment. To the south-east of the city lay another string of nineteenth-century villas which have been subsequently redeveloped for various purposes: Devon

County Hall was built in the grounds of several villas and another is now a recreational sports club. Not one of these large country houses is still private. Further out, where there were green fields in the early twentieth century, the city authorities moved residents of city centre slums, mainly but not exclusively the West Quarter, into the new estates of Burnthouse Lane and Beacon Heath. The commercial pressures to build housing have continued with such developments as the former Digby hospital in the 1980s.

Exeter's slum clearance and redevelopment began earlier than the twentieth century. The long Victorian response to cholera, discussed on pages 99 to 103, resulted in the provision in the 1880s of decent housing for working class families and the creation of Exeter's 'New Town'. It also caused the virtual demolition of Larkbeare House. Only a portion of the medieval building was saved and the rest pulled down to erect 239 houses. One local man stressed the need of those forced to live in large old buildings deserted by their wealthy owners and divided into multiple tenements. His concern was not with the loss of an ancient house but the lack of

Plan of the 'working men's dwellings' built for a six-acre estate in Exeter, now Roberts Road, in the late 1880s. No less than 239 houses were built. The scheme was organised by Daniel Radford, for whom, presumably, Radford Road was named. The mansion of Larkbeare was partly demolished to provide access.

WORKING MEN'S DWELLINGS,

LARKBEARE, EXETER.

Larkbeare at the time of its planned demolition in the late nineteenth century.

sanitation necessary for such large numbers of people. The result was, he argued, the physical and moral health of the working class was compromised.[371] The same argument was used in Plymouth and elsewhere.[372]

Plymouth's expansion was more clearly set by geography with the Sound, Hamoaze and Plym river effectively leaving only the north of the city free. Moreover, the estates at Mount Edgcumbe and Saltram also limit potential expansion. Commercial needs have squeezed available land between the old centre and Dartmoor National Park putting pressure on what were ancillary villages including Plympton and Plymstock. After the second world war housing estates were established in grounds of historic houses around Plymouth. Widey Court in the parish of Egg Buckland was an ancient property best known housing Charles I during the Civil War. In 1954 the house, which had some sixteen bedrooms, was demolished for a housing estate in a similar manner in which Radford in 1937 and later Whitleigh Hall were developed. At Widey Court two granite doorways were rescued but the rest of the building, including the Gothic garden house, was destroyed.[373] Radford, which comprised some fifty rooms, was demolished but the gate-piers and lodge were kept. Several features also survived in the grounds including a three-sided roofless tower, two granite arches and two pillars. A housing estate was built in the 1970s around the park created from part of the grounds.[374] The *Plan for Plymouth* of 1943 envisioned a collection of satellite villages for New Plymouth. Whitleigh, Honicknowle, Efford and Weston Mill were the result.[375] Hooe and Swilly were two other country houses converted to accommodate Plymouth's housing needs and the Whitleigh estate was another. This estate was built in the 1950s following the demolition of the Hall after a fire in 1941. The Hall, two farms and six cottages were demolished and rubble from blitzed Plymouth was used as hardcore for the eight miles of roads. The foundation stone of the first house was laid in April 1950 and it was

planned that 7,000 people would live on the 300 acre estate. Interestingly, the first tenants were labelled militant, ungrateful and meddlesome for objecting to the lack of telephones, doctors, schools and pavements. It was said they have expressed gratitude for the cleaner air, lack of noise and heavy traffic as well as better housing.[376]

In addition to those in and around Exeter and Plymouth, many other substantial houses and villas have been either pulled down and housing built, such as at Mount Boone in Dartmouth, Duncan House in Torquay and Barcombe Hall in Paignton, or merely been built in the grounds such as Chaddlewood near Plymouth, the Retreat at Topsham, Winslade at Clyst St Mary and Derncleugh near Holcombe. In contrast, the second building known as Buckfast Abbey, a castellated Gothic mansion built by Samuel Berry in about 1800, has been overwhelmed not by housing but by a new abbey from 1882.[377] In Plymouth Leighham's grounds are now an industrial park, and part of the grounds of Forde House at Newton Abbot have been taken over by local government and commercial buildings.[378] Many country houses have parts of their former grounds incorporated into modern housing estates with original garden features now gardens of new buildings. At Exmouth the lodge to Marley House is about all that is left to one of Devon's more impressive Victorian houses, at Knowle in Sidmouth part of a grotto survives in a bungalow's garden and there are impressive specimen trees from Winslade at Clyst St Mary in the gardens of many houses in the adjoining estate. There are many dozens of similar examples of such original features throughout the county, some unrecognised as such by their owners.

Commercial development elsewhere has also had a knock-on effect on buildings. For instance, it was the effect of commercial redevelopment at Withycombe Raleigh near Exmouth, and the subsequent move of population, that demolished the medieval chapel of ease, known as St John-in-the-Wilderness, in 1788. A new

Exeter's Rose & Crown in the mid 1830s, the High Street site was redeveloped in 1836.

Pen and ink drawing by Willem Schellinks, 1662, of Dartmouth with a portion of the garden at Mount Boone on the right hand side. Plants, probably exotics, are in pots. The naval college was later built on the site.

Interior and exterior photographs of Marley House, Exmouth. This late nineteenth-century mansion was demolished in 1930.

chapel was built in the village in 1720 with the consequence of only the tower and one aisle remaining. Nearly one hundred and fifty years later the church was rebuilt as the population increased with the village becoming a suburb of Exmouth.[379]

Conversions of older properties is an ongoing process, in great part related to their being economically viable. One of the more extraordinary schemes involved Abbotskerswell's St Augustine's Priory. This High Victorian Gothic building was converted to flats in 1986–7 and it had been intended to convert the chapel for a swimming pool.[380]

Leisure

One of the particular influences that has marked Devon in the last two hundred and fifty years is leisure: the introduction of tourism from the middle of the eighteenth century has changed the landscape more than many parts of the country. Coastal places that were mainly fishing settlements, such as Sidmouth, Budleigh Salterton, Exmouth, Dawlish, Teignmouth and Torquay on the south coast and Ilfracombe in particular on the north, were redeveloped to provide amenities that visitors expected. Promenades replaced bare stretches of foreshore, bathing machines jostled for space with drying nets, cottages were converted into hostelries, hotels were purpose-built and buildings were erected to provide refreshment and entertainment. Undoubtedly there were local tensions and even amusement amongst fishermen who were bemused by wealthy visitors being dipped in the cold sea: at Teignmouth in 1787 Charles Hubbard erected a tea house on the Den while local fishermen dried their nets nearby. For places like Teignmouth the prospect of tourism came with a decline in overseas fishing. The port emptied of male labour in the seventeenth and eighteenth centuries when ships left for Newfoundland in the early spring and tourism offered alternative employment when that diminished. The smells and roughness of fishing were at odds with the gentility

expected by tourists but there was at least one area in which both could happily co-exist. Only Shaldon had women who pulled fishing nets and male tourists appreciated the shape and forms of these muscular women, known as the Amazons of Shaldon, whose wet clothes clung closely revealing them 'naked to the knee'.[381] At Sidmouth the Marine Library was built in 1809 replacing The Shed, the earlier billiard room. The new library was the centre of amusement, gossip and social intrigue for the leisured class that frequented the new resort. In the late eighteenth and early nineteenth centuries these places replaced older buildings of a poorer standard and in a style of architecture out of fashion in favour of the smarter, more classical style of building. The arrival of tourism was shortly afterwards followed by the movement of retired people into Devon. East Devon was early on a favourite, particularly Sidmouth and Budleigh Salterton, oddly enough the coast which has become known as the Jurassic Coast. The green fields around the ancient centres were filled in the early 1800s with marine villas, many of them built in the picturesque cottage orné style, such as Sidmouth's Cotland House, Witheby, and Cottington which were themselves demolished after the second world war to provide modern housing. Beginning in the middle of the eighteenth century these small coastal villages and towns lost their seafronts to the amenities, their centres to more upmarket services, and their rural hinterlands to the spread of suburbia and its gardens.[382]

The growth of tourism also had its effect on land outside these resorts in such respects as the building of golf courses. This began particularly early in Devon. The county has arguably the earliest course in England: the Royal North Devon Golf Club at Westward Ho! was started in 1864. It also lays claim to being the first ladies club in the world. The 33 courses have maintained open ground but have necessarily also made great changes to the natural landscape particularly in the loss of arable and pastoral fields.[383] Race courses were also provided such as that at Haldon, and later Newton Abbot, which removed additional tracts of land from existing uses. That at Dean Marshes at Buckfastleigh closed in 1977 after nearly a hundred years in operation. Private ones have disappeared as well including one at Shute near Colyton.[384]

The development of tourism in the nineteenth century gradually made some services redundant. For example, it has been generations since bathing machines were found in Devon or separate beaches designated for men and women. Changing social attitudes removed the machines of the nineteenth century deemed necessary to preserve the modesty of those who wished to bathe from those who promenaded along the shore. Sidmouth was not the only place scandalised by bathers who swam without a machine nor were the ladies bathing in 1854 unusual in having reservations about men bringing their machines in close proximity to their own.[385]

There were of course earlier changes. Bowling greens were located in most towns but became prized by developers as open land and subsequently overwhelmed. The bowling green at Tiverton, located in the centre of the town, was thought in 1793 to have been 'perhaps the best and most frequented of any in the west of England'.[386] It was supplanted by the new cattle market.[387] Social change removed bull posts and bull rings in 1835, such as the bull-ring in the town square at Ashburton which had been operating since at least the late

seventeenth century,[388] at Great Torrington from 1686[389] and at Totnes on the Plains from the at least 1554 until 1815. In 1900 workmen found the old post and a great number of animal bones. The oak post was just over three feet in length. Bull baiting coincided with celebrating the 5th of November and one excuse for it was it tenderised tough meat.[390] Exeter's bull baiting was carried out at various locations and times including when the new mayor was chosen.[391] There were two sites in Plymouth: at the lower end of the Hoe and along the top of High Street. The last occasion was said to have been in 1830 at Milehouse.[392] Newton Abbot's bull-ring was demolished in 1826 and Cullompton also had two sites, the higher and lower bullrings.[393] Cock fighting has been found in such places as Ashburton, Barnstaple, Chudleigh, Churston Ferrers, Cullompton, Dean Prior, Hartland, Huntsham, Ivybridge, Littleham, Ottery St Mary, Plympton, and Tiverton among other places, although it was illegal from the middle of the nineteenth century it continued in Devon. Many took place in isolated barns but also at inns such as the Globe, the Half Moon Inn and the New Inn on Exeter's High Street, the Prince Eugene Inn at Totnes, the Golden Lion in Honiton and the Golden Lion in Barnstaple. That at Tiverton was located along the river and Exeter had one in Bampfylde Street.[394] One cockpit is known to have survived, that behind the Arundell Arms in Lifton,[395] but all other dedicated buildings were presumably demolished or redeveloped in the 1830s.

Chapter Six

Sense of improvement

A sense of civic improvement has lost many structures as well as the reappraisal and survival of others such as Chagford's Pound, where stray animals were held, which became a garden in the 1970s. These sentiments can both demolish and reconstruct. Two market crosses stood in the Square at Chagford until the mid nineteenth century when they were removed, probably when rebuilding the market house but possibly one of them was disliked for its 'popish' assocations, and the stones went to various locations including hedges. In 1928 they were retrieved and used to build the war memorial which was not uncommon. (see page 152) A sense of improvement cost North Tawton its ancient stone cross: it had stood in the centre of the village but was removed in 1887 when the Jubilee Clock Tower was erected.[396] Some improvements have been made for reasons of public

safety: the church steeple of St Mary Major in Exeter was deemed dangerous in 1581 when it was taken down and the tower was shortened in 1766 when that too was considered a public hazard. One hundred years later one reason given for demolishing the entire church was the structure was unsafe. A new one was duly erected and then demolished a century later.[397]

Improvement has also been undertaken in the sense of increased economic gain. For instance, in 1794 it was estimated that 'waste' land accounted for one fifth of Devon, a considerable portion being Dartmoor and Exmoor, and, during the agricultural boom years of the French wars, there were moves to make land available for farming. From 1777 to 1842 some 26,000 acres, nearly two per cent of the county, was enclosed by Parliamentary Acts in 66 different places. These were common land and included a change of use such as the 1200 acres at Hemyock in 1814.[398] It was seen as unproductive and controversies over the enclosures were concerned with rights of access rather than change of use: there was no concern in the eighteenth century in

Engraving of the east end of the medieval church of St Mary Major with the cathedral. This Exeter church had its steeple and tower pulled down in the sixteenth and eighteenth centuries before being demolished in the nineteenth century.

Beer by Robert Froude, 1807, with the collection of buildings later demolished in the cause of improvement.

destroying natural habitats and ancient monuments or concerns over losing areas of beauty.

Improvements were also made in respect to health, traffic and civic re-planning.

Health

A significant number of buildings have been demolished over concerns of poor sanitation and attempted improvement of public health. One example is The Hard in Beer, now a well-known small open amenity on the seafront, which was previously known as Charlie's Yard and comprised six thatched cob cottages. The residents' animals, including ducks, fed in the cesspool created by the village stream and in the last century Lord Rolle was reportedly so concerned that he moved his tenants to a row of new cottages on Common Hill.[399] In the nineteenth century throughout Devon many hundreds of other buildings were cleared because they were unfit for human habitation. The greatest single influence was the appearance of cholera in 1832.

A doctor recorded Exeter's outbreak in which more than 400 people died and he noted how the city was gripped by panic and terror. Many of the poor lived in squalid conditions in late medieval or Elizabethan town houses which when new had been considered grand and opulent buildings. But wealthy merchants had moved to the open and leafy suburbs and their former homes became tenements. One writer, who used the *nomme-de-plume* of the 'white slaver', described large families living in single rooms. The poor sanitation helped spread disease and after the outbreak local government officials began to clean the city by opening the streets to sunlight, water and air, by widening streets, covering drains and removing street obstructions such as steps, overhanging windows and arches. Buildings were demolished as new streets were carved out of the city centre.[400]

Plymouth had a similar history of cholera and in both cities it was argued that the medical and moral health of the poor was compromised.[401] In 1832 Plymouth had more than double the number of deaths and several equivalents to Exeter's West Quarter – two of these were Sutton Pool and 'The Marsh', the area around Union Street. They were described, within living memory of the outbreaks, as 'festering scenes of squalor'. The disease also struck in 1850 killing nearly two thousand people and in 1872 the number was higher. The living conditions were more congested than Exeter with poor people ('wretched, beastly and degraded creatures swarming

Nineteenth-century pencil drawings by N. W. Deckamant entitled 'Old Workhouse and St Andrew's Church' and 'In Westwell Street, Plymouth'. The workhouse was pulled down in the 1850s to make way for the new guildhall.

with vermin and wallowing in filth') in tenement buildings. In 1847 Reverend W. J. Odgers described in his *Report on the Sanitary Conditions of Plymouth* that twenty-seven streets housed 3,300 people without any drainage of sewerage and another 53 streets were only partially drained. He estimated less than one third of all Plymouth's houses were properly drained. Odgers also noted proper sanitation was optional for new houses and that there were still some 80 to 90 pig sties within the city bounds as well as 12 slaughter-houses. His report showed overcrowding, poor ventilation and inadequate numbers of toilets: many were without facilities and some streets, such as Stoke's Lane, comprised 10 houses with 102 people having no drains or toilets. In many places buckets were emptied at night emptied into the harbour. Even posh streets, such as Bedford Terrace, only had covered gutters.[402]

Various attempts were made at pulling down these buildings and erecting model cottages: towards that end the unsatisfactory Plymouth Improvement Commission was disbanded and two schemes of improvement undertaken. The area around Sutton Pool was cleared and a main line made through Old Town Street, Bedford Street, George Street and Union Street. Houses were pulled down, roads widened and new residential buildings built. One casualty was the Hoe Gate, the last vestige of the city's wall. The third appearance of cholera, in 1872, was followed by another bout of enthusiasm as it became clear that not enough had been done. In 1900 one writer remembered how Castle Street, or 'the Rag', had from the early eighteenth century into the nineteenth been infamous through a nightly population of 'the destitute and the dissolute'. He thought every house was a former inn and every inn a brothel. One local cleric, the Reverend Francis Barnes, was shocked on more than one visit to find men and women dancing in the nude. He sternly rebuked them and caused these 'furies' to decamp. The area was also known as Damnation Alley,

Photographs of a Notte Street house, and the Turk's Head, pulled down for improvement in Plymouth. The Turk's Head in Plymouth was demolished on the orders of the Board of Health in July 1861. The Abbey Hotel, later described by James Hine as a 'painfully modern structure', was built on its site.

the equivalent of Exeter's Castle Street and London's Drury Lane. In the latter end of the nineteenth century the Artisans' Dwellings Company was formed and more modern housing built on notorious slum areas such as The Cribs, also known as Doidge's Well, in Devonport, which included alleys and courts such as Bragg's Alley, Francis Alley and Trafalgar Court. Willis Street, Northbrook Street, Corry Street and part of Duncan Street took their place, now mainly within the Yard. Within these two generations hundreds of buildings, many of them late medieval or Elizabethan, were pulled down and thousands of their occupants moved to new buildings. As with Exeter, there was a great loss in ancient architecture but an enormous saving in the lives of the poorest of society.[403] But in 1905 one writer noted:

> On the outskirts of the town spring endless rows of unlovely tenements in which the same class of people crowd again, the people who have been disturbed in their former haunts and history repeats itself; slums rise again in other localities, but let us hope under better health conditions than in the past.[404]

In 1872 the living conditions of the poor were also graphically described by Henry Whitfeld, the editor of Devonport's *Independent*, in his pamphlet *Overcrowded Plymouth* and in a later book. Whitfeld wrote:

> families who swarmed in dirty hovels a dozen years before were festering in them yet – the rooms as miserable, the alleys and lanes more mouldy, and the atmosphere pervading them a little mustier. These remains were dens of fever and immorality... the rooms were small, dark, damp and dirty, and the occupants so debased that layers of straw on bare floors sufficed for sleeping purposes. A primitive water-closet, with no flushing apparatus, ordinarily sufficed for sixty or seventy persons.[405]

He was scathing about the gross inattention of the lord of the manor, Lord St Levan of St Michael's Mount, and Lady St Levan was also ridiculed for her solution to poverty being better church attendance. A letter to her, written by Whiteld in the guise of a pauper boy, must have scandalised local society:

> ... when yer ladyship spok of bringing us op as Christyuns, I says to my pal, 'Bill, what is a Christyun?' and Bill, he say, 'Oh, it's wun of them blokes as goes to chirch and chapel a Sundays, whiles we'm mendin our close as we sit in the bed, til we've a finished.' 'Well' I ses to Bill, 'I'd like to be a Christyun,' ses I. 'Rite yer are,' ses Bill, 'I'd like ter be a Christyun too, a very easy life they as, – Theyatre Ryal a Mondays, Grand Theyatre a Tusdays, over in the park a Wensdays, lodge a Thursdays, dance a Fridays, club a Saturday nites, and a soft cushing to pray on a Sundays, while the gurl is cooking a jolly good feed 'ome, with the Pawl Mawl Gasette or the Quiver in the hafternoons – Oh! I should like to be a Christyun'.[406]

Exeter was like Plymouth in that the movement to clean up slum housing slowly continued through the nineteenth century, aided by complacency as well as a lack of funds, including the demolition of seventeenth-century houses on the medieval bridge. These may appear picturesque to modern eyes but watercolours fail to capture the ripe smells from the leat or convey the wretched, and short, lives of the inhabitants. The houses were taken down in 1883 as well as many dozens more over the next fifty years as city authorities built more than a thousand homes in new estates such as Burnthouse Lane and Beacon Heath: Paul Street was cleared of a great number of old buildings which were unfit for housing.[407] After the immediate threat of cholera receded there was less pressure for change but efforts continued through into the twentieth century although public housing programmes after the second world war were not motivated by health concerns. In 1893 Plymouth had its Housing of the Working Class Committee and improvements continued with streets widened, buildings pulled down and new ones erected. The motives of one local man, 'Bully' Bates, have been questioned and his block of houses described as a 'cross between a barracks and a prison' but these buildings replaced ones with appalling conditions. Slum clearing also took place in Devonport where private initiatives, such as the Dockyard Dwelling Company, also built new houses.[408]

Of course rural parishes also had unfit housing but the problems in Plymouth and Exeter dwarfed those of smaller places. One observer found a small 'turf hut' at Rawridge near Upottery in 1820 in which a couple and their two young children lived: he wrote they had 'a savage way of life to the restraints of decency' and implored the lord of the manor to find them decent housing. He wrote 'pauperism, theft, illicit intercourse of the sexes and other vices increase as self-respect abates'.[409] Notable efforts were made, for instance, by the Duke of Bedford at Tavistock in the 1840s and 1860s and at Bridestowe where model cottages were built in the

early 1800s by the local cleric.[410] They still stand today. By 1926 another ethos was at work: national legislation concerned with the state of rural workers' cottagers sought to recondition dilapidated buildings and not demolition. One Westcountry inspector of a village reported it was:

best be described as a slum. I find it impossible to describe adequately in words the primitive squalor that obtains. The housing conditions beggar description. Out of fourteen working-class houses inspected, ten are beyond repair and are not only dangers to health but to life. They ought to be closed and demolished without delay, as they are liable to collapse at any moment.

Although no doubt efforts were not as stringent as would be wanted today, the emphasis was on the keeping and not destruction of older properties. By 1930 340 buildings were refurbished and saved, the number later rose to 1,446.[411] Another unusual example of renovation took place at Ilsington from 1937 to 1939.[412] These were the exceptions.

Two lithographs of Sidmouth by P. O. Hutchinson showing the attempts to cover gutters and sewers. The first was made in about 1831 and Hutchinson wrote 'at that time the spring of water from Cotmaton came all the way down as an open drain. A woman is washing clothes in it on the foreground and there was a flagstone to cross it, by way of a bridge. The two round columns are mounted by balls at the churchyard gate, now flank the entrance to Audley near Powys. The old woman, walking with a stick, was a Mrs Barratt. She was paralysed on the left arm and leg'. The second image was made the following year.

'View of the Brideston [sic] Cottages', 1808. Vancouver noted these cottages were built by Reverend Luxmoore at Bridestow to replace ones which 'were scarcely sufficient to afford a single night's shelter to a gang of gypsies'. He compared them with cottages in Chilworthy which were built using three 'mud' (cob) walls and a hedge bank. Vancouver wrote that 'the first range of these buildings were constructed uniform, and nearly in the following manner: room below, sixteen feet square, one door and one window in front; fire place with an oven opening into it with a flue; door opening back into a shed or lean-to, for covering fuel, labourers' tools, shelter for a pig, etc; another door from this lean-to opens into a small back yard, fenced off from a small garden attached to each tenement; under the stairs in the front room, leading up to the bedroom, is a panty fitted up with shelves; opposite to the fireplace, over which there is a mantle-piece, a sort of dresser is fastened to the wall with shelves, and these constitute the fixtures in the room below. The bedroom above is the same size as the room below. The walls of the first eight feet of these cottages are built with stone, the superstructure with cob, covered with a slate roof, and cost, upon an average, when finished in a plain and useful manner, from £38 to £40 each. The slate costs 10 shillings per thousand; a quantity fully sufficient for the making of a square of ten feet; the slate is bought rough at the quarry, and fashioned afterwards; one cart-load or ten horse-loads of stones will build a perch and a half of wall 20 inches thick; three cart-loads of clay are required for an equal portion of cob wall; eight bundles, or one horse-load of straw, is mixed and tempered with nine cart loads of clay, and consequently equal to the building of 4½ perch of cob of nearly the same thickness as the wall below. When the wall is 16 feet high, of stone only, the mason's demand is 2 shillings per perch of 16½ feet; if stone 8 feet and cob 8 feet, 1 shilling and 10 pence per perch; if cob only 1 shilling 6 pence per perch. In all cases, it is supposed that the materials are laid down in the rough, for the masons to dress and temper, and serve themselves. Four Winchester bushels of lime are used for every perch of stone wall; the lime ash-floor below coasts 6 pence in the square yard, tempering and laying down; and the floor above is made of rack deal, or any soft wood plank more convenient to be procured.' The row still stands today, situated outside of the main church entrance.

Photograph of a Devon agricultural worker's cottage before being reconditioned, 1926.

Traffic

One great reason for demolishing buildings has been street improvement. This became particularly important in the late eighteenth century when wheeled traffic, notably coaches, became more common. A good example is the development of Torquay's Fleet Street from 1865 to 1868. Local officials had also been unhappy with a number of wide spaces which were considered a nuisance because they were used for 'objectionable purposes'. The road was 23 to 28 feet wide, including pavements, and a plan was agreed to demolish buildings, including a row said to have been built of lath and plaster, and widen the street to 45 feet. A grand meeting was held on the steps of the London Inn to proclaim work was underway and a dinner for 200 people given in the Union Hall, but terms were not reached with the Cary family at Torre Abbey. Although more than £22,000 was spent, the plans were not completed. Local officials remained concerned by accidents in Babbacombe Road and Park Crescent and once again attempted to widen the junction. They purchased one end house and the frontage of Foulston's Regency market: these were pulled down and the widening finally completed in 1866.[413]

Street widening has in particular demolished many buildings. Exeter's North Street is one example of buildings being destroyed or pared back to accommodate increasing levels of traffic. In 1821 it was realised this street could no longer have a width of only nine feet and local authorities began demolition work.[414] It would be difficult to find many streets in the centre of either Exeter or Plymouth in which buildings were not taken down to improve traffic flows. This is just as true of every Devon town and probably village as well. Even underground monuments are not safe: when New Bedford Street in Exeter was laid immediately after the second world war 45 feet of the medieval underground passages were filled with rubble because it was thought modern traffic would collapse the road.[415]

A view of Honiton before the Shambles were taken down in the early 1820s.

Street improving was the cause for demolishing the Kingsbridge market house in the late eighteenth century: it was sited in an inconveniently place.[416] Markets are particularly vulnerable to traffic improvement schemes because they were situated in the midst of the streets. At Tiverton the early Georgian market house was taken down, along with other buildings, in order to improve traffic flow.[417] Chagford's market, The Shambles, was removed in 1862 and replaced by the building known locally as the 'pepper pot'. Exeter began planning new markets in the early nineteenth century because the traditional temporary stalls set up in the streets were inconvenient for traffic. It was not until 1835 that there were permanent food markets.[418]

Even churches have been demolished for street improvements. This is the reason Newton Abbot has one church without a tower and a tower without a church: the nave of the medieval church of St Leonard was demolished in 1836 in order to improve the flow of traffic in Wolborough Street but the tower was retained although not without controversy. That year a new church was built on a more convenient site but without a tower. In 1887 the tower features in the town's Jubilee celebrations but then years later there was an attempt to demolish the ancient tower but the intervention of the Society for the Protection of Ancient Buildings, with a postcard campaign of local people showing ninety per cent were in favour of keeping the tower, helped keep the tower intact.[419] Exeter lost several churches, including Holy Trinity, St George and All Hallows on Goldsmith Street, for street improvements.[420]

One of the most striking casualties of traffic improvement schemes are the city gates of both Exeter and Plymouth. Those at Exeter disappeared between 1769 and 1819. The North Gate impeded traffic and was taken down first. Then fifteen years later, in 1784, the East Gate was demolished. Interestingly, the city officials contributed towards making images of the gate.

Presumably, if it was considered, local officials deemed it too expensive to purchase properties on either side of the gate and redirect traffic around the gate. The West and South Gates followed a generation later but there was no outcry against either. It was not until 1823 when it was proposed to take down Broadgate, which stood between High Street and Cathedral Yard, that there were complaints of needless destruction. 'One of the old school' and 'modernus' wrote to a local newspaper against it but others won with the argument that the gap through the gate was so narrow as to be a public danger and inconvenient for coaches. One wag suggested painting the cathedral to make that more acceptable to tourists.[421] The destruction in Plymouth extended beyond the gates to the very walls themselves. By the end of the nineteenth century they had been reduced to a few stretches of banks of earth. One gate in particular was removed to make it easier for traffic to flow. The Frankfort Gate, also known as the West Gate, was situated between what is now Western Approach and Market Square and was taken down in 1783. Thirty years later the local authorities marked it with a plaque on which it was written:

Near this place formerly stood Frankfort Gate which, with others, formed the principal entrance into the town then enclosed by a wall erected for the greater protection thereof by the Mayor and Commonalty under the authority of the charter of Henry VI. But, in course of years, this mode of defence ceasing to be of any effect, the gate was taken down in 1783 and the street and avenues adjoining were considerably widened and improved. This tablet was put up by order of the Mayor and Commonalty 4th of June 1813.

The Hoe Gate was demolished eighty years later in 1863 in order to build better housing. The other gates were pulled down by the end of the nineteenth century: the Friary Gate was demolished in 1763, the Gasking or

Gascoigne Gate in 1768, the Old Town Gate in 1809, the Barbican or South Gate in 1831 and the East or Coxside Gate before 1890. Many were destroyed in order to make the passage of wheeled traffic easier.[422]

Other public buildings have been lost in addition to gates. Exeter's Great Conduit, a medieval building rebuilt in the sixteenth century, which stood at the Carfax, the junction of High, Fore, South and North Streets, was taken down in the 1770s because it was a nuisance to traffic. The conduit was the main source of water for the working population and was particularly regarded for making pea soup but was no longer conveniently situated for the increasing level of traffic.[423] Oxford also had a Carfax with a conduit which was taken down but it was rescued and re-erected at a country house as part of a design by Capability Brown.[424] Exeter's structure had no such champion.

Finally, traffic improvements have taken ancient monuments throughout the county. The Highway Act of 1835 allowed materials in waste or common ground to be used to repair roads and this was the cause of a

Exeter's Broadgate, pulled down to make way for coach traffic in the 1820s.

Drawing of the Frankfort Gate, Plymouth, demolished in 1789.

Drawing of Sparke's Gate, Plymouth, demolished to make way for the railway.

An earlier plan that was not followed: in 1914 Thomas Mawson proposed 'Exeter of the Future' which involved clearing much of the old city. The bombing during the second world war would have spared Mawson's buildings and destroyed the remaining older part of the city. It would have left Exeter with a twentieth-century city centre.

number of Dartmoor sites being destroyed. One such victim was Cranbrook Castle where the ramparts were denuded of thousands of loads of stones taken to mend nearby roads and the stone circle at Scorhill was another casualty when a farmer took stone for a gate post.[425] Another Dartmoor site also suffered from road improvements: a cairn near Merrivale Bridge was removed in the 1870s in order to make a new road.[426] Other damage was reported in 1902 to cairns, hut circles and a stone row.[427] Likewise wayside crosses have been taken: one in Peter Tavy was moved for this reason in the early nineteenth century as were others at Bovey Tracey and Halwell.[428]

Re-planning

Without doubt the greatest changes to the Devon landscape from re-planning came as a response to damage done during the second world war. It is questionable whether the redevelopment of the two cities would have happened if war had been avoided. Irrespective of whether both cities had outgrown their ancient street patterns, these schemes made the careers of many planners and others around them.

The timing of the two greatest plans is in itself extraordinary. *Exeter Phœnix, a plan for rebuilding* was printed in 1946 but *A Plan for Plymouth* appeared three years earlier in 1943[429] while Plymouth was still being bombed and the war had yet to be won. The great sweeping changes suggested at Plymouth, which were more fully followed than those planned for Exeter, were perhaps made with the assumption that the devastation would probably be even greater than that already suffered and therefore there would be fewer impediments to achieving the scale of change. In comparison to Plymouth, Exeter's plan merely tinkered around the edges. Whereas in Exeter the great need was to rebuild its retail outlets, particularly those in High and Sidwell Streets, Plymouth had a scale of destruction which allowed, if not actually demanded by the planners,

nearly a complete rebuilding of the city. The planners explained their 'daring' proposals were in response to comments made by the Minister of Works on a visit two years previously: Lord Reith was quoted as saying 'goodbye to the narrow and maze-like streets of the centre – broad ways and modern buildings will replace them'. It is interesting they believed Plymouth had been 'ripe' for rebuilding before the war because the streets and buildings were no longer appropriate to the needs of mid-twentieth century society. New Plymouth would, they argued, replace 'the outworn street plan, unsuitable for modern buildings and incapable of all but minor adjustments'.

As the planners hoped, they built New Plymouth in a simple geometric pattern. Just as the great fires at Tiverton in 1598, 1612, and 1731 were responsible for a new Georgian Tiverton, so too the war damage and the planners were the cause for Plymouth's centre being entirely a creation of the mid twentieth century. The current unpopularity of the result may have more to do with the architecture rather than the plan. Few today distinguish between the overall plan and the buildings. The style of architecture is, sixty years later, just as unfashionable as the late Victorian architecture which it replaced was in 1943: it is often said that the second fifty years of a building's history are when it is most at risk. The plan did not destroy many buildings, nearly all were already gone, but the loss lies in sweeping away the street pattern and the refusal to rebuild any historic buildings. R. N. Worth was one who mourned the loss of the 'organic' nature of Plymouth. The planners claimed that their task was 'to create something positive, practical and beautiful… something more ambitious than a correction of defects: it endeavours, with full knowledge of its deficiencies, to forecast a great modern city'. It is interesting they distinguished between 'Old' Plymouth, that around the Barbican, with the remainder. Their plan for the waterfront was to contain it within a wall and develop through demolition, refurbishment and erecting new buildings. That plan was not followed.[430]

The Exeter plan was not fully followed but still dominates the centre. The eastern end of High Street, in brick but dull, is more impressive than the rebuilt South or Sidwell Streets. Of the latter, only a fanatic for mid twentieth-century architecture could fail to become disheartened by the dreariness of the street. Whatever torments St Sidwell may possibly have endured during her lifetime, they seem insignificant to those a generation of modern shoppers have experienced in Sidwell Street. In contrast to Plymouth, criticism in Exeter at post-war building has focused on the failure to save Bedford Circus, which was damaged but not destroyed, the carving out of a by pass (Western Way) and the creation of the Guildhall Shopping Centre or particularly of the Harlequin Shopping Centre once termed 'mongrel Hollywood classicism and old fashioned art deco touched up with red and blue paint'.[431] The three latter schemes destroyed many early buildings, particularly in Magdalen and Paul Streets, and while being practical, remain visual eyesores. To be fair, those who were planning in the 1940s and 1950s were attempting to create a new vibrant city but it remains hard to justify the destruction of houses in Exeter's West Quarter when so many had already been destroyed.

One shared consequence of the schemes is both have main approaches that are at best undistinguished but could more properly be described as cheerless and uninspired. Plymouth's Exeter Street is depressing in the extreme particularly the closer one approaches Charles Church, now more a monument to insipid planning than to the war. The hopes expressed on its grand opening in February 1958[432] are strikingly at odds with its modern appearance. Exeter is equally unimpressive. Few who cross Exe Bridges are aware of a river underneath them and the ruins of the medieval bridge and the jagged tower of St Edmund's church stand as isolated and inaccessible from society as Charles Church does in Plymouth. The isolated groups of ancient buildings reflect a compromise between a public desire to preserve and the planners' wish to sweep all before them in the cause of utilitarianism. These traffic islands embody the cities beyond: history trapped by planners in the name of traffic improvement. Few visitors can appreciate they are arriving at an ancient city and not some dreary cow town in the American Mid West.

Only now, some sixty years later, are these plans being modified with both cities undergoing rebuilding schemes. Both plans originally included pedestrian areas, where, shoppers could walk 'without the danger of being slaughtered or maimed by rapid through-traffic'.[433] The new plan for Exeter, in redeveloping the Princesshay Shopping Centre, which was once famously dismissed as 'pedestrian in both senses of the word',[434] has attracted a controversy not experienced in the city since the early nineteenth century when it was divided on the location of the new market. Supporters of the new scheme argue that Exeter can now afford better architecture than that put up in the austere 1950s but opponents favour keeping the post-war buildings claiming devotion to both the plan and architecture, perhaps a sign that post-war buildings are becoming more acceptable or even fashionable. In fact one part of Plymouth's great plan, that of the Pannier Market, has recently been listed Grade II. But the general dislike of the two centres is also a statement of a distrust in modern architecture.

Chapter Seven

Fashion and taste

Capricious notions of good taste have resulted in the loss of great parts of Devon's heritage. For instance, in 1829 the subscribers of the Tavistock Library agreed to demolish their eleven-year-old building because the Duke of Bedford did not approve of the architecture. He felt it was not in keeping with its surroundings and provided space in the abbey buildings where the library remains to this day.[435] In January that year the rector expressed his surprise to the duke. He tactfully wrote he could not change his mind because his opinions were already public but would, in respect to the duke, remain neutral. Privately, he wrote, he hoped some consideration would be given to his views:

A building, that in itself, is certainly deserving of the greatest commendation as a true and chaste specimen of classical architecture. Were it about to be built, the question would be somewhat different: tho (as I speak dispassionately, as I did nothing in the business but pay my contribution) I confess that I might perhaps have been somewhat scrupulous to impose on future antiquaries by too great an assimilation of it to the abbey. But tho', in that case, it is near enough, were the style correctly imitated, to produce this effect, I yet think that it is sufficiently distinct & even detached from the abbey to be of a different form of architecture. It cannot possibly be identical with it: which would certainly be a violation of propriety, fitness or harmony; as when we see modern sashed windows in a Gothic building, or a Grecian screen as is or was in Winchester Cathedral. But juxtaposition of various styles of architecture, instead of being a defect is a beauty.... this juxtaposition of the Gothic & Grecian styles is constantly found in the pictures of the best Italian masters... At any rate I hope that it may not be pulled down till a good drawing of it be made, to show what once it was. If the site of it is wanted for a more useful purpose, this would be a better ground for the alteration than that of taste.

But in early March the subscribers agreed to pull down their building 'from an opinion generally prevalent that further improvements are contemplated likely to be very ornamental and beneficial to the town which the existence of the present library would be quite incompatible'.[436] The concept of mixing architectural styles is one which still rages, and while it is notable the debate was carried on in early nineteenth-century Tavistock, it is also interesting the issue was important enough to the duke to demand the destruction of a newly-built library financed by local people. His status as an arbiter of good taste was questioned. That same year, Miss Sophie Dixon, who most likely was herself a formidable personality, dismissed the duke and his showcase of Endsleigh, the Devon home he had built only twenty years before. On a visit to see this *cottage orné* perched on the Tamar valley she wrote, in her book, that the flower bed was tawdry and trifling, the introduction of rare garden plants into the wild a mistake, the grotto was destitute of interest and the £120,000 spent on it 'with its misarranged grounds and their fantastic decorations' a waste of money.[437] No doubt some in Tavistock, who may have felt bullied by the man who owned the town and most of those in it, sniggered at this chastening.

The notion of taste necessarily changes with each generation: for instance in 1862 one speaker at an Exeter meeting expressed the view that the mid Victorian 'tall, thin, flat-faced, flat-topped style' of its High Street buildings was uncouth and thought more favourably of the Elizabethan 'lofty gables, sharp-angled dormers and corbelled oriels'.[438] The previous year a Plymouth man deplored demolition of the Turk's Head by the Board of Health. He wrote that

If this or any other old building be in a ruinous state, and by projecting in an awkward ways endangers a single life, by all means let it go. But I am not at all certain that appearances are improved by the widening of streets in the older and poorer parts of the town. In the place of the picturesque gabled buildings, with its broken outline and quaint details, what do you usually get? Two gaunt shop windows of wavy sheet glass, with a thin door in the middle. A stuccoed superstructure, apparently resting upon nothing, enlivened by four square sash windows, with a cement moulding round each, the whole surmounted by a straight parapet coping, with an eighteen-penny urn – also in cement – stuck at each end. The thing is hideous from the beginning, seedy before it is 12 months old, and you show your antipathy to it by rushing through the street as fast as you can, fearing some unlucky accident you may be compelled to see it.[439]

In 1877 one Devon architect made 'a plea for the picturesque in Devonshire towns' and while his notions of saving old houses fits in well with today's ethos he exhibited other attitudes which would be questioned. He found Kingsbridge devoid of any picturesque interest, not a trait the modern visitor would agree with today. He approved of medieval or seventeenth-century buildings but rejected later buildings as too uniform. Likewise he found Buckfastleigh 'depressingly uninteresting' but there too we can find buildings from his time, and the last 125 years, that now appeal to modern tastes.[440] That same decade another Devonian criticised the architect of the earlier church 'restoration' at St Andrew's church in Plymouth: he wrote that John Foulston's 'sole object apparently was to eliminate every trace, so far as he could accomplish it, of interest and antiquity in the church'. In marked contrast to the lack of any criticism

from seventeenth or eighteenth century writers, this nineteenth-century Devonian was also dismissive of the Reformation's clearing out of religious objects and buildings: irrespective of whether there were needed reforms in church policy he felt there was no excuse for 'slaughter, pillage, rapacity and wanton destruction'.[441] By then there was a marked change of attitude towards those who had followed the Oxford Movement, discussed below, and its attempt to bring churches back to a medieval ideal. In 1905 the vicar of Shute wrote that he disapproved of:

Urns, cornices, capitals, balustrades, composed of stucco, with an iron stem in the middle to keep them together, one so useless and hideous that they need only to be mentioned to be condemned. I can hardly believe they give pleasure to anyone except those who get their living by making them.[442]

In 1910 Cecil Torr commented on Lustleigh church:

The whitewash was removed in 1871, and made way for much worse things – green distemper on the walls, blue paint and gilt stars on the roof, crude stencils on the side walls of the chancel, and on the eastern wall a fresco made in Germany. The trees and sky are hidden by glass that is exasperating in its colour and design. Lavatory tiles replace the granite paving of the chancel, and there is marble of the sort one sees on washstands.[443]

About ten years later one man unfavourably exclaimed, upon seeing Victorian church restoration, 'Oh, what a sea of pine!'[444] In 1932 the Council for the Protection of Rural England noted with distaste the 'disastrous use of red and yellow brickwork' at Sidmouth.[445] Some would view these houses as charming or quaint today.

A sense of aesthetics has guided the improvement of Cathedral Yard in Exeter for some two hundred years.

From the late eighteenth century through to 1821 the treasurer's house was gradually demolished. It stood on the north side of the cathedral but even though it had a window famed for its connection with Henry VII the authorities wanted a cleaner view of their cathedral. A number of other buildings were taken down, including medieval ones around the church of St Mary Major in the 1860s, and then that church itself nearly a hundred years later. The interior of the cathedral has had three periods of improvement: the mid to late-eighteenth century could be called 'exuberant antiquarianism', from 1805 to 1835 there was the 'Decorated Gothic' of John Kendall and finally in the 1870s the Gothic Revival of Sir Gilbert Scott. Screens are one of the most notable areas of constant change but there were many others also based on a changing sense of aesthetics. For instance, the Great West Window has been replaced three times since the Reformation: William Peckitt's stained glass window of 1766 was removed in 1904 for a memorial window to Archbishop Temple which was destroyed in the second world war. It was replaced by what has been described as a 'pedestrian' work. No doubt someone soon, if it has not already happened, will call for its replacement on the grounds of good taste.[446]

Fashionable trends are a cause for the loss and creation of a great number of buildings. Entertainment is a good example of this. Exeter's Royal Public Rooms, also known as the Royal Subscription Rooms, the Devon & Exeter Subscription Rooms and the Exeter Subscription Rooms, were built at the eastern end of High Street in 1820. It continued as the fashionable venue for concerts, exhibitions and balls until 1908 when it became The Hippodrome, a 'High Class Music Hall'. That lasted until the 1920s when the fashion for film brought a new change: the building was pulled down and on it was built The Plaza cinema in 1932 only to be destroyed in the bombing of the city in 1942.[447] It is now a non-descript retail building. All across Devon similar buildings were

Panelling at the Grange, Broadhembury, in the 1850s. It was exported to the United States several generations later.

erected to meet current needs and then subsequently redeveloped or demolished when those fashions waned. There is one stunning example of a single area which dramatically rose and declined in popularity: in the late eighteenth and very early nineteenth centuries Devonport, or Dock as it was then known, was the fashionable spot in the county. The importance of the navy to the country gave it a social cache to visitors, particularly with those who brought young unmarried daughters: the large number of naval officers made the balls and other social events there the ideal marriage market. The entries in the diary of Mrs Parry Price of Chester, who visited in 1805, show the social excitement.[448] But the end of the Napoleonic war, and the subsequent decline of the navy, brought with it a reversal in the fortunes of Devonport to where it seems impossible today to imagine it ever was fashionable. A similar tale could be told of many Devon seaside resorts, once highly fashionable in the nineteenth and early twentieth centuries, but now suffering from competition overseas and losing key amenities and buildings.

The fashion for old building materials resulted in architectural features being lost from Devon. In 1929 the oak panelling of The Grange in Broadhembury was exported to the United States as was that of a High Street building in Exeter at the same time. Curiously, it was purchased by Randolph Hearst and sent to California where it escaped the later destruction of its original Exeter building. It has since been acquired by Exeter City Museum and is now preserved, while every other feature of its former home has been lost. The American market was lucrative in the years before the second world war and French & Company sent agents to Devon to find building materials for its clients. The panelling of Number 229 High Street was one successful purchase and is now on show in Kansas.[449] Although these exports may be regretted today, at the time the objects found an appreciative home, unlike in Devon, and some have been saved whereas if left in their original locations they would certainly have not have survived. In this respect a comparison could be made between elements of Devon in the early part of the twentieth century and Afghanistan of the late 1990s where heritage was of no importance.

Churches

Nineteenth-century church alterations were remarkable, irrespective of whether they are thought of as renovations, refurbishments or modernisation the results were startling. In the early nineteenth century there was a fashion for lime washing the interiors of churches. In about 1819 at Broadclyst, for example, the painted screen and wall murals were covered.[450] There was so much applied at Moretonhampstead that the church was described in 1853 as 'an avalanche of lime'.[451] Some effigies were 'restored' so heavily that they bore little resemblance to their former selves. In 1877 one writer noted that in Devon some were:

irretrievably injured through a well-meant, but ill-judged zeal; some have not only been scraped carefully from whitewash, but have afterwards been tooled deeply all over, utterly destroying the ancient contour of the figure, and frequently robbing it alike of mail and ornamental accessories, or re-cutting them to another pattern, while incongruous restorations of the face and the extremities are generally added, occasionally with extraordinary exaggeration and grotesqueness.

The reason suggested for this was ignorance and the crude skills of local stonemasons.[452]

Churches were replaced at Teignmouth between 1819 and 1823. The reason given for the demolition of one of the ancient buildings was because it was dilapidated but the popularity of the coastal resort made the old fashioned churches redundant. East Teignmouth church was completely rebuilt and the old tower was destroyed. A replacement was later built to mark Queen Victoria's

Pen and wash of Bideford parish church, by Edward Ashworth, 'in its classic dress', c.1860, before his renovation.

Jubilee in 1887. West Teignmouth retained its tower. Not everyone agreed with the new buildings: the Reverend George Oliver called the latter a 'squat, puffed out and staring novelty'.[453]

As discussed on pages 33–34, not long afterwards the Exeter Diocesan Architectural Society promoted a 'simplification' of churches in which they were returned to an earlier style (whether or not it had been there in the first place) and the removal of later additions. For example, the church at Moretonhampstead in 1856 had the seats removed as well as the fifteenth-century screen and the gravestones on the floor[454] while at Plympton the carved stone pulpit was demolished with the pieces used to provide sleepers for the new pews.[455] The church at

Chudleigh was reputedly in a dilapidated state and ready for the hand of improvement when in 1843 the locals 'were fully awakened to the necessity of rendering the House of God more convenient'. The seating was greatly altered because it was considered 'an unsightly assemblage of irregular, unseemly boxes, of various heights, inclinations and dimensions'.[456] Nineteenth-century restorers of churches saw themselves as improving the buildings: Reverend Ellacombe of Clyst St George wrote he replaced the box pews because they were 'affording snug sleeping corners and hiding places for the thoughtless and ungodly'.[457] Curiously, one old man, who lived in Lydford, snored loudly each Sunday in his pew but was regarded as an 'institution' in the parish

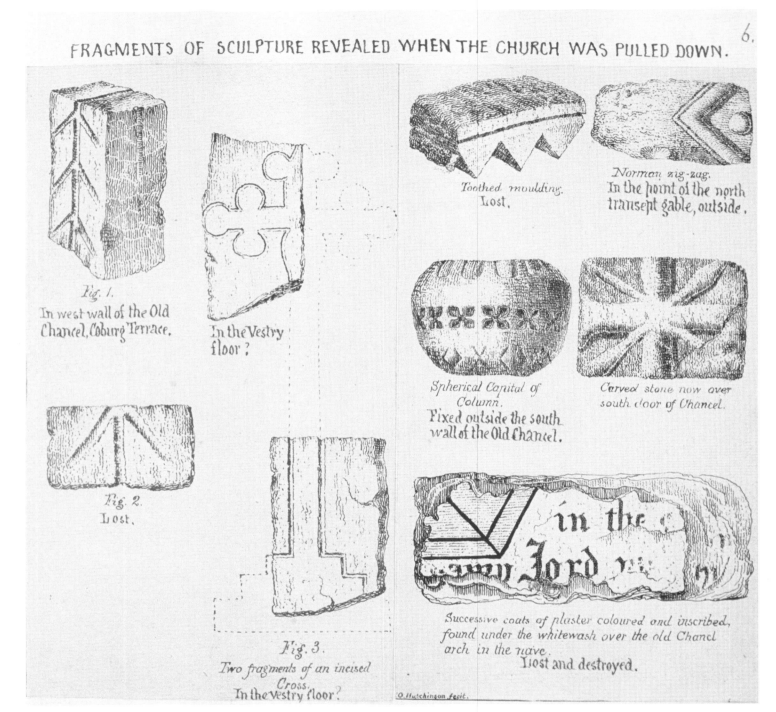

FRAGMENTS OF SCULPTURE REVEALED WHEN THE CHURCH WAS PULLED DOWN.

6.

Fig. 1.
In west wall of the Old
Chancel, Coburg Terrace.

In the Vestry
floor?

Fig. 2.
Lost.

Fig. 3.
Two fragments of an incised
Cross.
In the vestry floor?

Toothed moulding.
Lost.

Norman zig-zag.
In the point of the north
transept gable, outside.

Spherical Capital of
Column.
Fixed outside the south
wall of the Old Chancel.

Carved stone now over
south door of Chancel.

in the
Lord

Successive coats of plaster coloured and inscribed,
found under the whitewash over the old Chancel
arch in the nave.
Lost and destroyed.

O. Hutchinson fecit.

Drawings by Peter Orlando Hutchinson of carved stone found during the 'restoration' of Sidmouth's parish church in the nineteenth century.

and so was left to sleep during the service.[458] He was not alone. It was claimed in 1843 that even the Bishop of Exeter fell asleep and snored in public.[459]

It is unusual to find a church which was not greatly altered. When William Butterfield restored Morebath from 1875 to 1882 among his changes were replacing seating from 1534 and 1755 and the font that was possibly made in the early sixteenth century.[460] It is unclear why one medieval tomb, suggested to be that for Sir John Carew of Ottery Mohun of 1363, was removed during the restoration of Luppit church in the 1870s. Also at that time effigies were likewise reportedly taken from churches at Dartington, Paignton and Marldon.[461] An early twentieth-century study of fonts noted that crude restoration of Norman fonts at Buckland-in-the-Moor and Bickleigh near Tiverton had seriously disfigured the stone work.[462] There was also some rescue work: when the church at Sheepstor was restored in the mid nineteenth century the ancient screen was cut into separate sections, discarded and taken to a yard in nearby Horrabridge. It was subsequently rescued and placed in the church at Buckland Monachorum. That church, in turn, lost its parish stocks to Torquay and its ducking stool to Exeter.[463]

The church at Bridestowe has had an unhappy history with its carved oak benches destroyed 'in a deliberate holocaust'. In 1869 a local builder was given the screen in part payment for his labour and although he burnt it, he kept the oak tympanum that sat between the cornice and the apex of the roof tree. This measured thirteen feet six inches by seven feet high and was found after his death in a loft. It had the royal arms of Queen Anne but may have been made earlier.[464] Other histories are equally surprising. The Reverend Baring Gould, when a small boy, saved fragments of the screen from Lew Trenchard that his grandfather had placed on the wood heap. At Moretonhampstead the Earl of Devon, the patron of the living, was alleged to have taken part of the screen to Powderham Castle and the remainder went to Whitchurch. Powderham also had the stone screen at Greenway's Chapel in Tiverton: the earl had seen the stone lying in a heap in the graveyard and brought it home. Later, his descendants did not find either screen. At Rockbeare the screen was cut down to the level of the box pews in 1793 and then in 1887 the lower part was taken to Rockbeare Manor. The screen of Stoke Rivers went to Weare Giffard in 1832.[465]

Photographs of Malborough church during restoration, late nineteenth century.

The extent of the loss of ancient screens in the nineteenth century is staggering. This includes Ashcombe (sold in 1820), Ashprington (removed in 1846 and then destroyed), Axminster (removed in 1660 and parclose in 1875), Aveton Giffard (removed in 1869 but restored 1886), Bondleigh (removed 1839), Bratton Clovelly (nearly all sometime after 1820), Brixham (removed by 1861), Broadhembury (removed 1851 to a linhay which caught fire), Bulkworthy (mutilated after 1847 and removed in 1873), Broadclyst (removed after 1867), Churston Ferrers (removed in 1864), Churchstanton (sold about 1830), Clayhanger (after 1825), Coffinswell (removed by 1822), Dawlish (removed after 1825), Dean Prior (removed before 1875), Doddiscombleigh (removed after 1847), Dowland (removed after 1822), Dunsford (removed 1813), East Teignmouth (removed after 1822), Exbourne (removed in 1835), Fremington (removed 1845), Gittisham (removed 1845), Halwell (removed 1810), Hatherleigh (upper part taken down in 1820 and lower part in 1867), Hemyock (burnt before 1846), High Bray (removed after 1822), Ide (removed 1834), Iddesleigh (sometime early in the nineteenth century), Ideford (removed about 1846), Kentisbury (removed after 1847), Kingskerswell (before 1847), Langtree (removed after 1822), Lewtrenchard (1833 and since partly reconstructed), Loxbeare (removed 1832), Luppitt (removed after 1822), Marldon (removed after 1865), Malborough (removed later nineteenth century), Meavy (removed 1840), Monkokehampton (removed 1856), Moretonhampstead (removed 1857), Newton Abbot, St Leonard's (removed and sold 1836), North Huish (removed after 1822), Plymouth, St Andrew's (removed and sold in 1826), Poughill (removed after 1844), Peter Tavy (removed by 1852), Romansleigh (removed after 1822), Rockbeare (removed 1887), Sampford Courtenay (removed 1831), Sampford Peverell (in about 1826), Sheepstor (most removed in late nineteenth century, Shebbear (removed about 1887), Shirwell (removed after 1847), South Brent (removed in 1864 to rot in churchyard), South Tawton (removed about 1826), Stoke Rivers (removed in the late nineteenth century), Tetcott (removed after 1858), Tiverton (removed 1854, chapel screen removed 1835), Tormohun (removed after 1822), Uplowman (removed before 1822), Venn Ottery (last sections cut up in 1884), Warkleigh (removed by 1850), Wembury (destroyed by 1852), West Alvington (removed after 1869), West Buckland (removed in the early nineteenth century), West Ogwell (removed after 1822), Whimple (removed before 1822) and Woodbury ('ruined' in 1848).[466] The celebrated Harry Hems concluded the causes for their loss were 'apathy, greed, ignorance, fanaticism, or right down wilful wickedness, respectively or combined'.[467] But he overlooked one great force of the nineteenth century was the restoration, if not rebuilding, of churches.

Of course changes had also taken place earlier. The rood screen in West Teignmouth church was removed in the early eighteenth century because the minister wanted to make the building 'lighter' while the King's Arms and ten commandments, erected in 1666, were removed in 1790 simply because the wood was rotten.[468] The rood screen at Ashburton was taken away in 1718 and the pulpit and oak eagle lectern sold to the parish of Bigbury in 1777. Harry Hems built a new screen and stalls in the nineteenth century, to the designs of George Edmund Street of London, but there were still fragments of the original left in the town. Likewise the rood screen at Cheriton Fitzpaine was removed in 1793, that of Clyst St George in 1790 and Spreyton in 1758.[469] The greater number of changes took place however in the nineteenth century partly with the encouragement of the Exeter Diocesan Architectural Society.

Gardens

Gardens must change simply because they are constructed of living entities which must eventually die. In consequence there are more opportunities for change than with buildings but gardens are equally vulnerable to fashion. For instance, in 1793 the Reverend Polwhele noticed that in Lympstone there were 'some good brick houses' which had 'trim gardens where trees are cut into artificial forms'. Nothing else is known of this topiary which presumably was lost generations ago. Topiary, as discussed below, fell out of favour at the end of the eighteenth century but is also more likely to change because it is labour-demanding.[470] It is not surprising that not one historic maze in Devon has survived. It has been suggested there was a maze at Dartmouth and Hartland, both known as Gallants Bower, possibly as early as the fifteenth century.[471] If these did exist, they have long disappeared. Whatever influence changing fashion may have had in the late eighteenth and nineteenth centuries, when gardens were becoming less formal, the great difficulty with mazes is that they are also labour intensive. Devon had at least three mazes at the end of the nineteenth century. There were two at Pitt House in Hennock and Peamore House in Exminster which were both laid out in the second half of the nineteenth century. Neither were recorded in the tithe maps of 1839 and 1842 but had been planted by 1905. That at Pitt House may well have been planted that very year. By 1955 only the north and east boundaries of the maze at Pitt House still survived while that at Peamore disappeared between 1954 and 1967. The most important maze was at Holsworthy. It was known as The Labyrinth, as well as The Puzzle, and had been laid out by Viscount Mahon, possibly as early as 1821. It covered nearly an acre and some fifty years later it was said the maze was the only thing worth seeing there. It lay on the lower side of the rectory garden and was centred around a tree with a seat. The maze became so neglected that it was renamed The Wilderness and in the early twentieth century was sold and part of the land used for road widening. The remnant had made little sense by 1932 and in 1946 the rectory was sold and the site redeveloped.[472] The land is now used as a car park, still in the same shape, but with no remnants of the maze.

The disappearance of Parson William Davy's garden at Wilmead in Lustleigh is a particular loss. It was created in about 1818 on a knoll behind the house and he blasted the stone in order to clear the ground and create five terraces. Davy planted box and trimmed them to show Scriptural texts. He called it his *Living Body of Divinity* (in contrast to his published work *System of Divinity*). Some twenty years later the letters, which were some six inches in length, were still visible and visitors could read 'act wisely', 'deal fairly' and 'live peaceably'. It had vanished by the end of the nineteenth century. Many Victorian pixie gardens have also disappeared: these were box-edged, with narrow paths and they made a pattern. They were known as pixie gardens because the plants were grown to be marginally higher than the assumed twelve-inch height of the pixies.[473]

Many changes in garden fashions have occurred through minor alterations rather than great sweeping changes. Few formal gardens of the sixteenth and seventeenth centuries survive in England and a very much smaller number in Devon. Many, like that at Oxton, as discussed below, were changed in the late eighteenth century as England took up the new 'green' style of Capability Brown. The straight lines and manicured trees were seen as too artificial. One particular casualty in Devon, a county familiar with rain, were the ornamental stretches of water in the grounds of these private houses. There are remains of an eighteenth-century canal system still to be seen at Bicton; it may have extended a considerable way through the grounds of the now-demolished medieval house. Cheap labour during the Napoleonic war, in the shape of French prisoners of war, has been given as the cause for the redesigning of that landscape, with one consequence being the digging of a new lake below the house which had been built above the site of the former mansion. The formal gardens have been attributed to designs by Andre La Nôtre in the seventeenth century but surprisingly little research has been made of what is one of Devon's most significant ornamental landscapes.[474] Many other gardens had ornamental water: for example, the stream that runs below Castle Hill near South Molton has been depicted in a number of illustrations as being more formal than it is now.[475] There was also a canal at Painsford near Ashprington,[476] the Quicke family built a canal at Newton House in Newton St Cyres,[477] Sir Francis Drake had an ornamental canal dug out at Nutwell along the Exe river in the middle of the eighteenth century,[478] and it is likely that Poltimore had one and many others at country houses, such as at Great Fulford which still has a 'canal

Drawing of the canal at Painsford, Ashprington, mid eighteenth-century.

walk', probably existed as well. Water also features in the use of moats or fish ponds: Keynedon Barton near Sherford is one example of a medieval building with fishponds over which a causeway led to the house. Early fishponds survive at Haccombe near Teignmouth and at Dunkeswell Abbey.[479] The Templer family re-landscaped their grounds around Stover and ornamental water, with a canal system, was the overriding feature.[480]

The Balle family at Mamhead redesigned their landscape with trees imported from Italy at the end of the seventeenth century. Robert Balle chose to follow the fashionable formal style of gardening with terraces, trimmed hedges and fountains and other water features. The subsequent owner in the late eighteenth century, Lord Lisburne, was influenced by Capability Brown; he took away the formal features but left the trees which were then of a great size. In 1823 yet another new owner, Robert Newman, pulled down the house and inserted new terraces, enlarged one pond and created two new ones. The landscape now, like most historic Devon gardens, is a mix of work from the seventeenth century onwards but the dominating feature at Mamhead are the extensive plantations.[481]

It has been estimated that between 1086 and 1500 Devon had as many as 59 deer parks. These hunting reserves were scattered throughout the county and the owners were eminent families and the bishops of Exeter. There are possible remains of a 'standing' at the deer park at Dartington from which the hunt could be watched. In the sixteenth and seventeenth centuries there were at least 22 deer parks but increasingly land was turned to more productive uses. For example, by 1808 Brightley Park, in the parish of Chittlehampton, had been converted to arable farming.[482] Today the only deer park is that at Powderham Castle but the deer are still here. By 1950 Devon had four species of deer: Red Deer were in the north of the county, Fallow Deer were mainly in the east as were Roe Deer and the Sika, or Japanese, Deer in some wooded valleys of East Devon. In the mid 1970s they were

Nineteenth-century engraving of the grounds at Mamhead with its imported trees, the last remnant of the seventeenth century garden.

Nineteenth-century engraving of Okehampton Castle in ruins with the remains of the deer park around it.

joined by Muntjac Deer which escaped from captivity in Dawlish.[483] Deer have provided hunting on Exmoor and in other places as well: in the late nineteenth century the Duke of Bedford brought his hounds down from Woburn to Endsleigh in order to rid his tenants' lands of red deer.[484] Walls still exist in many places, for example those at Whiddon Park near Drewsteignton are impressive, and it is easy to imagine the deer at Okehampton Park alongside the castle. The remains of early deer parks can be viewed throughout Devon but the real inheritor of them are the many dozens of later eighteenth and nineteenth century parks created by local men who were influenced either by Capability Brown or the gothic movement in suggesting a fictitious medieval past.

Antiquities were also used as garden features: the Rolle family at Bicton transported the Seven Stones, an ancient circle of six upright blocks with a centre stone, from Peak Hill near Sidmouth in the nineteenth century to use as building material for their rockery.[485]

Country Houses

A considerable number of country houses have been pulled down and new ones built on the same site but not always because of a loss of finances as discussed on pages 62 to 67. Many were demolished simply because they were no longer fashionable. Good examples of this are Upottery, a small manor house which was replaced, as discussed earlier, in the 1840s and another is Wood near South Tawton, a Victorian villa pulled down in the early 1900s to build an Arts & Crafts house.[486] When the Reverend John Tripe changed his surname in 1780s to inherit the considerable fortune of his aunt Mrs Esther Swete he was in a position to pull down the late medieval house of Oxton in Kenton and build a new symmetrical mansion. The old formal garden, terraced with ancient yews, was also removed and Swete set out to improve nature with the invisible hand of taste by sculpting a cliff to imply it was an ancient quarry and carving out of the cliff face a hermit's cave, erecting what would hopefully be seen as a medieval gate and creating a lake by damning a stream. He appears to have had no qualms over his house but was quick to criticize the Carew family for tearing down their ancient home and

erecting 'a mere modern edifice, perhaps commodious within, but without, having no sort of claim to uniformity, or the graces of architecture; it stands, a tall mass, looking as though it had been disunited from some other building, built with the common stone of the country and thus even continuing un-stuccoed'. Swete claimed he would have felt obliged to have kept it for subsequent generations. Unfortunately Swete seems to have conveniently forgotten that Oxton had been his mother's maternal home for some two hundred years and also was an ancient building.[487] Shute near Colyton was pulled down in part: the Pole family built a new house above their old medieval home but unfortunately it stood in the way between the new site and the ornamental lodge. Half the building was demolished and the stone was used to build a bank alongside the new carriage drive.[488]

Occasionally entirely new landscapes, with new houses and grounds, have replaced existing ones. This happened with the building of Endsleigh, the *cottage orné* of the Duke of Bedford near Tavistock. The landscape was laid out by Humphry Repton and the Picturesque building, erected from 1810, was designed by Jeffry Wyatt. It replaced a pair of possibly thatched buildings known as Ingesley which Repton referred to as an 'irregular farmhouse, little better than a cottage'. The house overlooks the steep Tamar river valley with panoramic views to the south but Repton also inserted terraces to the south east and more intriguingly, he added the Dingle Dell to the north west. Locals were not allowed to continue living in the valley area but Repton thought it would be picturesque to have smoke rising from a chimney situated across the house: the suggestion of life was appropriate but not the reality.[489] A similar story can be told of Haccombe on the Teign estuary.[490] The Carew family demolished the ancient hamlet which stood below the house most likely because it obscured their view. The two rows of houses are shown on a map of about 1600 but not on the tithe maps of the 1840s. The land was instead used for arable and pasture.[491]

Haccombe in about 1600, showing a village straddling the lane leading up to the home of the Carew family. The village was subsequently demolished.

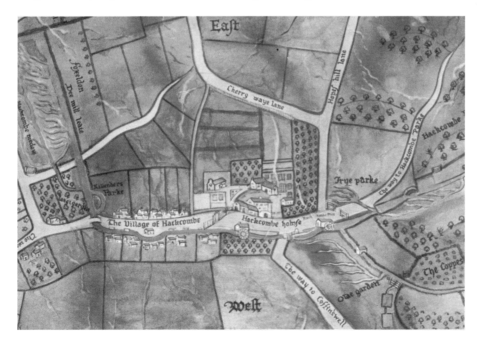

Follies

Follies can be found throughout Devon although these eccentric buildings, erected with no apparent purpose other than to provide amusement, can be confused with the remains of windmills or seamarks. Some are converted buildings such as that at Yeovale, in the North Devon parish of Alwington, which was the ruins of a medieval chapel moved by 1822 from the house to feature in the grounds.[492] Others have not survived partly because of the expense in their maintenance. A number of these have been lost at Castle Hill near South Molton. Their disappearance is partly due to the great number which were built in the grounds. Visitors today admire the triumphal arch across the valley and the ruins of the castle above the house but are ignorant of eighteenth-century features long gone from the landscape: these include a Chinese temple and bridge, hermitage, a Palladian villa known as Clatworthy, a temple to Venus and, most interesting of all, a model village. The latter was known as Shamtown and even had a tower stuck onto one of the cottages. They have been reshaped, dissolved with time, had their materials scavenged and the temple at Holwell suffered a fire. Although these were buildings erected simply for pleasure the cost of them was high: in 1771 it was estimated that the expenses in building Holwell Temple was over £823.[493] The Reverend Swete also had a folly at Oxton in Kenton: his Gothic arch was reconstructed several times until it achieved the right degree of suggested antiquity. Unfortunately the arch was taken down in the 1960s when there was no enthusiasm for picturesque follies and because it was impractical for tractors.

Engravings of the follies at Castle Hill: the castle, the villa at Clatworthy and the Hermitage.

Chapter Eight

Natural Disasters

Natural disasters, in the way of fire, flood and storms, have accounted for considerable changes to the county's landscape. Damage from earthquakes has been slight,[495] in the eighteenth century shocks were felt in 1727, 1752, 1756, 1757, 1775, 1789 and 1792 but these have only been curiosities. The most damage seems to have been to a pinnacle on the church tower at Widecombe-in-the-Moor.[496] Along the coastline, particularly in South Devon, cliff falls have been much more common. For example, six acres fell at South Down near Beer in 1788, another fall happened at Peak Hill near Sidmouth in 1811 and at Chit Rocks in 1849, in 1885 there was a tragic fall of stone at Dawlish[497] and a large landslip at Teignmouth in 1853 caused the railway to close.[498] At Beer a number of caves, which were associated with smuggling, have been lost. One was called 'The Chapel' because of its size and 'Tom Tizzard's Hole' was used by a man of that name as his home. When the 'The Old House' collapsed an onlooker was reported as saying it sounded 'like a thousand tons of stones falling down'.[499] Devon's most famous landslip is at Dowlands near Axmouth in 1839. On Christmas Day a tract of land, a mile long and several hundred feet wide, collapsed some two hundred feet into the ground and land also rose offshore. Two labourers' cottages were destroyed amongst the general changes to the topography: banks of soil and stone covered fields and meadows. The chasm can still be traced nearly two hundred years later and it was then, as now, a site for visitors. In the first week thousands of visitors were charged six pence to view the devastation. Curiously, the landslip, as destructive as it was, has embellished the landscape in spite of the loss of the cottages.[500]

But there are other natural disasters besides fire, flood and storms. The introduction of new diseases have had devastating effects. That best known in recent time is Dutch elm disease which destroyed many thousands of trees in Devon in the early to mid 1970s; by August 1972 some 500 trees were dead[501] unlike other parts of Britain such as Brighton and Pembroke which escaped. The disease appeared in Plymouth by August and was noticed at Torbay two months later before being found across the county. Many particularly significant trees were lost including some of the elm trees planted in the mid seventeenth century at Tawstock near Barnstaple as a memorial to four brothers who died of plague.[502] The Devon landscape had been filled with elms. Polwhele, for example, noted in 1793 that a feature of Clyst St George was its elm trees[503] but many other places as well had prominent elms.

Another great change has been the introduction of new species of garden plants into the countryside, most notably buddleia, rhododendrons, laurel and Japanese knotweed, which have overtaken some native species. The Veitch firm, for example, recommended that rhododendrons be planted at Stover House near Newton Abbot in 1842 to fill in gaps[504] but they had no idea of the consequence. These have since overwhelmed the planting scheme. Most recently in the summer of 2003, there have been alarming reports of an introduced oak disease brought about through the plantings of rhododendrons.

Prominent trees have been lost when they reach the end of their lives: the Great Tree of Holsworthy, an elm tree under which St Peter's Fair was traditionally proclaimed, was cut down from its site in Lower Square in about 1890 because it was not safe. A scion of this tree, the Chasty Elm Tree, stood one mile from it in 1934.[505] Possibly the notable plane tree on North Hill in Plymouth, which stood near the Pound, had reached the natural end of its life when it was cut down in 1849 and mostly used for firewood. Some wood was used to make a garden seat.[506] Trees planted near village crosses are particularly noticed when lost but there have been many reasons for their disappearance. In many villages, such as

View of the landslip at Dowlands near Axmouth. In 1839 John Harvey, a bookseller who lived in Sidmouth, wrote 'the convulsion of which we now give a brief description, occurred on the south coast of Devonshire, at the distance of two miles east of the mouth of the river Ax, and the town of Seaton, and about one and a half south-east from Axmouth village. We will not enlarge on the geological interest it has excited throughout the country, or the curiosity which has been evinced by the thousands of persons who have crowded to examine it, but enter at once on the subject.

It commenced at three o'clock on the morning of Tuesday, the 24th of December, 1839, when the family of Mr Chapple, who occupies the farm of Dowlands about half a mile distant, was aroused by a crushing and low rumbling sound. Nothing, however, further occurred until four o'clock on the morning of Christmas day, when some labourers of the farm, who tenanted two cottages built on the slope of the debris of the undercliff, were awakened by noises similar to that which had been heard the night before. On getting up and endeavouring to open the door, the man who dwelt in one of them, discovered that it was so wrenched and distorted, that he could not accomplish his purpose without violence and the assistance of a crow-bar. He then saw that the ground was sinking beneath him – that it was subsiding in terraces towards the sea – that it was gaping with fissures – and that the walls of his dwelling were cracking and tottering as if ready to fall. He then hastily got his family out, and proceeded to his landlord and gave the alarm, for no one knew how far it would go, or where end. During the whole of Christmas Day the disruption continued; making a roaring and grinding noise resembling some kinds of thunder, and causing the earth to tremble at a great distance from the actual disturbance. An immense tract, extending east and west one mile in length, and many hundred feet in width, subsided or sank down so as to form a ravine or chasm more than two hundred feet in depth. Parts of several fields, included in this area, descended with great regularity and precision; so that their surfaces, still bearing their crops, are now at the bottom not much broken up, and only thrown into a slanting position, instead of being level, as they were before. The hedges which divided these fields can be traced on along the fallen portions, as well as across the high country which has remained unmoved. This regularity, however, is not universal. Towards the eastern and western extremities of the chasm – particularly towards the former – the devastation has been extraordinary and complete. Columnar masses, resembling vast pinnacles or towers of chalk, are in some places left standing, whilst the more broken and crushed parts have sunk around them; immense banks of flint and broken rock rise in hillocks on every side, whilst the ground is rent and scored in seams many feet wide and deep. An entire orchard is to be seen in one part, which has descended to a level much lower than it before occupied; some of its trees are overthrown and uprooted, whilst many others are still standing, and will bear fruit next season. A wood of forest trees has also been broken up in the same way; the cottages before mentioned are in ruins, and their gardens destroyed; and the devastation around, although dreadful and terrific, is full of beautiful grandeur.

This chasm, however, is but one moiety of the phenomenon. It ranges east and west, and parallel with the sea shore, and in running through the district, cuts off from the main land a portion of the original country measuring one mile in length, a half a mile in width. This huge mass, so cut off, has been forced on its foundations many yards in a southerly direction towards the sea, inclined somewhat from its former lever, and rent and depressed into terraces. The bed of the sea also, the whole way along in front of it, has been lifted up to the height of forty feet above the surface, to a great distance out from the original line of coast, now forming reefs and islands, inside which are bays and small harbours, into which boats have been, and have found good soundings. These reefs of thrown-up rock are covered with marine productions, such as corallines, sea weeds, and shells. The western basin somewhat resembles the Cobb at Lyme; but it has the advantage over it in being larger in size: the eastern basin is entered through a long narrow channel, which then widens into a larger bay.

We must now enter into an inquiry as to the causes of so vast and violent a revolution. It was at first supposed to have been an earthquake, according to the usual acceptation of the term, that is, a dislocation of the earth by the agency of subterranean fire. A closer examination, however, of the component materials of the district, and a mature consideration of other accessories acting thereon, will incline to decide otherwise. It is most probable that water, and not fire, has been the cause; and, in order to make this apparent, it is requisite to mention the geological construction of these hills.

The upper stratum, running through the cliffs, is chalk. This rests on the green-sand formation, much consolidated, and alternated with seams of chert, a species of opaque flint. Beneath this comes a deep bed of loose, sandy marl, or 'fox-mould' as it is locally termed, and it is this unstable and friable soil that contains the chief causes of the disturbances under consideration; and lastly this stratum is supported by the blue lias, a formation partly composed of beds of tough and impenetrable clay. These being the component strata, let it be borne in mind, in order to the understanding of this explanation, that all the soils above the lias are pervious to water, but the clay in the lowest resists it. The rain and other atmospheric moisture which falls on the upper surface, and the springs of water which may tend towards one point, will filter through the chalk and sandstone, and be mainly absorbed in the spongy fox mould. It cannot descend lower, because the clay of the lias resists it. Now, where the edges of these soils are exposed along the cliffs, so as to lay them bare and unsupported, this water will be seen oozing in springs out of the sandy mould immediately above the clay – which it carries away with it – slowly and almost imperceptibly perhaps, but surely and inevitably. Such a process, going on through the course of ages, must necessarily undermine the super incumbent strata; and when a season occurs more wet than ordinary, and such indeed as England has experienced during the past summer, the catastrophe is hastened on with a sudden crash, even such as we now describe. The precipitate and violent subsidence of such a great mass, had power, by its overwhelming weight, to act laterally, and it was this lateral force which served to thrust upwards the bed of the sea, previously seven fathoms beneath the surface, now into reefs forty feet above.

Although the effect produced is as terrific and ruinous as if the fires of Vesuvius had been the agent, yet we have endeavoured to show that fire had indeed no part in it. Several other places on the south coast of England exhibit the remains of similar convulsions, wrought, without doubt in a similar way, but in what age it is impossible to say, as no record of such an occurrence exists to inform us. The Undercliff in the Isle of Wight may be instanced as one; the Pinhay Cliffs, only three miles east of Culverhole Point (the subject of this paper) as another; and a third on the cliffs between Beer and Branscombe. It is not a little remarkable that Providence should not have suffered a single life to be lost during so great a revolution, although it commenced in the middle of a dark night, when the inhabitants of the two cottages, which were shortly reduced to utter ruin, were in their beds.

The concourse of persons which has flocked to the scene of devastation is incredible; many thousands have been there, congregated from almost every county in the kingdom, even the most distant. The crops of the two farms which have suffered (that is, Dowlands and Little Bendon) were getting so spoilt and trodden down by these visitors, that the tenants, in order to save something from the wreck, and in some sort remunerate themselves, held it necessary to levy a toll of sixpence per head on all trespassers. In this way, it is supposed that they are reaping a silver harvest, far richer even than if the catastrophe had never occurred. The crowds during the first week were too numerous to be counted.'

Woodland in the late nineteenth century, parish meetings were held at the trees. One blew down in 1869 and knocked the cross at its base.[507] Chagford's Cross Tree, an ancient oak which had been planted near the parish church, was felled in 1975 because it had honey fungus. A replacement was planted near the original location. There was also a Cross Tree, also known as the Cross Elm, planted outside the church at South Tawton. It was replaced by an oak in 1953.[508] A tree stood in a similar position in Bere Ferrers until at least 1907 but no reason for its loss has been ascertained.[509] In comparison, Moretonhampstead lost its tree at the church cross because of a storm whereas Meavy still has its cross, or at least part of it, near the ancient oak and church. At Halberton in 1577 a tree was substituted for the cross.[510]

Finally, one of the more unusual natural disasters was to Devon's most famous wooden bridge on 27 June 1838. Only eleven years before the bridge across the Teign estuary at Teignmouth had been built comprising 34 arches and 1,671 feet in length. Over the course of those years the timbers were eaten through by shipworms and the centre arches collapsed. It was rebuilt, still in wood, and reopened two years later in 1840.[511]

Floods

Water has been a cause of great loss in Devon. Minute quantities, in the form of damp for which Devon is known, have caused inestimable damage particularly to carved wood. Occasionally there are vivid descriptions: for instance in 1793 churches such as Bridford and Trusham were reported as being so damp that the walls were green.[512] These incidents are not as newsworthy as major floods causing damage such as that at Alphington on 2 July 1760 when some twenty houses were destroyed when the Alphin Brook suddenly rose.[513] One passing visitor recorded in her diary that:

the poor people were in their beds, and one old woman in hers drowned by the rain being prodigious heavy; it

came pouring in such torrents from the hills behind, and hurled down so great a quantity of stones of such amazing size, that soon broke down walls built only of a composition of clay and straw, called cob. The houses were instantly overflowed and tumbling to pieces; all were in the utmost consternation, as one may easily imagine, from the ruinous state their habitations are still in.[514]

Flooding at the vicarage at Thorverton in 1821 greatly damaged the parish registers amongst causing other destruction.[515] Often the details are very thin such as when Lady Howard's Oak was swept away in 1888[516] and there is only a casual reference to a flood carrying away an 'aboriginal cyclopean bridge' at Dartmeet sometime in the early nineteenth century.[517] One of the most famous floods hit the North Devon coast in the early seventeenth century: water began to rise in the early hours of the morning of 20 January 1607 at Barnstaple and caused widespread damage. It was claimed to have been higher than any previous flood. The waters burst through the locked doors of houses along the quay and threw down walls in its way and there were three casualties: the home of a tucker collapsed and killed him and two of his children still lying in bed.[518] The flood extended along the length of the Bristol Channel and it may have been the cause of the destruction of a number of buildings in Lynmouth used to smoke-cure herrings.[519]

Floods along the county's rivers were commonplace such as in 1348 when the river Exe badly damaged Exe Bridge,[520] in about 1412 the church of St Thomas, then near the river, was destroyed by a flood and rebuilt at the Reformation in its present location,[521] and floodwater destroyed some 53 houses in Tiverton in 1625.[522] The flooding of the Exe in 1960 at St Thomas resulted not in the loss of life but in reconstructing the flood defences. Dartmoor too has had a great number of destructive floods: one destroyed two bridges (Hill Bridge and Mary

Tavy Clam) on 5 July 1880. Ten years later another flood washed away the long clapper under Bair Down as well as the bridge. Mary Tavy Clam was once more carried away and there was considerable damage at Tavistock.[523]

Incursions of the sea during storms have caused great losses at many places including Exmouth. A flood there washed away five acres of the Warren in 1817 and caused no known damage to property but many rabbits were drowned.[524] Another flood damaged boats and unroofed many houses on 30 November 1823 and nearly a year later, on the stormy night of 22 November 1824, the sea burst through the embankment and flooded some seventy acres. Women were brought out of their beds 'in a state of almost nudity' and there was considerable damage to property.[525] A storm in February 1838 washed away up to one quarter of the Warren with exceptional high tides.[526] At Teignmouth the sea broke through the railway in 1855 and 1859,[527] a phenomenon not unknown today. Brunel, who designed the line, was said at the time to have been scornful of the danger of the sea and laughed at suggestions of potential problems. One passenger later remembered being stuck overnight in Dawlish when the line washed away: he slept on the floor in an inn's coffee room because of the number of passengers to accommodate.[528] More recent floods have the ability to make us remember the loss of life rather than property: the opposite is true of floods that occurred generations ago. The events at Lynmouth

Storm damage to the railway near Teignmouth.

on the night of 15–16 August 1952, which resulted in the deaths of 31 people and damage to 93 houses, is a good example of this.

Deliberate flooding by man, rather than that of nature, has also caused widespread destruction. The creation of Burrator Reservoir in the 1890s resulted in the loss of the Meavy river valley which included Longstones, the eighteenth-century home of the Elford family, which was later purchased by Sir Masseh Manasseh Lopes. The remains of the house are visible and that of the garden walls can be seen when the water levels are low. Fernworthy Reservoir also took hut circles and a prehistoric site was flooded when the Avon Dam Reservoir was made. The creation of Roadford Reservoir from December 1989 caused the flooding of 308 hectares and destroyed a number of medieval hamlets including three farms.[530]

Storms

Great storms have been responsible for destroying many buildings throughout Devon. Those in vulnerable situations such as windmills, which are particularly sited in windy locations, are more prone to damage. One in Brixham for example had its cap and sails blown off in a gale in about 1870 and another in Exmouth was destroyed by a storm in 1818.[531] Many storms have taken place in winter such as those of 1795, 1814, 1836, 1838, 1853, 1866, 1881 and 1927.[532] As noted above, coastal damage has been a feature of Devon's storms including that of 1731 which nearly destroyed Ilfracombe's pier. It needed to be largely rebuilt.[533] The storm of 9 March 1891 was particularly fierce and destroyed 63 ships including many from Devon or along its coastline.[534] The 'Torbay Cyclone' of January 10–11 1866 caused the loss of some 50 vessels and the lives of 100 people.[535] In the last five hundred years thousands of vessels have been sunk and some storms have had a very local impact such as that of 4 October 1821 when thirty-one seamen lost their lives at Clovelly. The boats were destroyed as well

as the lives of the nineteen widows and sixty-one children left behind.[536] Occasionally ancient ruins have been revealed such as a bread oven and old walls in the sand at Dawlish in the eighteenth century but even then there was no recollection of the buildings.[537] The Parson and the Clerk have been recognised features of the coast between Teignmouth and Dawlish for centuries but they have precarious positions and in 2003 a large chunk of red sandstone fell into the sea. In 1922 Cecil Torr of Wreyland remembered the Parson falling into the sea and that local people, who had tried to set the stone back up, ordained another stone as the Parson and one more as his new Clerk.[538] Chit Rock, on the western end of Sidmouth, was another prominent feature of the Devon coastline. It blew down on 22 November 1824 in a storm which caused great damage to the town. It was, reportedly, swept away 'in an instant'.[539] It was this storm that Sydney Smith famously illustrated with the redoubtable Mrs Partington of Sidmouth. He wrote:

In the winter of 1824, there set in a great flood upon that town – the tide rose to an incredible height – the waves rushed in upon the houses, and everything was threatened with destruction. In the midst of this sublime and terrible storm, Dame Partington, who lived upon the beach, was seen at the door of her house, with mop and pattens, trundling her mop, squeezing out the seawater, and vigorously pushing away the Atlantic Ocean. The Atlantic was roused. Mrs Partington's spirit was up; but I need not tell you that the contest was unequal. The Atlantic Ocean beat Mrs Partington. She was excellent at a slop, or a puddle, but she should not have meddled with a tempest.[540]

With the destruction of the pillar also went the annual custom of choosing the King of Chit Rock. Each year a fisherman was elected and he was marched to Chit Rock where the men attempted to climb it, cheered, waved their caps and drank to the King with grog.[541] Chit Rock is

Lithograph of Chit Rock, 1824, entitled 'Chit Rock, Sidmouth, this rock fell during the dreadful storm on the 22nd November 1824', showing the great differences between Turner's work and the rock pillar itself.

remembered as Sidmouth's great landmark but this has not been the fate of 'the Great Knob', a stone stack which stood to the east and is thought to have tumbled down in the eighteenth century.[542] Was this a name given by local fishermen? Equally unexplainable is the name Devon sailors gave to a cove at the entrance to the harbour of St John's in Newfoundland: Wash Bollocks. There were several other local stacks which tumbled in the storm of 1824 including Two-Penny Loaf, Great Picket Rock, Tortoise Shell Rock and Man-of-God Rock. King and Queen Rocks also stood off Chit Rock but fell sometime

in the eighteenth century. It may be no accident that Sidmouth had a second salacious association with its other great 'nob'.[543] In 1811 J. M. W. Turner visited Sidmouth and some twelve years later produced a painting which included Chit Rock. Interestingly, just over a hundred years later a Sidmouth man thought he discerned a message in Turner's painting in that 'the spirit he invokes is that of coast erosion' but, in sharp contrast, a more recent writer has pointed out this is Turner's most sexually explicit image: he 'elevated' Chit Rock 'into a massive phallus' in an allusion to the sixty-five year old

Viscount Sidmouth and his marriage that year to a much younger woman. The Viscount was then subjected to public ridicule and bawdy comment. A generation later Ruskin thought the picture showed 'the back of a breaker, just heaving itself up, and provoking itself into passion, before its leap and roar against the beach'. Turner's two initial drawings of Chit Rock bear little resemblance to his later painting. It would be interesting to know whether the story of Sidmouth's Great Knob of the eighteenth century had inspired Turner.[544]

Destruction has been very localised including Bideford's

Globe Theatre, a travelling company that performed on the riverbank, which in 1882 had been under threat of closure by accusations that it was damaging the morals of local people. It survived only to be destroyed by a storm two years later.[545] Often it has been church towers have borne the greatest damage including when lightning struck the church tower at Cruwys Morchard in 1689 and melted the bells.[546] Lightning also struck Marystow in 1729,[547] South Molton in 1751,[548] Buckland Brewer in 1769,[549] Manaton in 1779,[550] Inwardsleigh and Parkham in 1789,[551] Great Torrington sometime between

Engraving of Sidmouth based on the painting by J. M. W. Turner, c.1830, with its phallic representation of Chit Rock.

Four rock formations which were destroyed in the storm of 1824: Tortoise-shell rock and Man-of-God which stood under Peak Hill, Great Picket Rock near Otterton Point and Two-Penny Loaf near Ladram Bay.

Tortoise-shell Rock and Man-of-God Rock, under High Peak Hill.
Looking south.

Man-of-God Rock.
Sidmouth beyond.

As the contour of the cliffs and headlands in this neighbourhood is continually varying in shape and feature, owing to the ceaseless action of the sea and the atmosphere, I here jot down sketches of some of the rocks on the coast, before the waves sweep them entirely away, as they did Chit Rock in 1824.

Great Picket Rock.
Otterton Point beyond.

Little Picket Rock.

The Two-Penny Loaf, a rock so called by the fishermen, stands at the base of the cliff, in a slight indentation of the shore, known as Chizzlebury a Chisilbury Bay, and between Ladram Bay and Otterton Point.

Two-Penny Loaf.
Rock at the foot of the cliff a mile westward from Ladram Bay.

A view of what the Great Knob may have looked like, from an aquatint entitled 'Rocks at Branscombe', 1818.

1786 and 1829 and more probably in 1799,[552] Peter Tavy in 1803,[553] Kingsbridge in 1828,[554] Kelly in about 1834,[555] Lustleigh sometime before 1887[556] and Holsworthy in 1890 and 1914.[557] A very early record for a storm destroying a church tower concerns Down St Mary in 1413 but there is no mention of lightning.[558] Neither is there for a gale which caused a pinnacle on Lydford parish church to crash through the roof in the late nineteenth century.[559] One writer in the early nineteenth century believed churches along the edge of Dartmoor were particularly susceptible: he noted a number of pinnacles had been seriously damaged.[560] Another writer regarded Moretonhampstead to be 'the land of thunder' because of the prevalence of storms: in the late eighteenth century one storm carried off a chain and forty feet of wire from the clock.[561] On the morning of 21 October 1638 a fierce thunderstorm famously had a disastrous effect on Widecombe-in-the-Moor: lightning struck the church during Sunday service and killed at least four people. Many others had serious burns from

which they later died. Even a local dog was killed: he had tried to escape by running out of the church but never made it through the door. The tower and internal fabric of the church were seriously damaged and the storm was the subject of several national pamphlets.[562] More recently, a storm on the night of 25 January 1990 blew down the medieval timber spire of the church of St John the Baptist at Hatherleigh: it landed on the nave and caused widespread damage.[563]

Of course localised storms have damaged many buildings other than churches: in about 1727 lightning hit a farmhouse in Blackawton and melted the pewter in the kitchen and the slate slabs were torn into pieces. Some of the stone passed through the wooden floor.[564] It appears that a tornado, described as looking like 'a large cloud like a woolpack', fell upon Rowden Wood near Tavistock on an August morning in 1768 and created a passage some forty feet wide through the woodland. It had come from Bere Ferrers, where it destroyed an orchard, and passed on to Dartmoor.[565] In the early sixteenth century a new quay was being built at Seaton when a storm 'as never in mind of men had before been seen in that shore' utterly destroyed it.[566] Much less serious was the storm of 14 October 1877 when 260 large cauliflowers were blown out of a Torbay field.[567]

There have been a number of 'Great Storms' and the phrase is usually given to those that are personally experienced such as the recent storms of 1987, 1989 and 1990 when many thousands of trees were lost in Devon.[568] That of 26 November 1703 also caused widespread damage. Appropriately enough, the morning after it raced through Tiverton a storm petrel, a West Indian bird, was found in a local orchard. It was claimed that most of the houses in that town were unroofed.[569] The storm destroyed twenty elm trees in Cathedral Yard in Exeter that were shortly replaced afterwards with lime trees.[570] The school house at Great Torrington was also severely damaged.[571] Perhaps the most famous casualty of the storm was the Eddystone Lighthouse. It had been begun only seven years before and the builder, Mr Winstanley, went out to the lighthouse just before the storm hit and never returned.[572] Other eighteenth-century storms of note were on 8 January 1734 which also unroofed many Exeter houses as did that of 4 February 1775, on 7 January 1775 at Starcross and on 28 August 177 throughout South Devon.[573]

In 1891 the 'Great Storm' caused widespread damage throughout Devon. Two hundred feet of the breakwater at Brixham was washed away and unusual damage included the Ladies' Bathing Pavilion being carried away at Dawlish and gravestones at St Petrox's church at Dartmouth Castle dropping into the sea. Gardens were particularly hit: the lime tree avenue at Maristow was destroyed, the trees in the American Garden at Combe Royal were 'laid almost bare', 1,000 trees were reported thrown down at Membland and 2,000 at Mount Edgcumbe. Some of Lord Edgcumbe's favourite ancient trees in his private garden were destroyed including an elm, a chestnut tree and a Turkey oak. An old cork tree

and what was described as a 'famous' holly tree in the English and Italian garden also fell to the ground. Perhaps the most individual loss was an ancient sycamore or plane tree at Buckland Abbey in which seats and a table had been placed in the crook of the branches for serving tea.[574]

The events of 1891 were not unusual in trees being one of the main losses. For example, in November 1677 gentlemen planted avenues of elms in Brixton near Plymouth to raise money to support the poor. Unfortunately storms interrupted these plans by repeatedly removing trees.[575] In December 1929 a storm fell an oak which stood directly across from Buckland Abbey on the neighbouring hillside: it had allegedly harboured Sir Francis Drake from an angry stag and he is meant to have had it shot and placed the antlers above the fireplace.[576] Noteworthy trees are continually lost to storms. Until 1903 the 'Dancing Tree', also known as the 'Punchbowl Tree', stood near the south gate of Moretonhampstead churchyard. This elm tree had its branches pollarded and trained for a platform to stand in its branches. Nearly 20 couples were said to have been able to dance on it, with a fiddler playing in the branches. Notable occasions were held: in 1800 a concert was held for George III's birthday and in 1807 French prisoners of war gave a concert to local people. By 1862 the tree was decaying and then the great blizzard of 1 October 1891 ruined its shape. In 1903 it finally blew down altogether in a storm.[577] Interestingly, a replacement tree was planted in its location and this purple beech is known as the Cross Tree (see page 127). This may not have been the only Dancing Tree in the county: Reverend Baring Gould claimed in 1907 that an oak on the road between Exeter and Okehampton, near Dunsford, which was still standing, was 'woven and extended and fashioned into a flat surface'. The Fulfords of nearby Great Fulford were supposed to have an annual meal and dance there with their tenants. Another, he wrote, had stood in Lifton and the great oak at Meavy

Photograph of Moretonhampstead's Punchbowl Tree (alias the Dancing Tree), late nineteenth century. It was damaged by a storm in 1891 and finally blew down in 1903.

was another where there was a platform. In 1862 it appears that there may have been other Dancing Trees.[578]

Individual items have been lost that are in themselves inconsequential but taken collectively form a considerable body of loss. For instance in 1861 the weathercock at Kentisbeare church fell in a storm. Its history was discovered within the bird in a note: 'Edward Blackmore made the thighs, legs and feet and this under-part new July 16 1804 and repaired the tail, chollies, pipe, etc., the original part was made in 1764'.[579] Few other weather vanes have survived, the victims of storms and wear and tear.

Fire

In July 1920 a carnival was held in Torquay to raise funds for the local hospital. Two men from HMS *Royal Arthur* appeared as Ancient Britons and covered their bodies with oakum, the loose fibre made from untwisting old tar ropes. When one struck a match to light a cigarette both men caught on fire and the '2 blazing torches, as they were later described, ran through the crowd in desperation but subsequently died.[580] Historians are more likely to note damage to property in assessing the impact of a fire, rather than the cost in human lives, but recent tragedies have a sense of human loss that earlier ones lose. Fire is an expected risk for some business ventures, such as the firm established in Plymouth in the early nineteenth century by William Bryant and Francis May who made Lucifer matches. After a few years they succeeded in burning down their factory and reopened the Swan Vestas company in London.[581] The amount of timber in dockyards puts them at risk: Devonport had slight fires in 1778, 1779 and 1812 and then on 27 September 1840 one destroyed two battleships and a frigate. The damage reportedly cost £200,000. Among the losses were various figureheads of ships and other mementoes including what was reputed to be a flag under which Nelson died at the battle of Trafalgar. There was also an explosion at the powder works in 1821 and in 1920 another fire swept through the yard.[582] Perhaps the most dangerous business was one on Dartmoor which ran from 1846 to 1897: the gunpowder factory at Powder Mills near Postbridge had at least explosions in 1848, 1885 and 1887.[583] It has been suggested that fire was a particular threat to Devon: the Reverend Polwhele wrote in the 1790s that it 'has been the fate of more towns in the West than any other part of the kingdom'.[584] The fear is nearly impossible to appreciate for those living in the twenty-first century. One consequence of the great fire at Chudleigh on 22 May 1807 was locals noted events in relation to whether they happened either before or after the fire in much the same way as those who survived the early 1940s refer to 'the war'.[585]

Fires during wartime have destroyed great numbers of buildings (see pages 157–169) and fire was one reason given in 1904 for the loss of many local manuscripts: it was claimed that year that sextons were instructed by their rectors to burn parish registers because 'troublesome people came worrying round, wanting him to search for them for nothing'.[586] At Barnstaple the town's ancient records were kept in an outbuilding in the middle of the nineteenth century and were used to help to light fires.[587] Nearly all of Great Torrington's records were destroyed by the great fire of 1724[588] but there were

Anonymous watercolour of Creedy Park, Sandford, 1900, destroyed by fire in 1915.

others, particularly in 1759, in which documents may have been lost.[589] The fire at Creedy Park near Crediton on 4 November 1915 was particularly painful because the owners had recently improved and redecorated over the previous six months. Among the losses were four panels of tapestry brought out of Paris in the late eighteenth century after being hidden in a cellar during the French Revolution. During the fire policemen cut the tapestries from their frames with penknives. There were a number of paintings destroyed, including a landscape and two seascapes, but the greatest loss was John Norden's great map book of 1598. It comprised a collection of twenty-five maps which had passed through the hands of at least eight men before being copied by the Reverend G. T. Llewellin, the vicar of Sandford, in the 1800s. Curiously,

the cleric made notes on the great fire of Crediton in the eighteenth century, which it survived, only to be destroyed through fire in the following century.[590] In 1884 it was claimed that Plymouth had lost a great many early documents because a Totnes man, Nicholas Goodridge, burned the record chest in the council chamber. He paid £300 to make amends.[591] As unthinkable as it may be, it was suggested that a lawyer at Moretonhampstead recommended his clients to burn their title deeds.[592] In 1787 fire destroyed Tawstock House, the home of the Bourchier-Wrey family, and most of the documents were lost. Curiously, one seventeenth-century collection, the papers of Henry Bourchier, fifth Earl of Bath, were saved because of a dispute between his widow, Rachel, Countess of Bath, and her second husband, Lionel

Lindridge in 1793, the house was destroyed by fire in 1963.

Cranfield, third Earl of Middlesex: that marriage broke down and the second husband refused to return the Bourchier family documents to Devon from Kent where he lived. It was this argument that saved the papers, including household and estate accounts, maps and love letters, from later destruction. They remain safely in Kent.[593]

The causes vary but it is difficult to accept the reasoning behind one of the most damaging fires to Devon's heritage. Many estates, such as Great Fulford, have stories that stewards burnt family papers but these are invariably difficult to corroborate. However, the descendent of one of the county's most famous Elizabethans is rumoured to have arranged the family papers for posterity, selected those to be saved and placed the remaining manuscripts, those which she felt did not reflect well on the family's name, on a bonfire. Her censorship has forever deprived future generations of a fuller, and probably more balanced, understanding of one of the county's great men. In addition to arson, some fires can be attributed to unfortunate accidents such as happened at Cullompton in 1798 when the locals were celebrating the naval victory over the French: a rocket landed on a thatched roof and destroyed seven houses.[594]

Fires have taken many individual buildings, such as Torquay's Cricket Club Pavillion in 1906 and the second Eddystone Lighthouse in 1755.[595] One prominent building lost to fire was Axminster's carpet factory. It was erected

An interpretation of the severe weather endured by the Eddystone Lighthouse.

by Thomas Whitty in the middle of the eighteenth century and was proudly shown to George III and his family in 1789[596] but was destroyed in a fire on 23 January 1828. The stock and furniture were saved but little else. It was rebuilt but eight years later the owner was declared bankrupt and the stock, looms and machinery, along with a number of weavers, moved to Wilton.[597] The number of individual buildings lost to fire is impossible to estimate given they were a common occurrence in villages every year. Most fires were unreported or only sketchy details have survived such as the fire which destroyed the vicarage at Harpford in 1763 or the mansion at Dunscombe about the same time.[598]

Human suffering features in records as well as the manner in which men and women coped with disaster: for instance in 1831 the cleric at East Anstey calmly requested additional copies of church forms from Exeter because his parsonage had burnt down the previous week. He casually mentioned he had found accommodation in a nearby farmhouse and hints he will have to move because it was exclusively reserved for the landlord during the shooting season.[599] Pleas for public assistance with the victims of fires are concerned with human suffering, particularly those concerned with the Tiverton fires discussed below.

Churches, and particularly their towers, have been set on fire: that of St Thomas near Exeter was burnt down on 30 January 1645[600] and fire greatly damaged All Hallows on the Walls in Exeter in 1646.[601] Lamerton church was burnt in 1877 only a year after it had been renovated: a small lamp, specially constructed in order to keep the new organ from being damp, was blamed.[602] One of the more recent notable losses has been the parish church at Buckfastleigh which was destroyed by arson in 1992, Exeter Cathedral suffered from arson in 2002 and Braunton church was damaged in 2003. Fortunately the ancient font was saved at Buckfastleigh but not the early nineteenth-century box pews or the Jacobean pulpit.[603] Only a quarter of county's earliest parish registers have

survived and fires at churches, vicarages and other buildings caused many losses. These include fires at Woodleigh in 1662, Belstone in about 1772, West Woolfardisworthy in 1789, Clayhidon, Dodbrooke, High Bickington and Tamerton Foliot by 1831, Knowstone in 1890, Bondleigh in 1915. Ashbury lost its early registers in a fire at Ashbury House and at Cornwood in the parish clerk's cottage.[604]

Country houses were particularly vulnerable to fire and it was a lucky building which did not have fires causing at least partial damage such as that at Killerton in 1924.[605] Other fires caused complete devastation: Northcote in East Down was burnt down in about 1700,[606] Hembury Fort House in 1752,[607] Escot in 1808,[608] Heanton Satchville in about 1820,[609] Peak House in Sidmouth at the turn of the century,[610] Creedy Park in 1915,[611] Shobrooke in 1945 and Bystock Court near Exmouth in 1907.[612] Other houses were also burnt including Tawstock, the ancient home of the Bourchiers, earls of Bath, in 1786. The current building, now a private school, was built on the same site overlooking the Taw to Bishop's Tawton. The owner, Sir Bourchier Wrey, is said to have designed it.[613] Membland Hall near Holbeton in the South Hams was demolished after a fire in the 1920s. The house had been rebuilt by a member of the Baring family but only some of the ancillary buildings survive.[614] Clovelly Court had two destructive fires. In 1798 the house was rebuilt because of the damage and in 1943 it was a Red Cross Convalescent Home when a second fire destroyed the building a few days after Christmas. The main part of the house was reduced to a shell and all that remained was a medieval wing.[615] Yarty House in Membury was destroyed by fire in 1851 with the exception of its dovecote but that was subsequently demolished.[616] In 1895 fire swept through Oldstone, the mansion near Blackawton, which had been the home of the Cholwich family in the early seventeenth century. The house had been a holding of Torre Abbey since the thirteenth century and was once a substantial building

Yarty in Membury, 1830. The artist noted that 'Yarty House, which was the abode of a farmer Mr Newbury, was early in the morning of the 11th January 1851 totally destroyed by fire with all the adjoining farm buildings except the dovecote in the middle of the court yard'. He also observed that it 'is fast falling down – it is taken down as far as the ground floor window and but few of the walls remain with the doorway in the centre of the front which was opposite of the east – over the entrance is a shield with helmet mantle and crest in stone'.

with a range of exceptional buildings. In February 1895 it was owned by the Dimes family when fire destroyed the building. The house lies in ruins but the late eighteenth-century shell grotto and folly (or barbican) have survived.[617] Fire also gutted the centre of Castle Hill near South Molton in 1934. Locals still remember the height of the flames.[618] One of the most recent losses has been Lindridge near Teignmouth: in April 1963 a fire destroyed this mansion, one of the grandest to have been built in the county.[619] One of Devon's best-known fires was at Dunsland which the National Trust had acquired in 1954. An extensive renovation was nearly finished when fire struck on 14 November 1967. The damage was so severe that it was not possible to reconstruct the house and after some features were removed the building was

demolished. It has nearly erased all memory of it from the landscape.[620]

The Escot fire happened while the family were at home. The owner's subsequent account expresses the desperation he felt:

The 27th December 1808 while the family (including Sir William Pole and Mr Coult, Mr Amyatt, Mrs Phillipps & Miss Jenkins, with the boys and Miss Phillipps who were home for the holidays) were at dinner, just as the first course was ended, which was about 5 o'clock, a tapping noise was heard at the parlour door, which being opened nobody appeared. Soon after the tapping was repeated when Foulope returned and told me I was wanted. I went to the door where I saw Mrs Locke, the housekeeper, who said the Chintz Room was on fire. I ran up to it, but the smoke issuing from it into the dressing room adjoining was so thick & suffocating that I could not enter it. I instantly called for water and returned to the parlour to quiet the alarm of the family by telling them that a window curtain was on fire and I thought would soon be got under. I then ran upstairs again and made another attempt through the best dressing room to enter, but found it still more impracticable. I then ran round thro the sitting room to the opposite door of the Chintz Room, which I opened & the smoke not yet having set that way, the current of air being stopped, I saw the bed-place enveloped in a deep smoke, the window curtains half burnt, but the side of the room where the fireplace was, for about a foot from the wall free from smoke. I ran back into the pink dressing room and taking a jug of water from the wash hand stand endeavoured to extinguish the burning window curtain next the door. I saw no smoke issuing from the chimney. I returned to the gallery and endeavoured in vain to get assistance of water, but the smoke and darkness there was so thick, that I could neither see or be seen and the water had been carried to the top of the house from an idea that the chimney was at risk. I then went downstairs and desiring Mr Amyatt to take care of Lady K. and the children. The fire gained ground rapidly and all attempts to extinguish it from within appeared to be hopeless. I then went to secure my papers.

The Dinner Bell having been kept ringing from the time the fire was first discovered, numbers of the neighbouring farmers soon arrived to our assistance, among others Francis Pyke, a respectable farmer of Talaton Moor, who was very active, but he had not been employed long before he fell thro' a window of the area at the back part of the house & was killed on the spot, leaving a widow and 4 children. All the gentlemen of Ottery & the officers of the barracks, with a military guard & the barrack fire engine soon arrived but the fire

engine was no sooner attempted to be played than it burst and could not be repaired.

In about two hours the house was nearly burnt. A great many things were saved owing to the exertions that were made, particularly by Mr Whitelock our apothecary who had seen the blaze of light from the room, as he was coming to the house & who going round to that side from whence it issued saw the fire, at which time it had not he says yet seized the window curtains of the room.[621]

Five days later Kennaway wrote once more about the fire and it is clear that only two walls of the house were safe, the rest of the house had been completely destroyed. Interestingly, he expressed no sorrow on the loss of his home, nor of the contents, and seemed more concerned by financial implications. His letter was to James Wyatt, the architect, to ask whether he would design a new house. The two men had previously met at Escot and it may be that Kennaway had already considered erecting a new building or Wyatt may have visited Escot en route while working on the Exeter Law Courts, Bicton, Powderham, Nutwell Court at Lympstone or nearby Rockbeare. Wyatt did not live to work on Escot, he died only a few years later.[622] The house that was lost had been built in 1690 for the Yonge family and was a building of some note.[623]

Fires at individual buildings may be most prevalent but it is surprising how many towns have had considerable portions destroyed in one event. South Molton had two large fires: 24 houses were lost in a fire which coincided with the great storm of 26 November 1703 and in 1841 a further 70 houses were burnt. But there were at least 27 other fires in the nineteenth century in 1825, 1826, 1827, 1828, 1833, 1835, 1836, 1837, 1840, 1842, 1844, 1845, 1852, 1853, 1859, 1861, 1861, 1863, 1867, 1870, 1874, 1878, 1879, 1887, 1889, 1891 and 1892.[624] The introduction of building regulations relating to fire precautions and effective means of putting out fire has lessened the effects of and the fear of it. Previous generations were terrified by the prospect of devastating fires and many tens of thousands of buildings in Devon, and even some entire villages and towns, have been destroyed by sudden and uncontrollable fire. Serious fires include Axminster (20 houses in 1800), Bradninch in 1665 and 1832, Broadclyst (60 houses in 1870), Chudleigh (some 166 houses, most of the village, in 1807), Chulmleigh (95 houses in 1803), Clyst Honiton (most of the village in 1825), Clyst St Lawrence (10 houses in 1847), Crediton (460 houses in 1743 and other fires in 1766, 1769 and 1772, 33 houses in 1841, 30 houses in 1842), Dalwood (12 houses in 1825), Cullompton (264 houses in 1839), East Ogwell (a good part of the village in 1598), Exmouth (15 houses in 1838), Great Torrington (27 houses in 1598 and a greater fire in 1724), Halberton (17 houses in 1817), Honiton in 1672, 1699, 1747 and 1765, Lynton (13 houses in 1898), Moretonhampstead (15 in 1816, 40 in 1845, 21 in 1854), North Tawton (30 In 1832, more than 60 in 1834), Ottery St Mary (50 houses in 1767 and nearly the entire town in 1866), Plymouth (1377, some 600 houses in 1403, 1549), Sheepwash (1743), Sidbury (10 houses in 1820), Silverton (16 houses in 1878), Stoke Canon (12 houses in 1841), Tiverton (nearly the entire town in 1598, 1612, and 1731, 21 houses in 1831, 14 houses in 1833, 1849 and 1850), Thorverton (17 houses in 1816) and Winkleigh (18 houses in 1800).[625]

The destruction of these places both fascinated and horrified fellow Devonians. In many instances sightseers gathered to gawp at the devastation while the former residents stumbled through the ruins of their lives. The history of one particular town shows how prevalent fires could be. In Tiverton there were serious fires in 1598 (some 400 houses), 1612 (some 600 houses), 1661 (some 45 houses), 1726 (4–5 houses), 1730 (15 houses), 1731 (298 houses), 1738 (10 houses), 1739 (10 houses), 1762 (20 houses), 1785 (55 houses), 1788 (some 20 houses), 1794 (120 houses), 1795 (8 houses), 1797 (12 houses) and 1815 (6 houses). More than 1,600 buildings were

lost. The fire in 1598, which began with a woman cooking her pancakes over a fire made from straw, also took the lives of some 50 people.[626] In the fire fourteen years later every building was destroyed with the exception of the church, parsonage, school house, almshouses and 30 houses of poor people standing in the town.[627] Medieval Tiverton disappeared and a new Jacobean town was built in its place. But, as seen by the details above, the town continued to lose buildings and was redeveloped in 1731 and 1794. The visitor to Tiverton today sees a town which appears Georgian in its origins. Two other Devon towns also could appear to have been built in the eighteenth century: Honiton lost some three quarters of its buildings in 1747[628] and Crediton 460 houses, a great portion of its buildings, four years earlier. Chulmleigh's fire in August 1803 removed 95 houses, more than two thirds of the town. A generation later it was described as a 'dull town'.[629] In 1801 there were 360 houses in Chudleigh but the fire six years later destroyed 166 of them. Four years later the number of houses increased to 370, ten more than a decade before. One of the casualties of the fire of 1801 was the market house, 'a long straggly building in the centre of the town'. A new building was erected elsewhere, which was itself taken down because it was 'wretchedly planned and badly built', but on the site of the original building a granite pillar marking the loss was erected.[630]

Town fires took many domestic buildings as well as some notable public ones: for example, the market house was burnt at Ottery St Mary in 1767,[631] Crediton in 1743,[632] Chudleigh in 1801,[633] Hatherleigh in 1840,[634] and Tiverton in 1731 where the new one was dedicated to the memory of the fire.[635] Cruwys Morchard lost to fire its almshouse in 1841 and its school two years later: the effect must have been devastating to this small mid-Devon parish.[636] Totnes had its theatre burnt down in 1860 but it was Exeter that has the more notable history. In that city three successive theatres were destroyed in 1820, 1885 and 1887. In the

The Tiverton market house, 1783, erected after the fire of 1731.

latter fire more people died than were killed during the blitz in 1942.[637] Local records are full of references to industrial buildings being burnt such as the three water grist mills at South Brent in 1698 or the yarn mill at Broadhempston in 1846.[638] Another building which could be described as a public building, although it was privately owned, was Fordland House or Cottage outside Ide. This was the home of the White family, including of John White Abbot, the artist, and in the nineteenth century was, in the words of one local man who went there, 'a pleasant resort for musical and tea parties for its rustic scenery, pleasant bowers and numerous enveloped summer houses'. It was also known for skating. There was a fire in the very early twentieth century.[639]

The use of cob and thatch, combined with houses tightly packed together, contributed to the high incidence of fire. Travellers commented on these building materials: for instance one Royalist cleric in the 1640s noted that in Bradninch 'almost all the houses be clay, without any timber in the wall except the doors, roof and windows which is the fashion of the country'.[640] The popularity of thatch was responsible for many fires quickly spreading and throughout Devon there were moves to force homeowners to replace it with slates. For example, in the sixteenth century a number of thatched houses in Paris Street in Exeter caught fire.[641] Gradually slate replaced thatch and brick replaced cob. In Ottery St Mary many of the cob houses lost in the fire of 1767 were rebuilt in

Pen and ink sketches of Fordland, by John Harris in the 1820s and George Townsend in the 1850s, showing the house and some of those who patronised it.

brick. Later writers commented upon how much more attractive these places were including the Reverend Stebbing Shaw who in 1788 thought the buildings of post-fire Honiton 'now wear a pleasing aspect'.[642] By 1882 the last thatch had disappeared from the centre of Exeter although nearby places, particularly St Thomas, still had thatched cottages.[643]

Fires in the countryside have also destroyed many acres of Devon, some deliberately through swaling, and others apparently through accident. For instance in 1886 a considerable part of Wistman's Wood was seriously damaged. Two gentlemen were thought to have caused the fire by carelessly dropping a cigarette.[644] The countryside was also damaged through fires started in more unusual ways: a fire in Stoke Canon was caused by the sparks of a train's locomotive.[645]

Many towns have been 'improved' after disastrous fires. Trinity Square in Axminster is named after the fire on Trinity Sunday in 1834 which destroyed a range of some 30 buildings. A series of extensive fires in the town removed a considerable number of buildings with the result that open spaces were left around the church and churchyard.[646] Ashburton had a serious fire at the end of the eighteenth century and the streets were subsequently widened. Some survivors of the fire were demolished in order to effect the street improvements.[647] A knock-on effect of the destructive fire at Buckfastleigh's church was the subsequent demolition of the Victorian chapel of ease: it was argued that it was inadequate to meet the needs of the parish so it was destroyed in 1998 for a new church.[648] In effect, one fire cost Buckfastleigh its medieval and Victorian churches.

Chapter Nine

Religion

Changing religious practice over the last five centuries has been a major influence on the landscape. The most prominent building in most parishes at the beginning of our period was the church and these have had tremendous internal and external alterations. Changes in the nineteenth century are discussed more fully on pages 114–117 within notions of fashion and aesthetics but modifications to buildings could easily have been noted here. For instance, at Holcombe Burnell in about 1740 it was decided that more room was needed at the communicants' rail and to achieve this the woodwork for a monument to Thomas Dennis, built in about 1602, was

burnt.[649] Likewise, when in 1832 a gallery was added to the church of Hatherleigh workmen were instructed to destroy the newly discovered wall painting they uncovered.[650] There is an extraordinary range and number of changes and some are wholly unexpected such as the repairs made at the parish church of Marystow in West Devon to fix the hands broken off two memorial effigies. They had been deliberately mutilated but unfortunately during the repair Sir Thomas Wise was given his wife's hands and she his.[651]

The Reformation

Devon's monasteries faced abrupt changes in the late 1530s. Bedford House in Exeter, founded by the Black Friars (the Dominicans) by 1232, was dissolved in 1539 and over the following four hundred years the site was occupied by a series of prominent buildings. The Earl of

The parish churches of Cullompton and Hatherleigh had similar wall paintings of St Christopher which were both destroyed. In the early nineteenth century building work on the church at Hatherleigh revealed a wall painting. The artist explained 'in the year 1832 as the workmen were scraping off the whitewash from the wall adjoining the new gallery on the north aisle in order to refix a monument scripture sentence from Judah 55 Chapter 6 & 7 verses was discovered written in old black letters in a good state of preservation. This on being removed, and several more layers of whitewash scraped off an old painting, in distemper, appeared to view, supposed to be a figure of St Augustine, first archbishop of Canterbury, or as some say St Christopher, upwards of eight feet high with fishes &c at his feet. The annexed drawing is a rough copy taken on a scale of one inch to the foot'.

Bedford had his Exeter townhouse there until the eighteenth century when Bedford Circus was built in its place. Those buildings lasted until 1942 when they were hit by bombs and subsequently demolished.[652] In the early 1950s Princesshay, a shopping centre, was built but is now designated to be demolished. Nothing now remains of the original buildings. Buckfast Abbey has had a strange history. It was founded just before the Norman Conquest and then re-established a century later. Some two hundred and seventy years after it was dissolved, and demolished by the Petre family of nearby Torbryan, a castellated Gothic mansion was erected on the ruins, in about 1806, by Samuel Berry as a domestic dwelling and only a few generations later, in 1882, Benedictine monks acquired the site and began rebuilding the abbey.[653] Buckland Abbey, founded by the Cistercians in 1278, was dissolved in 1538 and best symbolises the county's role in the Reformation. Three years later it was granted to Sir Richard Grenville whose family converted the buildings for domestic use: the church was turned into a dwelling. Sir Francis Drake purchased the buildings in 1581, shortly after his circumnavigation of the globe that brought him his great wealth. The Grenvilles and Drake modified the buildings but kept the tithe barn among other farm buildings.[654] The conversion of what had been a Catholic building into a private residence was a strong political statement by Grenville and subsequently Drake. The buildings of Dunkeswell Abbey, which the Cistercians founded in 1201, were allowed to be used as building materials including by the Simcoe family who in the early nineteenth century built a villa and church on the site of the abbey church. Within the earthworks can be seen the remains of a pair of fishponds.[655] Forde Abbey, formerly part of Devon, was converted into a private dwelling by Sir Edmund Prideaux in the mid-seventeenth century. Hartland Abbey, which began as a collegiate church in about 1050 and was re-founded in 1169 as an Augustinian monastery, became a private dwelling when it was dissolved in 1539. The house was not greatly

remodelled until 1705 and then again in 1779 when the Great Hall and chapel were demolished. The only part of the original abbey to survive is part of the cloisters.[656] Newnham Abbey near Axminster, founded by the Cistercians in 1246, was dissolved in 1539. By the end of the eighteenth century the buildings were in ruin and had been used as a quarry for new buildings. Damage was also caused by fire and during a particularly wet year the east wall of the chapel fell in. Sculls and parts of skeletons were once seen tumbling into the nearby brook.[657] Tavistock Abbey, founded by the Benedictines in about 970, was dissolved in 1539. The ornaments of the shrine of St Rumon, made of gold, silver and precious jewels, were sent to the Tower of London, lead was stripped from the roof and six bells were sold as well as paving stones, candelabra, choir stalls and tabernacles. The site of the abbey, together with much of the local

land, was granted to John, first baron Russell. The abbey church stood in ruins until about 1670 when the stone was used to build a schoolhouse. The main refectory and the remains of the cloister and chapter house were demolished between 1716 and 1725 and on the site of the refectory there was built 'a pompous dwelling house', now known as the Bedford Hotel. Some of the infirmary

The remains of Tavistock Abbey in 1807.

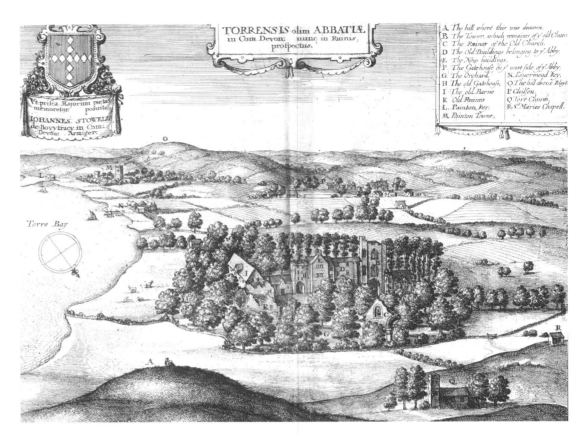

Etching of Torre Abbey, 1662, showing the extent of the buildings

buildings survived the Dissolution including the misericord, a dining hall used by the sick, which from 1691 was used for religious purposes. The ruins of the abbot's lodgings can be seen in the front garden of the vicarage, one tower of which is known as Betsy Grimbal's Tower. The Tavistock Library occupies another of the remaining abbey buildings.[658] In 1598 Thomas Ridgeway adapted two wings of Torre Abbey, which had been founded by Premonstratensian canons from Welbeck Abbey in 1196, for domestic use. Lysons reported in 1822 that little was left of Torre Abbey but in fact the west and south ranges survived to roof level although the south range had been 'faked up' to look like a Georgian house, as seen from the harbour, in the 1740s and the great hall had been converted to a chapel later in the eighteenth century. Curiously, the church tower was demolished at that time but the following generation, in the early nineteenth century, built a new 'Gothick' tower and ornamental arches, and the ruins of the church and

chapter house were used in the early nineteenth century as landscaped features. Reverend Joseph Reeve eulogised the ruins in a poem 'Ugbrooke Park' and an extract was set in stone. The tithe barn and the fourteenth-century red sandstone gate remain.[659]

The county's priories also had abrupt changes. These include Cornworthy Priory, founded in the late twelfth century and dissolved in 1573. The gatehouse still stands in what is now a large field devoid of any other buildings.[660] Part of Frithelstock Priory, founded by the Augustinians in the early thirteenth century, also survives but only as a collection of walls. These ruins are adjacent to the parish church for which the prior and his canons were responsible. Nearby Cloister Hall, a farmhouse, is on the site of the priory buildings and may incorporate some of its original fabric.[661] The best surviving building is that of St Nicholas' Priory in Exeter. It was founded by the Benedictines in 1087, was dissolved in 1536 and the church and chapter house were dismantled shortly

The ruins of Frithelstock Priory in 1830.

afterwards. The foundations and flooring of the church were removed and some stone used to repair the city's wall and Exe Bridge which caused one local man to remember a prophecy that the river would one day run under the church of St Nicholas. The Mallet family acquired the two remaining buildings, comprising the refectory and west range, in 1562. They were divided into tenements and the area became the centre of the city's Huguenot population at the end of the seventeenth century and that of the Roman Catholics in the 1790s when they built their chapel on the site of the Chapter House. Exeter City Council purchased the West Range in 1913[662] and the Refectory by Exeter Historic Buildings Trust in the mid 1990s. The ruins of part of Canonsleigh Priory, founded in 1160 and dissolved in 1539, were used as a garden ornament in the late eighteenth century.[663] Perhaps the most inglorious end was that of the chapel: the stone from the building was burnt for its lime to dress the fields. At least one other religious building, one

connected with the bishop's palace at Chudleigh, also had its stone reused by a kiln.[664] Pilton Priory, founded by the Benedictines between 1181 and 1187 to the north of the parish church, was dissolved in 1536 and there are no existing buildings other than the church and Bull House, the home of the prior. Pilton Abbey is a nineteenth-century building unconnected with the priory. Totnes Priory was founded in about 1088 and the buildings demolished in the 1530s. The Guildhall is built partly on the site.[665] Barnstaple Priory was founded in about 1107 and the buildings remained at least until the middle of the seventeenth century. In 1819 substantial foundations of the building were discovered by builders erecting a tanning yard.[666] Kerswell Priory was founded between 1119 and 1129 but all that remains is a farmhouse possibly on the site of the church. In 1985 a substantial outbuilding was demolished.[667] The twelfth-century priory at Polsloe was, as explained earlier, given to the city of Exeter in the 1930s and in 1980s was

Photographs of the archaeological dig at St Katharine's Priory, c.1933, which revealed a skeleton and the Priory in 1933.

converted for use as a community centre.[668] Otterton Priory was founded by 1087 by the Benedictines and acquired by the Duke family following the dissolution. The Priory is the remains of their converted home. Finally, Cowick Barton was possibly built on the site of the twelfth-century priory.[669]

Much can be told of the fortunes of more minor Catholic buildings. A local man demolished one chapel, built to serve Bishop Grandisson's palace in Bishopsteignton, to use as building material.[670] Richard Clarke did the same with a chapel in Uffculme in order to erect Bridwell.[671] In Chagford a chapel was pulled down because it obstructed the view from a neighbouring property and the stone rebuilt the house and garden walls.[672] A chapel in St Thomas was partly demolished and the stone used for an Exeter church.[673] A building thought to have once been a chapel of ease in Sidmouth was later used as a public house, known as The Anchor, and in about 1805 converted to a private dwelling.[674] A chapel at Branscombe later served as a barn as did another at Tedburn St Mary,[675] at Belstone one became a stable,[676] one at Burlescombe became a farmhouse,[677] another at Christow was an outbuilding,[678] and still one more in Luppit was turned into a mill house.[679] The Marwood family purchased Combe Raleigh's Chantry House, a late medieval priest's house possibly associated with a late fifteenth-century chantry. They leased it as a private dwelling house.[680] Only part of the chapel's tower at Copplestone survived into the 1850s; it had been partially removed in 1793 and the cellar turned into 'a very good sitting room'. Unfortunately the stone pulpit was broken into pieces and then used as flooring.[681] In Tiverton one chapel was used as the bridewell and another was converted to serve as a coffeehouse, the guildhall and prison.[682] When at the end of the eighteenth century Sir Francis Drake renovated his house of Nutwell in Lympstone he merely converted the chapel into a library.[683] Finally, a medieval chapel on South Brent Hill has been thought to have been transformed by an Ashburton man for his amusement: Nicholas Tripe, whose large house was subsequently the Golden Lion, allegedly fixed sails to the ruined based of the chapel so he could watch them move from his bed in the morning.[684]

Individual parts of the fabric of churches were removed or defaced in different phases under Henry VIII, Edward VI and Elizabeth I. Some of the changes were direct responses to national instructions such as that of 1536 to removed cult figures (Pilton lost two images of Our Lady of Pilton and Our Lady of Lorell) and that of 1538 to remove images connected with pilgrimages or offerings. Consequently, the image of St Urith was taken from Chittlehampton while at Plymouth removed items included a cross from the hand of St Saviour. The church at Rewe near Exeter lost velvet and satin clothes, rings, silver ships, beads and money that had been offered to saints.[685] In some instances it is unclear when changes were made: it may have been during the rule of Edward VI, or possibly as late as 1561, that the screen at Ottery St Mary was mutilated by the projecting woodwork being chopped off and niches filled with fragments and mortar.[686] At Exeter Cathedral the new dean appointed in 1537 was accused two years later of having defaced Bishop Lacey's tomb by removing the brass effigy, of destroying images of saints and of defacing religious books. Then, thirteen years later in 1551, there were additional instructions to remove altars, statues and relics: among the losses at the cathedral were some 12 crosses, 24 chalices and 123 copes. Two years later a bonfire was lit in Cathedral Yard where many more items were destroyed. The building was effectively denuded of many of its richest treasures.[687] From 1548 to 1550 a number of saints' images were removed throughout Devon: St George was taken from Ashburton and Exeter's Holy Trinity and St Lawrence and a number of saints were removed from North Molton, Whitchurch and Morebath.[688] Thirteen religious pictures and the tabernacle from the altar of the church of St Mary Steps were some of the items placed on a bonfire in Exeter's Cathedral Yard in September 1559.[689] Under Elizabeth many more items were removed throughout the county so that by the 1570s rood lofts, for example, were nearly gone. It was during her reign, in 1568, that Chudleigh finally removed its altar stone.[690] Items were not only demolished but sold: Woodbury and Whitchurch made

money from its tabernacles while Crediton and Morebath sold the gold from its images.[691] It may have been from one such sale that a cloth belonging to Bishop Grandisson made it to the Azores.[692]

Items were also targeted outside churches. By 1500 there were several thousand ancient stone crosses in Devon erected for a variety of purposes. A portion have survived. Their destruction began at the Reformation because some were seen as idolatry objects: the stone cross at Woodbury was damaged in about 1550 and Barnstaple's palm cross was pulled down and the materials carted away three years later.[693] Other stone crosses were removed in subsequent years because they were inconveniently situated. Since the early sixteenth century other uses were found for them. One study tried to identify former crosses originally used in churchyards, markets, as boundary stones and along waysides from stone which was merely similarly shaped, particularly granite columns, which may have been rubbing posts such as one at Bridestowe. Understandably in a rural county, many have been used for gates (Bishop's Nympton, Bovey Tracey, Chagford, Churchstow, Cornwood, Ermington, Harford, North Huish, Okehampton, Peter Tavy, South Huish, South Tawton, Totnes, Ugborough) and as troughs (Ashburton, Bampton, Bridgerule, Hennock, Ipplepen, Modbury, North Huish, Ottery St Mary, Paignton, Tamerton Foliot, Throwleigh). Other uses include as materials for buildings (Chivelstone, Churston Ferrers, Crediton, North Bovey, North Huish, Plymstock) including a pig house (Walkhampton) and pump house (Great Torrington), in walls (Ashburton, Buckfastleigh, Shaugh Prior, Woodleigh), as steps (Holbeton, King's Nympton, Membury, South Molton), pavement (Bow) and within hedges (Shaugh Prior, Trusham). The base of the village cross at Hartland was used as a foundation stone for a new chapel. More surprising uses are as footbridges (Drewsteignton, Spreyton), lamp-posts (Newton Abbot, Newton Ferrers), road signs (Bicton), memorials to

William III (Newton Abbot), George V (Sheepstor) and Queen Victoria (Buckland Monachorum, Newton St Cyres), war memorials (Alphington, Ashprington, Berry Pomeroy, Chagford, Dodbrooke, Haccombe, Holne, Ipplepen, Rewe, Shillingford) and memorial stones (Buckfastleigh, Gidleigh, Harpford, Heanton Punchardon, Plymtree). They were used as ornaments notably as garden features (Buckland Tout Saints, Christow, Clyst Honiton, Dawlish, East Portlemouth, Filleigh, Heavitree, Okehampton, Plymtree, Shillingford, Silverton, Stokenham, Ugborough) including as a base for sundials (Buckland Monachorum, Churston Ferrers, Dawlish, East Portlemouth, Torquay) and birdbaths (Chulmleigh, Newton Abbot). Some are now museum exhibits (Exeter and Plymouth). It has often been difficult to identify whether random pieces of stone were once used as crosses: for example, a large granite kerb stone in Gandy Street at Exeter was supposed to have formed part of a cross in 1849. A previous owner paid a guinea for it in 1770 when it was sold along with other stone from Exeter's medieval bridge where it had been used as a key stone. It may have come from St Nicholas' Priory.[694] Some crosses have regained their status as religious objects: one was reused to ornament the Methodist chapel at Sampford Courtenay and the shafts of two crosses support the font at Dolton. Many crosses had stone pedestals and these stones have had a similar though less easily defined history. It should be pointed out that some now in Devon were taken from Cornwall including one on the village green at Kenton.[695]

Holy wells were another casualty of the Reformation. By 1500 Devon had more than two hundred and thirty five, many of which were dedicated to saints, associated with religious buildings particularly parish churches where the water was sometimes used for baptisms and visited because for their healing qualities.[696] For instance, water from Coverney, or Covety, Well at Great Torrington was used to treat eyes and the rags hung up on nearby bushes.[697] The religious changes of the sixteenth century made these venerated springs redundant and only wells thought to have natural, and not supernatural, medicinal qualities were permitted.[698] While the water itself has continued to flow at these sites the stone structures for many of them gradually deteriorated or were dismantled: the holy well at Leigh was moved by the Duke of Bedford to ornament his country house of Endsleigh, and renamed The Wishing Well, and it has been suggested that the stonework for the well at Lew Trenchard was moved to the manor house also as a garden feature.[699]

The Civil War

The attacks of the sixteenth-century were followed an onslaught in the 1640s, giving rise to some popular confusion as to whether Thomas Cromwell in the 1530s or Oliver Cromwell in the 1640s and 1650s was responsible for change. Certainly it was remembered: in 1877 one Devon writer noted that the 'fanatic zeal of Puritan iconoclasts' was responsible for destroying effigies[700] and it was recalled in 1843 that the stained glass and the royal coat of arms of James I in the church of Ottery St Mary were destroyed by Parliamentary soldiers stationed there from 1645 to 1646.[701] By 1643 Exeter Cathedral ornamental writing over the communion table was expunged on the grounds it was superstitious and a picture of Moses and Aaron on each side of the Ten Commandments was defaced. In 1706 one visitor at the cathedral had the marks from the guns of the Parliamentary soldiers shown to him. Stained glass was destroyed and the queen of Edward the Confessor was flattered by having her statue mutilated in the mistaken belief she was the mother of Christ. At Bovey Tracey the royal arms of Charles I were taken down and the font sawn into different parts by the vicar. At Cornwood the new incumbent pulled down the rood loft and broke the stained glass.[702] The communion table at All Hallows on the Walls in Exeter was burnt as late as 1658.[703] The early sixteenth-century monument to Katherine Courtenay, who styled herself 'Katherine Plantagenet, the daughter, sister and aunt of Kings',[704] was claimed to have been destroyed during the civil war in the church at Tiverton but there already was substantial damage by the 1630s. Tristram Risdon, the early historian, wrote that it 'lamented me to write time hath not so much defaced [it] as men have mangled that magnificent monument'. Perhaps the damage was done during the Reformation.[705]

It is a moot point as to whether the image of Gogmagog, the pagan giant, which was annually cut or dug into the grey limestone of the cliff side of Plymouth's Hoe for the May Day celebrations, was discontinued because of pressure from the town's ruling Puritans. The last mention in Plymouth's records is in the late sixteenth century but there are two later references: in 1602 Richard Carew, who lived only five miles away at Antony across the Sound and was almost able to see Gogmagog from his grounds, wrote of two figures with clubs, possibly similar to the Cerne Abbas Giant, as did Thomas Westcote, the Devon writer, in 1630. According to Westcote the images were of different sizes with one 'surpassing the other in every way'. The second figure was Corineus who, according to an ancient legend, wrestled with Gogmagog. He may have been added later given there was only one image noted in the earlier references. Presumably the religious brethren of Plymouth disapproved because of its associations with May Day frolics but they would not have been supportive of any pagan figure, particularly if it had attributes similar to those of Cerne Abbas. The figure had been a Plymouth feature since at least the late fifteenth century and the legend was well known enough to come to the attention of Geoffrey of Monmouth who was writing in the eleventh century and Edmund Spenser in the late sixteenth century.[706]

Damage was also done through plundering: Roundhead soldiers were reported to have broken into the church at Newton St Cyres and taken the communion cup as well as eight shillings and two pence from the poor men's box.[707] It is unclear whether the loss of the manuscripts of Sir William Pole, who was writing a history of Devon, were destroyed through malice or by mistake. His house of Colcombe Castle near Colyton was burned in the war.[708]

Church-houses

Nearly every rural parish in Devon had a church-house in the sixteenth century. Brixham had four buildings known as church-houses; in 1600 two were situated at the entry

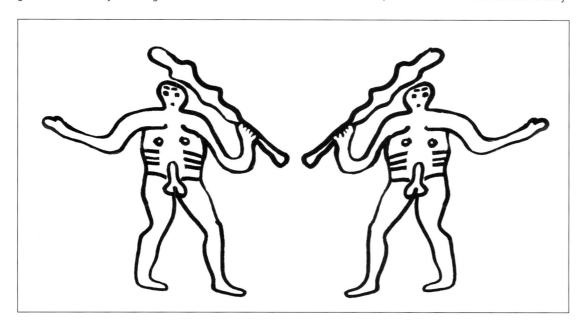

Did Plymouth have two figures similar to the Cerne Abbas Giant which offended the religious fundamentalists of the early seventeenth century or were they merely covered over during the rebuilding of the town's defences at the Restoration?

to the churchyard and the others were elsewhere and curiously described as being used by churchwardens.[709] These buildings, in many ways the precursors to the modern village hall, were used to raise money for the upkeep of their church by staging church ales, events where participants would pay for their food and drink. Their decline in the seventeenth century is due to the Puritans who objected to the rowdiness with which these events were associated. Occasionally they were also known as the Guild House, such as that at Holsworthy.

Over the past four centuries these buildings have met various fates. The church-house at Diptford was used as a poorhouse, then an inn and afterwards a school while that at Ideford was a poorhouse, school and private house. Many have been demolished such as at Branscombe in about 1890, at Exbourne the stone was used to build a school in 1830 and at Littleham near Bideford the building was demolished in 1843 and the materials used to build a parish room. This also happened at Blackborough where the building was pulled down and a yew tree was then planted on its site. The land was incorporated into the churchyard. Others demolitions include those at Hatherleigh, Holsworthy, Kentisbeare, Membury, St Thomas and Witheridge while those at Harpford, Plymtree and Whitestone were destroyed by fire. One study has attempted to trace the histories of these several hundred buildings. Some were used for other public purposes: a considerable number became poor houses or almshouses (Belstone, Bratton Fleming, Brixham, Chawleigh, Cheldon, Clawton, Combeinteignhead, Cornworthy, Dean Prior, Dowland, Exbourne, Holsworthy, Ilsington, Manaton, Pinhoe, Sutcombe, Winkleigh). Some were used as schools (Braunton, Bridgerule, Buckland Monachorum, Chudleigh, Colyton, North Molton, Widecombe-in-the-Moor), a school dining room (Lustleigh) and a reading room (Winkleigh). Many have survived as public houses (Ashprington, Broadhempston, Manaton, Walkhampton) and some are still known as the Church House (Holne).

Others took other names such as the Mermaid in Ashburton and the Red Lion in Broadclyst. Still others were house conversions (Bratton Fleming, Cheriton Bishop, Highhampton, Ilsington, Nymet Tracey, Rose Ash, South Brent) and one became a Boy Scouts' headquarters (Heavitree).[710]

The return of fittings

Some religious items were later returned: one of the aims of the failed Prayer Book Rebellion in 1549 was the restoration of images and attempts were made during Queen Mary's reign to return items but her rule of a mere five years from 1553 to 1558 brought only a temporary respite. Some items had not been destroyed but were merely brought out of storage and in other cases money was spent on replacement: Exeter's St Petrock's church for example had a new rood screen between 1555 and 1557 and roods were reinserted at Ashburton, Braunton, Crediton, Exeter, Morebath, South Tawton and Tavistock. Images of saints were replaced at Braunton and Woodbury. Many other parishes show a more cautious or pragmatic approach to their churches.[711] Religious items still turn up that may well have once been put aside for safety such as a medieval alabaster angel found in a box whilst workmen were digging in a cellar in Pinhoe near Exeter. Other fragments have been found which may have been discarded such as a series of alabaster carvings found in South Huish church during demolition work in the late 1860s.[712] With the swing of the pendulum in many if not most places items were repaired, brought out from hiding and new ones purchased. Had Queen Mary lived longer more parishes may have been like St Petrock in Exeter which employed a mason to fix noses back on disfigured statues. Richard Frand of Ermington left money for the replacement of images for Exeter Cathedral in 1556 but he would have had to change it shortly afterwards. It is likely that many Devonians watched from the sidelines as conflicting religious instructions were issued from London for more than a generation. Religious life under Henry VIII, Edward VI, Mary and Elizabeth was potentially dangerous and in one parish, which may have been typical, it can be seen that the parishioners hedged their bets. At Morebath near Bampton local people in the 1540s duly took down their images and removed the altars. Some items were destroyed but many others were taken away: it is unclear whether these villagers were acting as good Catholics, looters or souvenir seekers. But during the reign of Mary these religious items were returned and the altars re-erected. A few years later, during Elizabeth's rule, the screen was taken down, the altars destroyed once more and the chalice replaced.[713] It is unknown whether items were again placed into safe keeping because there was not an opportunity to do so. There may be more to this than religious devotion: this process was an expensive one. The parishioners were financially responsible for the continual modifications to their church and for replacing the highly-priced religious artefacts. Many no doubt resented repeatedly paying for the changes in religious law introduced hundreds of miles away.

Unease

In about 1700 one writer collected stories of local uneasiness in reusing redundant Roman Catholic buildings; this survived in manuscript form until the late eighteenth century when the Reverend Richard Polwhele used it for his history of Devon.[714] There was a tradition in other parts of the country that God would punish those who committed sacrilege upon the Catholic buildings.[715] At Holcombe Burnell a chapel, which stood near the manor house, was pulled down and an 'upping-stock' was built near the barton. In 1793 it was reported that the local people claimed that one particular stone could never 'be kept firm in its place'.[716] Cheriton Fitzpaine had a chapel which was converted to use as a cider house and the owner was said to have lost his property because of his 'profanation'.[717] A chapel in Whimple was converted to domestic use but it was later

said that any one who subsequently lived there did not flourish.[718] This was also the case, so it was said, with the man who converted a chapel in Broadclyst: one James Baker, who allegedly had been a wealthy man, 'never thrived afterwards' and later had his leg shot off. He died lonely and in poverty.[719] Another chapel in the same parish was converted first for use as a school and subsequently as a brewhouse. That had unfortunate results: Polwhele related that:

the proprietor and his family were doomed, it seems, from the moment of its profanation to conflict with various evils. Their nights were disturbed by strange noises and apparitions, and their days marked by continual crosses: they had, moreover, to lament, that they were denied the comfort of good ale: their beer, whatever was its quality, invariably turned sour.[720]

There was a worse fate for the Whyddon family: a font was used by them for the pound house and their punishment was the extinction of their line.[721] Finally, Polwhele related that at Ludwell near Dawlish an ancient chapel dedicated to St Mary survived to the end of the eighteenth century because the owner made his son promise never to demolish it.[722]

There is no record of any disquiet when the chapel at Oldridge near Exeter was demolished: it was claimed that the stones were carried to Trowbridge to repair a kitchen and the communion table was used as furniture in a nearby alehouse.[723] In 1899 the Reverend Baring Gould recounted the tale of a Manaton rector who was allegedly offended by his parishioners' carrying coffins three times around the churchyard cross: his solution was, supposedly, to break up the cross one night and hide the fragments.[724] In some other cases religious items were reused without any apparent qualms: a Silverton man used a church cross in his hedge but at Halberton a local man incorporated a statue of the Virgin Mary in his bread oven. His bread was baked upon the inverted figure.[725]

Redundant buildings

Changing religious practice has made a great number of churches of all types redundant: in the past 35 years more than fifty established churches alone have been made redundant within the diocese. For instance, the church of All Hallows on Goldsmith Street in Exeter was pulled down in 1906 because the congregation was small. It had been empty for many years, partly through a fall in population, and local authorities were able to push through its demolition. A significant number of other churches in the city have also closed, and the buildings dismantled, because of dwindling attendance.[726] One other significant factor for small congregations in the established churches was the opportunity to choose other places of worship. The rise of the dissenters in the seventeenth century was accompanied by the erection of dozens of other buildings for religious worship. Many of these have also subsequently suffered from small congregations and

been replaced. Such Nonconformist buildings as the Weslyan chapel at Broadhempston, built in 1822, has been converted for domestic use. Similar conversions have been made at Branscombe, Chudleigh, Hennock, Luppitt, Marwood, Parkham, Tawstock, Tiverton and Westleigh. Some chapels have been superseded by newer buildings and one, the Unitarian chapel built in 1790 in Devonport, was closed because it was opposed by the dockyard authorities. But many of these redundant buildings were converted as workshops (Bulkworthy, Chulmleigh, Moretonhampstead, Tavistock), a hostel (Buckland Monachorum), an office (Newton Abbot), commercial use (Exeter, Tavistock, Torquay), and a garage (Monkleigh). Others have become derelict (Chivelstone, Crediton, Inwardleigh and Woodbury).[727] A recent notable loss is that of the Dartmouth Methodist Church which was built in 1874 to 1875 and after a series of unsuccessful schemes for redevelopment in the 1980s it was destroyed by explosions in February 1991.[728]

Chapter Ten

War

War has been an intermittent influence on the county's landscape although it is difficult to access the extent of the earliest damage. Perhaps one of the more continuing destructive forces has been the use of Dartmoor as a military training ground from 1875 to the modern day. Damage has included a stone circle and menhir being used as target practice.[729] However, the level of losses from the second world war has made war the most visible destructive force to Devon's heritage.

Until the Reformation details of any loss due to war are often very thin. For example, it is largely accepted that the Vikings burnt Exeter in 876 and 1003 but little is known of the extent and subsequent reconstruction of the city.[730] In 1403 the French likewise attacked and burnt Plymouth before sailing to Salcombe but there are few details on damage. The following year they sailed to Dartmouth but were beaten back at Blackpool. It is uncertain whether they returned a month later: the French claimed they destroyed the port but this may have been an exaggeration.[731] The accounts of the Civil War are mainly from propaganda pamphlets and the misinformation is not always apparent. These publications were avidly sought, at least by the middle and upper classes: the Earl of Bath, the county's leading Royalist, sent pamphlets from London to his wife at their home at Tawstock near Barnstaple with the note 'though it be stale here, yet it will be fresh for poor country folks'. On another occasion he noted the newssheets would 'furnish her with knowledge stuff to entertain her gossips'.[732] During the second world war newspaper reports were heavily censored with many attacks barely noted to preclude the enemy benefiting from details of success or failure. Finally, in each of these wars it is more conventional to note the damage to property than the loss of life: the deaths of many tens of thousands of men and women, both civilian and military, were often unrecorded.

It is not until 1549, during the Prayer Book Rebellion, that information is somewhat detailed. In that uprising the village of Clyst St Mary and some barns in Crediton were burnt and buildings outside Exeter's walls were 'beat and brake down'.[733] At Plymouth the rebels burnt a steeple, supposed to have been that of the former friary of the Carmelites, in which the town's 'evidence', that is the records, was kept.[734] Surprisingly, throughout the long Spanish war the county did not experience an assault, unlike those by Devonians in Spain, although the Spanish did burn Mousehole in the far west of Cornwall. The activities by Drake and other privateers largely kept the theatre of war away from Devon. The following generation saw a collapse of effective naval protection of the coast and no part of the country experienced more ship losses than Devon. Whereas in the late sixteenth century the English were the predators, in the early seventeenth century they became the prey. These constant attacks off the Devon coast by North African pirates began in 1625 but even so there is no evidence that these men actually landed in the county and took captives as they had on the Continent and Ireland. One report that 'Turks', as they were generally known, had taken Lundy turned out to be groundless: the reported pirate ship was merely a Dutch one anchored off the island. Devon's losses were in ships and men, unlike those in Spain where Elizabethan Devonians had raided and burned coastal settlements, Cadiz among them. An unknown person in Barnstaple however was responsible for spreading a rumour that a Cornish fishing port had been attacked and sixty men, women and children taken from the parish church: in 1625 an Irish mariner heard this story in North Devon and retold it to a Welshman who in turn reported it to London. The story created alarm at the time and has confused historians for several hundred years. There is no evidence that the raid on

'Munnigeasa in Mount's Bay', a confused combination of Marazion, which is in Mount's Bay, with nearby Mevagissey, ever took place nor any others in Devon.[735]

The Civil War

Devon's first experience of destruction on its own territory after the Prayer Book Rebellion took place nearly a hundred years later with the Civil War. The two largest urban areas particularly suffered because of their long sieges but much more is known about the war at Exeter because Plymouth has yet to be adequately studied. Nevertheless, the main outlines are clear: the Royalists tried to take Plymouth, which had declared for Parliament, and in 1643 the town rebuilt its Elizabethan walls and gates and added new defences. For two years they tried to capture Plymouth but failed. There was some damage including the sails of the windmill on the Hoe being shot off by Cavalier cannon[736] but the surrounding areas suffered more: Saltram, Borringdon and Leigham were ransacked, Ham House was set alight as was Radford House and at least one house in Stoke Damerel was pulled down.[737] In contrast, Exeter moved between the two sides by initially supporting Parliament and then taken by the Crown. The city was Parliamentarian until September 1643 when the Royalists captured it and stayed until April 1646. During those years Exeter was besieged and along with the surrounding suburbs and countryside was devastated. As mentioned earlier, in January 1643 a Roundhead mob was responsible for considerable destruction to the cathedral: they defaced the images of Moses and Aaron (the damage can still be seen today), smashed the window glass and struck off heads of memorials including that of Queen Edith, wife to Edward the Confessor. It was reported they tore down the organ and paraded with the pipes allegedly telling the choir 'boys, we have spoiled your trade, you must go and sing hot pudding pies!' The Roundheads attacked the Royalists in St Thomas and burnt the suburb including Hayes Barton.

This probably included a barn which was mentioned in 1691 as having been burnt by soliders of the Exeter garrison. The Royalist capture a short while later brought recriminations: one Roundhead supporter, aptly named Mr Prigg, had his house and shop in Broadgate pillaged. The goods of other merchants were also attacked but it is questionable whether there was much looting beyond that directed towards particular individuals. At the start of the siege in the autumn of 1643, with the city surrounded by Parliament supporters, there was further destruction in surrounding areas: on one day the Cavaliers burnt hundreds of houses to clear the area outside of the walls. They returned less than a week later and burnt another eighty buildings. By the spring of 1646 the damage by both sides amounted to the levelling of all houses outside the four main gates: the parishes of St David, St Sidwell, St Thomas and Holy Trinity lay in ashes. The city too was bombarded and one notable casualty was the church of All Hallows on the Walls. It was eventually pulled down.[738]

But there was also destruction throughout the county: large country houses in the vicinity of Exeter, such as Ashton, Canonteign, Peamore and Powderham, were occupied in the sieges and in some instances damage is known to have been considerable. Artillery was shot at Great Fulford from a small earthenwork which in the nineteenth century was identified as laying across from the house. It may be the building now known as the Deer Linhay, a barely visible line of cob, or an earthenwork lying just above it. The house was also looted. Throughout Devon many individual buildings suffered as war raged around them. One example is Court House, the Modbury home of the Champernownes, which was heavily damaged and finally demolished in about 1706. The lane, in which it was commonly said the Royalists fled from the Parliamentarians, was known as Runaway Lane. The approach of armies caused considerable alarm particularly given the propaganda spread by opposing sides: the Earl of Bath received a petition from the town of Barnstaple asking him to stop soldiers from occupying the town. These men were alleged to have committed 'outrage and violence' on their march. Even so a significant number of houses in the surrounding suburbs were destroyed. The owner of one was described as a 'wicked woman who had the worst and the smoothest tongue that ever her sex made use of to mischief'. She later pursued one Royalist leader for compensation with a 'malignancy' that was 'venomous and devilish'. The nearby church at Pilton was damaged and the tower was not rebuilt until 1696, more than fifty years after it was attacked. No doubt to some degree armies plundered as they passed through areas: Lord Goring's men had a particular reputation for it. Perhaps the best-known example of destruction in Devon, at least outside of Exeter and Plymouth, is that of Great Torrington where the last great battle was fought. On 16 February 1646 the church was destroyed through an explosion of some eighty barrels of gunpowder kept in the building and scores of men imprisoned there, possibly as many as 200, died in the blast. There was also damage done to surrounding properties and two houses were later rebuilt. Six years later the church was re-erected, the roof and tower had been most heavily damaged, but the vicarage was still in a ruinous state as late as 1744.[739] The steeple was later replaced.[740]

The Second World War

For nearly three hundred years, from the 1640s until the 1940s, Devon had little experience of war within its own boundaries although its men, mostly through the navy at Plymouth, were heavily engaged in war elsewhere. The county received no material damage from the invasion of William of Orange in 1688 (nor that of the Duke of Monmouth a few years before). However, in 1690 some 300 to 400 Frenchmen attacked Teignmouth: accounts of the damage differ but as many as 116 houses were destroyed as well 172 others plundered. The French also burnt ten ships and some fishing boats.[741] There was no destruction from war in Devon during the eighteenth and

nineteenth centuries: the longest known period in the county's recorded history. There were also no attacks in the first world war and it was not until the 1940s, just short of three hundred years after the Civil War, that it was once again changed by war. Devon's two cities suffered considerable damage but, curiously, the nature of their devastation was a direct consequence of their different characters: one was destroyed because of its strategic importance and the other for its heritage value.

Destruction in Plymouth began in 1940 and continued until 1944. Its strategic importance to the navy resulted in a bombing campaign of some 59 attacks that took the lives of more than a thousand people and destroyed thousands of buildings. Landmark civilian buildings, such as the Central Library, an extraordinary number of churches

Two memorial windows to 'the siege of Plymouth, 1643–45, the good women courageously bring strong waters to the men' and 'King Charles the First summoneth the town of Plymouth to surrender'. They were designed by J. Fouracre in the 1890s and erected at the Plymouth Club situated at Windsor Terrace off Citadel Road. The building was bombed in the war and the window was destroyed with it.

The devastated centre of Plymouth.

(not just Church of England but Baptist, Congregational, Methodist, Unitarian, Roman Catholic and Salvation Army as well) and the guildhalls at both Plymouth and Stonehouse, were destroyed as were many naval buildings. Great areas were levelled and the ancient city, with its medieval, Elizabethan, Georgian and Victorian layers, disappeared in nightly attacks over a few short years.[742] Another notable casualty was the Edgcumbe family house at Mount Edgcumbe which was destroyed in 1941, the fire taking with it family treasures and portraits. It was not rebuilt until 1958.[743] John Foulston's Royal Hotel and Theatre, as well as his Princess Square, not to mention his Athenaeum with its Doric portico built to resemble the Temple of Theseus at Athens,[744] were heavily damaged or destroyed and the Pier, built to a design by E. Birch in 1884, was severely damaged.

Plymouth particularly suffered in books and original documents. One of the great losses was the Athenaeum. The first strike was in March 1941 when the glass roof of the Scientific Library was destroyed and then in the following month the entire building was ruined. Fortunately about a hundred of the rarest books had been sent to Wrangaton near Ugborough for safety.[745] The Proprietary Library lost its collection of manuscripts that had been proudly listed in 1853. Among the losses were the 25 volumes relating to Dr John King from 1690 to 1731. These included an account of his journey to Exeter, Plymouth, Okehampton and Great Torrington in 1692. Some material held in a deed box in Lloyd's Bank was saved. Strangely, one survival from the city was the collection of material donated by Reverend Sabine Baring-Gould: two volumes of folk songs and twenty-one volumes of extracts from parish registers had been borrowed by a local historian and they were saved. Some documents were destroyed when the new Guildhall and Civic Offices were bombed and the records of the workhouse were also lost when that building was bombed.[746] A collection of documents held in the Devon & Cornwall Room at the Main Library was destroyed,

including a deed dated 1329. Half of the records were grants, leases, fines and bonds relating to Plymouth and the remaining half were concerned with property in and around Plympton.[747] All the books were however destroyed with the exception of some 300 to 400 volumes. Some rare books had been sent to Endsleigh.[748] Losses at individual buildings were also great: the early parish register for East Stonehouse was destroyed in 1941 along with the registers for St George and St Paul. Catholic records were destroyed when the Bishop's House in Plymouth was hit.[749]

In 1941 Plymouth was, according to Joseph Goebbels, the Nazi minister for propaganda, 'the image of horror'.[750] Many local people may have agreed with him. The city's monument to the second world war is the ruined Charles Church. Although now unsympathetically encircled by traffic, the shell is a vivid reminder of the damage wrought by German planes. The church had been started in 1641 and finished in 1708. Three hundred years after it was first constructed, on the night of 21–2 May 1941, bombs fell and demolished the fabric of the building: all woodwork was destroyed, only one bell was not cracked and all the monuments were damaged. In the months that followed gravestones were vandalised and various items of value disappeared.[751] In 1943 it was suggested

Plymouth's Pier, destroyed during the second world war.

Some of the churches damaged or destroyed through bombing in the second world war comprising, clockwise this page, Cockington, St Sidwell in Exeter and St Marychurch and, on the opposite page, St Andrews in Plymouth, Bedford Chapel in Exeter, Charles Church in Plymouth and Clyst St George.

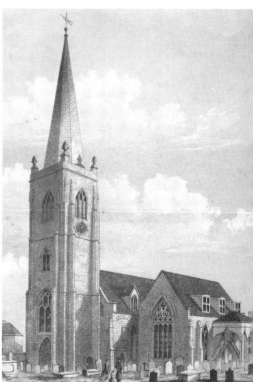

A series of drawings of Paragon House in South Street, Exeter. The building was possibly late medieval in origin and was either rebuilt or renovated in the late seventeenth century. It is typical of the many hundreds of houses which were destroyed but little noticed at the time.

to leave the church in its state as a memorial of the war and in 1957 it was purchased by the city.[752] In spite of the dreariness of its surroundings, the church still has the ability to inspire.

The devastation and horror of the war cannot easily be understood by subsequent generations. One Frenchman, who was in Plymouth on the night of 20 March 1941, when the city was particularly damaged, later recalled being in a shelter:

We were jammed elbow to elbow in our stronghold. Many shelterers clenched their teeth and stood silent, while others smoked or whistled. Then someone set the example of breaking into song and a cacophony followed; for anything would do, hymns or popular ditties or both together. Still the sound of voices failed to drown the uproar outside, and therefore everybody tried to sing a little louder.[753]

Exeter suffered in a different way. It was chosen as a response to the Allied bombing in March 1942 of Lübeck,

an ancient city known for its architecture but with little strategic importance. Hitler is said to have consulted the Baedeker guide to England to identify five similar English cities which included Bath and Norwich. The first bombs fell on a raid the night of 23 to 24 April but did comparatively little damage. In the following nights other raids were made and then in the early hours of 5 May fire bombs fell and, although less than a hundred people died,

Exeter High Street, after the bombing of the second world war and subsequent clearing.

LOST DEVON: CREATION, CHANGE AND DESTRUCTION OVER 500 YEARS

thousands of buildings were destroyed during an hour and a half including 1,500 houses. As with Plymouth the Main Library was destroyed and the city's books with it. Also lost were the Lower Market, much of High Street, the grand workhouse and Dellers' Café. Bedford Circus was seriously damaged and the cathedral suffered as well. A great number of religious buildings were damaged or destroyed in that raid or subsequently including Bedford Chapel and the churches of St James, St Lawrence and St Sidwell. Some four hundred shops, including a great stretch of High Street, were lost. It was said the next morning in Germany 'We have chosen as targets the most beautiful places of England. Exeter is a jewel. We have destroyed it'.[754]

Exeter also suffered a great loss of documents. Ancient papers held by the city council and main library were sent to Bicton and Sydenham for safekeeping.[755] When the probate registry at Bedford Circus was destroyed it also took centuries of locally-proved wills. Those registered in London have survived but not the many thousands housed in Devon. Also, when the library was hit it destroyed books

housed outside the muniments room and it also took some manuscript records and ancient deeds. Unfortunately it also took the actual accession lists of the records without which it is possible to know the full extent of the damage. Finally, a bomb hit the south quire aisle of Exeter Cathedral and damaged a great number of diocesan documents, mainly bishops' transcripts going back to the early sixteenth century. The Fire Brigade doused the documents with water and volunteers later tried to dry them with some success. The papers were transferred to Rougemont Castle where the staff of the record office later shook the dust and rubble from the bundles. Manuscripts which were considered valuable had been removed from the cathedral before the war but this did not include these particular papers. The documents appear to have been regarded as being of little importance by the church hierarchy: the bishop instructed volunteers to throw them away along with the rubble and the dean's later account of the bomb damage omits any mention of the papers.[756] Also records for the parishes of Allhallows on Goldsmith Street, St Paul, St Stephen, St Martin and St Lawrence were heavily damaged to the extent that they are now unfit for use. Some church papers for Pinhoe perished but not through bombing: the registers were buried for safekeeping and were too heavily damaged by damp to be used.[757] It may have been a tradition in Pinhoe to bury its artefacts: it was said that the stone cross was buried during the Civil War.[758]

One class of loss, often not listed or considered, are the contents of buildings which were bombed. In the city's late seventeenth-century workhouse on Heavitree Road were nine portraits, including William III and Ralph Mitchell, the building's architect, which were lost. There was also a painting of the building which was described in 1854 as having been the work of a pauper 'who evidently had a taste for the fine art but did not understand perspective'. Other buildings also had art which was destroyed including the College Hall of the Vicars Choral in which there were five half length portraits.[759]

The Women's Window in Exeter Cathedral, put up in 1886, to a design by John Hardman & Co. from subjects suggested by Miss E. Marriot of 'Seven Women of Holy Scripture'.

One prominent feature which was lost was the ornamental ridge tile, probably made in the early seventeenth century, which adorned a merchant's house in Fore Street. This rider on a horse had been a notable landmark and its destruction in the bombing, after a successful campaign to preserve the building from demolition in the 1930s, has been greatly missed. Similar tiles were on buildings in Plymouth, Tavistock and Totnes. Only Chagford retains its tile, once known as the Tithe Pig or the *Agnus Dei*, in *situ*.[760] That of Exeter disappeared into dust in the early hours of 5 May 1942. Two memorials remain: the hall of the Vicar's Choral in South Street and the almshouse in Catherine Street are reminders of the devastation and loss. A few years later it was said the city paid a heavy price for being acknowledged one of the country's most beautiful places.[761] Yet it could be argued Exeter was only mutilated by war in that it is still identifiable whereas Plymouth was changed so drastically by bombing that it is hardly recognizable with the city of 1939. Arguably greater than the devastation of the war years were subsequent changes made by planners in rebuilding both cities, as discussed on pages 109–110.

A great number of other places also suffered. Like the rest of the country, iron railings were taken throughout Devon and only in a few instances have they been re-erected. A number of churches were destroyed or badly damaged. That at Cockington was hit by a bomb in 1943 and suffered damage to the glass and roof. The parish church of St Marychurch in Torbay was hit in 1943: 26 children and teachers were killed and the church had to be rebuilt.[762] The church of Clyst St George was attacked and one casualty was the parish register: in 1793 the Reverend Polwhele had proudly noted that for some two hundred and fifty years all local baptisms, marriages and burials were noted in the book and that even during the Commonwealth years there had been no interruption.[763] The village of Aveton Giffard was attacked on the afternoon of 26 January 1943 by seven Focke Wulf fighter

bombers. They dropped bombs and then attacked with machine guns. The church and rectory were hit and one five-year old child was killed. The church was reduced to a shell and completely rebuilt from 1948 to 1957.[764] The damage seems particularly tragic given the efforts of the rector in 1884. Remnants of the ancient screen had been stored in the rectory cellar during the church restoration in 1869. Harry Hems, the Exeter craftsman, later reported that:

Lovingly the fragments were spread out on the rectory lawn; and one by one, like a child's puzzle, piece by piece was fitted together, until the whole story of what the good old screens were once was made clear upon the greensward. 'You must put everything in situ again,' said I. 'I will,' was the rector's prompt rejoinder. And so the forlorn looking fragments – for they were forlorn then – were carefully packed, and despatched to Devon's capital, where they were tenderly cared for by that band of modern art-workers who toil – much as men toiled in the old times – beneath the benign shadow of the 'Luckie Horseshoe'. The whitewash and the relays of paint which successive generations of apathetic churchwardens had put upon them (coats of many colours, like Joseph's garment is recorded to have been) were soaked off. This colouring be it remarked, was one of it ancient, but had been put on at various periods during the last hundred years or so. Then came the mending and the piecing; but in no instance re-working: all the work is today precisely as the original craftsman fashioned it; and one place, where he failed, from some now altogether unaccountable cause to complete his moulds, remains still in the same unfinished state as my medieval predecessor left it.

They were finished and re-erected in the summer of 1885[765] only to be completely destroyed in 1943 along with the rest of the church. One other church suffered badly but the damage was caused by Allied planes: the

LOST DEVON: CREATION, CHANGE AND DESTRUCTION OVER 500 YEARS

church tower at Dunkeswell was demolished in 1947 and subsequently rebuilt because of the vibrations from the Navy Liberators and Catalinas based at the United States Naval Air Station.[766]

A long list can be made of other places which suffered air attacks or where stray bombs were dropped between July 1940, when the first bomb fell, to the last in May 1944: this includes Appledore, Axminster, Barnstaple, Bere Alston, Berry Pomeroy, Bishopsteignton, Black Torrington, Bovey Tracey, Braunton, Brixham, Brixton, Buckfastleigh, Budleigh Salterton, Chittlehampton, Churston Ferrers, Clyst Honiton, Colyton, Cornwood, Crediton, Cullompton, Dartington, Dawlish, Diptford, Dittisham, East Allington, Exminster, Galmpton, Gittisham, Harberton Ford, Hartland, Honiton, Ide, Instow, Ivybridge, Kenton, Kingsbridge, Kingsteignton, Kingswear, Lynton, Malborough, Marldon, Modbury, Okehampton, Ottery St Mary, Paignton, Salcombe, Seaton, Sidbury, Sidmouth, Slapton, South Molton, Staverton, Stoke Fleming, Stoke Gabriel, Tamerton Foliot, Tavistock, Teignmouth, Tiverton, Totnes, Uffculme, Ugborough, Westward Ho!, Whimple, Widecombe-in-the-Moor, Woolacombe and Yealmpton.[767]

One of the most extraordinary examples of war damage happened in the South Hams from December 1943 to June 1944: villagers in Sherford, East Allington, Strete, Stokenham and Slapton had to evacuate for American troops. Eventually they learned this was for the D Day landings of 6 June 1944. Private possessions were taken for safekeeping and churches were emptied of removable articles of value. Organs and stonework were sandbagged for safety. On the door of each church was placed a message by the bishop which read:

to our allies of the USA this church has stood here for several hundred years. Around it has grown a community, which has lived in these houses and tilled these fields ever since there was a church. This church, this churchyard in which their loved ones are at rest, these homes, these fields are as dear to those who have

left them as are the homes and graves and fields which you, our Allies, have left behind you. They hope to return one day, as you hope to return to yours, to find them waiting to welcome them home. They entrust them to your care meanwhile, and pray that God's blessing may rest upon us all.

Damage from bombing was in some cases severe: the church at Slapton was directly hit and the southern wall destroyed. The rood screen was later reinserted in a clumsy way. The church at Blackawton was vandalised, possibly after the troops left. Many other buildings were damaged by target practice and hedges destroyed.[768]

Another casualty relates to the Reverend John Swete, the best-known promoter in Devon of the Picturesque Movement of the late eighteenth century. He diligently wrote twenty journals of his travels throughout the county discussing which views were more romantic, gothic, beautiful or picturesque and left these to his descendents. They were kept until April 1942. A member of the family had three volumes by the side of his bed one night and the remaining ones were in another part of his house in Newton Abbot when a German bomb fell in the garden. Mr and Mrs Swete were rescued along with seventeen journals. The remaining three books were never seen again.[769] Some of the rescued volumes bear the scars of the shrapnel.

A number of airbases were opened during the war only to close afterwards. One main site was RAF Harrowbeer at Yelverton on the edge of Dartmoor. Initially flights were made for air sea rescue but spitfires were also flown by Polish men for escort duty and afterwards others were flown by men from Czechoslovakia, Belgium, France, Canada, Australia and New Zealand. Another main site with a similar history was Dunkeswell, initially for the RAF but then taken over by the Americans.[770] Other airstrips were opened before the war but were superseded such as Little Haldon, Folley Gate near Okehampton and Denbury. The latter is now the site of

HM Prison Channingswood.[771] Harrowbeer became redundant once the foreign aircrew left. As with any war, the influx of men alters the population and in the 1940s foreign soldiers left behind babies and some men returned to wed Devon women. Newton Abbot still has its Polish community whereas Brixham eventually lost its substantial number of Belgian fishermen and their families.[772]

One strange casualty was at Hatherleigh. At night a curfew bell was rung at nine and in the morning during the summer at 5 and in the winter at 6. In the early nineteenth century it was supposed the custom had continued from the medieval period and only stopped in 1939 when the ringing of church bells ended across the country.[773]

A category of loss mostly unconsidered is that of the destruction of private homes and businesses. Many thousands of personal items were destroyed including important pieces of art and documents. These losses are often unrecorded because their owners died along with their possessions, a chilling reminder of the effect of war.

The destruction of buildings and manuscripts in war has changed what can be learned about the past in that it has eliminated resources from examination. But in a limited way the destruction of the second world war also created opportunities for studying the past. From 1945 to 1947 trial excavations were undertaken in Exeter to capitalise on the lack of standing buildings in many parts of the city. One writer later remembered, apparently with some affection, a group of female archaeologists. Not all locals were as supportive: Lady Eileen Fox, who led the excavations, recalled how some passers-by thought it a

Miss Ethel Lega-Weekes, the well-known historian as drawn by Harold Murray in 1949.

waste of public money. She also suffered from the attentions of one local historian and remembered:

I was at the mercy of the local cranks, such as the witch-like Miss Lega-Weekes, a learned old lady, who kept popping up unexpectedly at the side of the trench to ask me difficult questions.

Interestingly, the only labour that could be had during the 1946 season was a group of six Italian prisoners of war who were housed at nearby Poltimore. The men cooked their mid-day meal of spaghetti in an old air raid shelter donated by the city.[774] It would be interesting to know their thoughts as they ate their lunch, in a foreign city devastated by their allies, and sifted through the evidence of centuries of Exeter's past. The descendants of the culture which created Exeter helping to distinguish two thousand years of Devon's past lost in the dust to war as well as fire, flood, vandalism, theft, indifference, fashion, improvement, development and religion.

Conclusion

In the last five hundred years key elements of Devon's heritage have been lost for a great number of reasons. Fire, storms and floods have destroyed some, others have gone through natural wear and tear, and the rest, most likely the vast majority, have been lost through the pursuit of fashion or war, in redevelopment or civic improvements. Much is irreplaceable. Plymouth before the second world war was filled with an interesting mix of buildings that befitted one of the country's great ports. But that is a memory for a very few and soon there will only be images and words for future generations to try to imagine 'Old' Plymouth. It will never be rebuilt as it was. Likewise, the destruction of thousands of original documents in Exeter in 1942 has put parts of the county's history forever beyond our reach. These documents had unique details of the past which no others can now tell us. Many losses were avoidable: the campaigns of destruction pursued in the name of Jesus in the 1500s and 1800s equals those of religious fundamentalists in third world countries today. Civic improvers and redevelopers are also often zealots, destroying with one hand in order to rebuild with another. It is not feasible to safeguard existing heritage without having a sufficient understanding of these forces. The only effective way to protect the present for the future is to understand the past.

Yet it is not possible to save everything. For example, fonts and altars from deconsecrated churches have particular circumstances: Church of England policy requires destruction unless another church provides housing. Thus those of St Sidwell's church in Exeter were recently destroyed and the fragments placed in the foundations of the community centre. These can be seen as both artistic creations and religious objects with conflicting views on whether it is appropriate to preserve or destroy. Society needs to debate and decide what needs to be saved for future generations based on individual merits. In many instances fashion dictates this. The eighteenth-century pursuit of classical buildings made earlier vernacular styles unfashionable, just as the classical was during the Victorian enthusiasm for gothic. It is only recently that society has appreciated nineteenth-century building. To counter this, and the waves of destruction, the Georgian Group was formed and afterwards the Victorian Society. The current unpopularity of twentieth-century building will pass, but not before thousands of buildings will be demolished only to be mourned in the future. Buildings also need guarantees of financial viability. Not one country house can exist on ticket sales to the public nor is every one appropriate as a hotel, flat or office. Solutions need to be reached based on particular circumstances of each building and through a reasoned assessment of what society can and should maintain for future generations. The recent discussions over the future of Poltimore House centre on its development as a regional arts centre. Is this its last chance before the building crumbles to the ground?

A vibrant society also needs to grow and cannot stay still. We need to understand the relationship between creation and destruction. Buildings generally rise over the remains of others and we would not have our favourite buildings without the loss of others. But it should be a matter of considered thought of when to destroy, save or refashion.

At the beginning of the twenty-first century documents continue to be destroyed, distinctive buildings are demolished and natural habitats erased. Parts of our heritage have problems particular to them. Unless, for example, there is a great religious revival in the next generation it is likely many parish churches will be faced with redundancy and society will have uncomfortable questions on their future. Most rural churches are maintained by small groups of dedicated parishioners. Even so, a considerable number of established churches

An example of the various fates of one type of object: some of this early heraldic glass has been destroyed through war, other pieces have been obtained by museums and one example remains in situ.

From left, At Bampfylde House in Exeter when that building was destroyed in the second world war.
Still survives at Ashton Church.
Was at Cowick Barton in Exeter but now housed at the Victoria & Albert Museum.
And below, formerly at Cowick Barton, now part of the Burrell Collection, Glasgow Art Gallery and Museum.

in Devon have recently been made redundant and some have been demolished. In Exeter not all of the remainder are as fortunate as St Martin's which is in the custody of the Churches Conservation Trust: St Mary Arches has recently lost its eighteenth-century organ, St Pancras has been caged for a generation in a shopping mall with passers-by oblivious to its delights and the restoration of St Martin's church tower, while badly needed, coloured it bold pink and it now pricks the skyline in an unfortunate manner. The conversion of another church has implications for the future. St Petrock's church was faced with closure and recently was developed for community use with a portion retained for worship. It is a difficult building to convert with an unusual internal arrangement and the distinction of being the only one within the county, and probably much further afield, of historically being encased by secular buildings with only the tower showing. Glimpses of its importance are there to be seen but the conversion has removed the very heart of the church and with it any sense of dignity. Through a thin partition there is a din from the homeless centre into the church and an atmosphere of irreverence if not irrelevance. There is a dilemma of whether it is possible to combine the needs of a modern care centre with the function and preservation of an ancient building. It must be said that on the one hand the changes are reversible, the building has possibly been saved from redundancy, there is a heavy use for the centre and it is commendable that the Church of England is involved with the homeless. It is true that religious buildings, like all others, must continue to develop but society is much more aware of their historical significance. One must question the propriety of using this particular building for such a purpose and wonder what implications it has for others in the diocese. In the past thirty-five years more than 50 established churches in Devon have already been considered for redundancy and nine have been demolished. Others have been converted for housing

(Harracott in Tawstock, Brownston in Modbury, Paignton, Swimbridge), a farm building (East Putford), a parish hall (Horrabridge) and recreational purposes including as a sports hall (Torquay) and for the Torbay Operatic and Dramatic Society (Torwood). St Saviour's in Tormohun was transferred to the Greek Orthodox Church and others were retained for worship.

Interestingly, had St Petrock's church been made redundant, which was a likely outcome, and turned to secular purposes it would have gone through the local planning process but established church buildings still in religious use are altered within Church of England administration. When planning legislation was first passed these buildings were exempted and listed separately because they did not receive state aid. In 1977 however they were allowed to receive government funds. It is questionable whether this exemption is still appropriate and it could be argued that the importance of these buildings (nationally the Anglicans hold 50% of the country's grade 1 listed structures)[775] merit the same planning process as other buildings. It is not easy to find appropriate uses for redundant religious buildings and this issue is likely to become more pressing, particularly in rural parishes, in the years ahead. Four other faiths (the Methodists, Roman Catholics, Baptist Union and United Reformed) are also exempt as well as properties belonging to the Crown. This includes government departments, including English Heritage, and the Duchy of Cornwall. Consultation on change is made on a voluntary basis. It could be argued that these groups merit different structures but this privilege is uncomfortable particularly in Devon where the Duchy of Cornwall owns a considerable amount of land and properties on Dartmoor and in Bradninch.

It is commonplace to point to the loss of buildings and suggest it would not happen today. But has society changed its attitudes towards preservation? In about 1750 the cleric at Tavistock wrote bitterly about the destruction of the abbey:

The Chapter House and Cloisters were demolished by a worthless upstart of this town, who valued himself upon laying the foundation of a pompous dwelling house for himself and family in the cloisters adjoining to the school and Chapter House, turning out their remains and stone coffins to public view, with that inhumanity, contempt and ridicule of which none but such a wreck would be capable.[776]

He was unusual. It was not until the 1820s that a local campaign was first made for the protection of a local building (Exeter's Broadgate) and until then destruction was seen not merely as change but progress. In 1861 a local newspaper gave a voice to a Devon building on the verge of demolition:

I was designed and put upon my foundations rather more than 400 years ago, and have to thank the Crusaders, who beat the Infidels in the Holy War, for my name [the Turk's Head]. In my youthful days the good town I'm about to quit for ever hadn't as many hundreds as it now has thousands of people, but I had more friars of orders grey, black, and white, than there are persons of every shade in all modern Plymouth. Some of them were early patrons of mine, and ever and anon gave me a call, liking well my sign, but better still my sack and my jovial company. A church, a monastery, and a town cross were my near neighbours, and I thrived well in their company; and of my surrounding contemporaries (solid, gabled, mullioned, and put together much as I am), there was hardly one that kept its head (or tiles) much higher than mine, for the tall and overhanging timbered houses, like my old friend in Notte Street, had not yet been thought of.[777]

This Plymouth inn was nevertheless destroyed. Could it happen today? It could, and in some instances, should. Not every structure has to be saved merely because it is old but judged on its merits. In 1816 the ancient bridge

at Chudleigh was taken down. This bridge, of two large arches and one small one with angular recesses in which pedestrians waited for passing traffic, was no longer capable of taking the increased level of traffic. By the early nineteenth century there were 'six Royal mails, a number of stage coaches and a variety of other vehicles'. Although paltry by modern standards, the bridge was considered outdated. In the nineteenth century one local woman commented 'whatever these historians thought of it, this county bridge was narrow, the walls low, the approach at each end was by a sharp turn, its passage was altogether dangerous for the long heavy laden coaches'.[778] Hopefully today we would build a second bridge. All buildings need to be judged on distinctiveness and their value to society. Fortunately what has changed is the introduction of legal protection for the historic environment and public awareness of its importance.

What is desperately needed is more research. For instance, we know very little of oddities like Exeter's medieval statue of St Peter and why it survived the Reformation and the Civil War. How did it manage to last four centuries? One of the most significant of Devon's industries, lace-making, has yet to have a thorough history. Much of what has been written concentrates on the nineteenth century and it would be surprising for most to learn that in the seventeenth century men too made bone lace and it was done by individuals in places far from Honiton, or the rest of East Devon, such as

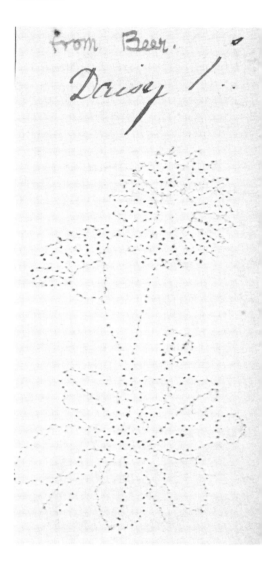

Examples of Victorian lace from East Devon.

from Beer.
Daisy!

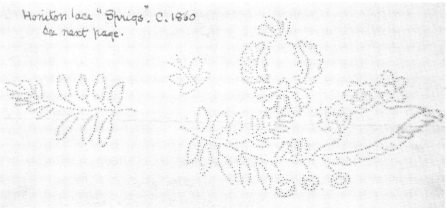

Honiton lace "Sprigs" c.1860
See next page.

Kingsbridge. Not long afterwards the county justices tried to engage 'masterless men' in making bone-lace. As fascinating as these snippets are, the subject needs proper investigation.[779] Even more serious is the lack of a comprehensive study of the cloth trade. Arguably local history has never been more popular but no public institution in Devon has a dedicated research and publication programme and efforts fall instead to individuals. Much of what we know is by accident. Many archaeological finds have come about through chance surface finds and it is not often that archaeologists can be certain of what will be found. Unusual artefacts also turn up: for instance in 1827 a collection of late Elizabeth English silver, subsequently dubbed the 'Armada Service', was accidentally uncovered in a cave in Brixton near Plymouth. These thirty dining dishes had probably been hidden for the nearly two hundred years since the Civil War.[780] Also, surviving documents dictate what is known about the past: for example, the only record of the 'churching' of a woman in Devon comes from early seventeenth-century Gittisham. Her experience may have been typical but we shall never know.[781] There is much we are ignorant of and, yet, the collections gathered in libraries, museums and archives now make research possible on a scale not dreamed of by previous generations.

A great danger is the deliberate telling of false history. Some stories have been told in an obviously humorous way, such as the account of the treacle mines at Tamerton Foliot and Dunchideock,[782] but which unfortunately are still believed by some. Some exaggerations can be expected: for instance, a Totnes spring became so popular from 1605 for its alleged medicinal qualities that it could not supply demand until it was realised the virtues were overrated. It was redundant within a generation.[783] Some are instances of inaccuracies rather than deliberate misleading: an inaccurate report was printed that a specimen of *cynoglossum omphaloides*, a relative of the hound's tongue, was found among the rocks at Teignmouth and resulted in a number of Georgian botanical tourists searching in vain for it. It was eventually reported the plant never grew there.[784] Other stories have their origin in ignorance: in the late nineteenth century the erosion of one numeral carved in stone to mark the restoration of Peter Tavy church had the villagers believing their church was restored in 1027 and not 1827. They were not happy being told the truth.[785]

Others are more planned: in Bideford it became generally accepted that three local women executed for witchcraft in the late seventeenth century were the last to have been killed in England. A later writer pointed out that the guide book had been too keen to promote an exciting story: there were further executions elsewhere in the eighteenth century.[786] One story of deceit is that of Barnstaple's early charters: the town contrived a history of fifteenth-century charters which fooled Westminster and gained liberties it was not entitled to.[787] T. E. Lawrence, after his experiences in the Arabian Desert, is alleged to have started a myth about Radford House outside Plymouth. He was stationed at Mount Batten in the 1930s and suggested that a granite shaft in the stable blocks was of Roman origins. It was subsequently known as the Roman Altar.[788] More recently, in 2000 a couple retired to Devon and purchased what they thought was a former hunting lodge of Edward VIII. The estate agent showed them the king's gun cabinet and informed them the Queen Mother had been photographed on the lawn. They agreed to pay £130,000 more for the house because of the royal connection but subsequently discovered the story was false.[789] These stories have a tourism impact. Visitors to Borringdon Hall Hotel are told that Elizabeth I visited the manor house in 1588[790] but she never travelled to Devon. At Bradfield in Uffculme visitors believed that Philip of Spain, husband of Queen Mary, stayed at the house en route to London[791] although he too never came to Devon. Through the 1980s and 1990s it was commonly repeated that 'Bridge over Troubled Waters', written by Simon and Garfunkel, was about Bickleigh Bridge. Tourists' visits were enhanced by the tale but it was admitted to be false some twenty years later. Finally, for more than a hundred years the history of Mol's Coffee House in Exeter has been enlarged to become a tale of Sir Francis Drake, Sir John Hawkins and Sir Humphrey Gilbert, and occasionally Sir Walter Raleigh, drinking a cup of coffee in 1596 while planning England's campaign against the armada. Unfortunately this was eight years too late, several generations before coffee was drunk in England and when each man was either far from Exeter or already dead. Neither coffee nor spirits were served at that time. The tale was begun by a Victorian to increase the number of visitors to his gallery and then accepted quite happily ever since. It has done a disservice to the building's history as an Elizabethan Custom House and then a Georgian Coffee House run by women.[792]

There is however much to be encouraged about; in spite of constant destruction Devon has a rich heritage. Many individuals have saved key elements of the past and their efforts should be remembered. In the 1880s wooden panels were discovered during the demolition of a cottage at Whitford and brought to Shute Barton: it was supposed they were from a medieval priest's house.[793] At the same time another wooden panel, with an image thought to have been of a pope, was rescued from a rubbish heap during the restoration of the church of Widecombe-in-the-Moor.[794] In 1878 Exeter's Harry Hems rebuilt the font cover at Shaugh Prior church: this fifteenth-century carved wood, now seen as the glory of the parish, had been removed during church renovation from 1867 to 1868, stored in the loft of Mrs Mumford of Undershaugh and retrieved some ten years after the urging of a visiting cleric. Hems is alleged to have found it in a farmer's linhay and the farmer's wife said the 'rotten old thing should be burned'. At other times objects were destroyed, but fortunately in these three

instances local men and women chose preservation.[795] New sources are becoming available every year. One example is a series of potentially important maps of East Devon, possibly drawn in the seventeenth century, that has recently been relocated. For at least last ten years they were misplaced after being deposited at the Kent Archives Office.[796] After conservation work the maps will be available to be examined for the first time. All across Devon local historians are delving into records and examining artefacts on a scale unknown in the county's history. Some exciting work is being undertaken. For instance research is currently being made into the history of Devon's cold baths. These eighteenth and early nineteenth century sites are only now being recognised for what they were. We may even have others from the late seventeenth century.[797] In ten years we shall know a great deal more about these and, hopefully, a great number of other subjects.

Many individual items are lost for uncertain reasons but they may still survive somewhere in Devon or elsewhere. For instance it would also be useful to know the current whereabouts, if it exists, of Haccombe's map of about 1600. It has not been seen since the Carew estate was sold in the 1940s but it might be in private hands.[798] Other important maps are missing such as Kingsbridge's great map of the late sixteenth century which was redrawn and published in the *Gentleman's Magazine* in 1799 but has not been seen since. Dartmouth has also lost early maps: two survive from the seventeenth century but two others were last in the Guildhall. An interesting map of Awliscombe from 1763 is also missing.[799] Does Barnstaple's lost chronicle of the late sixteenth century still exist? A remarkable statue of Thomas Baron, mayor of Exeter in 1705, was once in the church of St George, then at St John and subsequently removed to St Mary Arches in 1937. Another stone monument, that to Benjamin Oliver, was also in St John's church.[800] A statue of Neptune once stood on Exeter's Victorian Public Baths. Have they found new homes or were they destroyed? It is not known whether the records of the Bampfylde family at Poltimore have survived or those of the Savery family at Shilston. As late as the 1930s there existed an early Stuart portrait of Lady Lucy Reynell of Forde House in Newton Abbot but it has not been seen for at least a generation. Was it destroyed in the second world war? An unusual mazer bowl was discovered on or near the site of Wolmerstone Chapel in Crediton in 1791 but its current location is also unknown.[801] In 1908 the church of St Petrock's in Exeter had a chained library of sixteenth-century books kept in a glass case but where is it now?[802] It is possible, if not probable, that some of these items have owners who are unaware of their significance.

What of the future? Many losses are beyond our control, at some point war will once again kill and destroy although it may not be Exeter or Plymouth but some place unthinkable to us like Colyton or Totnes.

Much of what we have about us today will, for a variety of reasons, not survive for future generations. Buildings are only rarely rebuilt in the same way, documents hold unique information and once native habitats are lost then they can seldom be brought back. Yet, we must recognise the process of change is the process of history; society must change. Nearly forty years ago one president of the Devonshire Association exhorted his members 'we must adapt rather than destroy, improve rather than merely preserve'[803] and this remains the challenge. We need also to differentiate between change and progress. Over the last five hundred years a great number of people have worked towards ensuring that Devon has kept its heritage. William Crossing, Beatrix Cresswell, Raleigh Radford, Ethel Lega-Weekes, Arthur Everett and W. G. Hoskins are just some of the many Devonians toward whom we all owe a great debt. Now, at the beginning of a new century, it falls to others to learn, cherish and protect the best of Devon's past.

Abbreviations

DAT	Devonshire Association Transactions
DCNQ	Devon & Cornwall Notes & Queries
DCRS	Devon & Cornwall Record Society
DEI	Devon & Exeter Institution
DH	The Devon Historian
DRO	Devon Record Office
E&E	Express & Echo
EFP	Exeter Flying Post
EPG	Exeter & Plymouth Gazette
NDRO	North Devon Record Office
PDAS	Proceedings of the Devon Archaeological Society
PI	Annual Reports and Transactions of the Plymouth Institution
PLSL	Plymouth Local Studies Library
TEDAS	Transactions of the Exeter Diocesan Architectural Society
WA	The Western Antiquary
WEH	Western Evening Herald
WMN	Western Morning News
WSL	Westcountry Studies Library

Illustration Sources

Page 7 WSL, p&d006619; page 8 WSL, p&d01323; page 10 WSL, SC2354; page 11 *Österreichische Nationalbibliothek;* page 15 WSL, oversize unlisted print; page 16 Francis Stevens, *Views of cottages and farmhouses in England and Wales, etched by Francis Stevens* (1815), 7; page 17 WSL, p&d05550; pages 20–21, 24–5, 28–9 WSL, no reference; page 31 WSL, p&d042792; page 32 WSL, p&d06873; page 38 WSL, p&d05546; page 39 WSL, p&d05545, J7903; pages 40 & 41 WSL, John Smale Short, *Historical Memoirs of the town and parish of Hatherleigh, Devon, collected from the best authorities,* early nineteenth century, pages 401, 407 and 409; page 42 WSL, A. W. Searley, *Some Devon Churches,* volume 7, page 175 & 455; page 43 WSL, p&d09453; page 44 WSL, p&d09454; page 50 WSL, sb/tot/0001SEA, page 201; page 51 WSL, SC1745; page 52 DRO, 547B/982; page 53 WSL, no reference; page 54 DEI, no reference; page 56 Exeter City Museums, Antiquities Archive; page 57 Henry Francis Whitfeld, *Plymouth and Devonport: in times of war and peace* (Plymouth, 1900), 281; page 58 Exeter City Museums, Antiquities Archive; page 60 WSL, SC1388; page 61 WSL, p&d000399; page 63 WSL, sale catalogue, Eggesford, 1913; page 64 WSL, SC1381; page 65 WSL, oversize drawing, no reference & p&d05584; page 66 WSL, photograph album by Edward Pocknell; page 67 WSL, SC1001; page 69 WSL, A. W. Searley, *Some Devon Churches,* volume 7, page 510, 512; page 70 WSL, A. W. Searley, *Some Devon Churches,* volume 6, page 117 & SC444; page 71 WSL, SC999 & A. W. Searley, *A book about Kingsbridge,* volume 1; page 72 Arthur Charles Ellis, *Historical Survey of Torquay* (Torquay, c.1930), 289; page 73 WSL, SC880; page 75 WSL, B/Axminster 677.643; page 76 WSL, SC920; page 77 WSL, SC255; page 78 WSL, p&d004973; pages 79 & 80 WSL, A. W. Searley, *A book about Kingsbridge,* volume 1; page 81 WSL, SC1349; page 84 A. W. Searley, Arts & Crafts, volume 1, page 3 & A. W. Searley, *Some Devon Churches,* volume 7, page 466; page 83 WSL, p&d 09450; page 82 WSL, p&d09449; page 83 WSL, SC1798; page 88 WSL, p&d044330; page 89 WSL, A. W. Searley, *A book about Kingsbridge,* volume 1; page 90 WSL, p&d08619 & p&d07599; page 91 WSL, p&d00534; page 92, Daniel Radford, 'Working Men's Dwellings', *Devonshire Association Transactions,* 1890, XXII, 141 & WSL, p&d41636; page 94 WSL, p&d06873 & *Österreichische Nationalbibliothek;* page 95 WSL, s/dev/1907/cor, pages 46–7; page 98 WSL, SC799; page 99 WSL,

p&d008726; page 100 DRO, Z19/31/2; page 101 Henry Francis Whitfeld, *Plymouth and Devonport: in times of war and peace* (Plymouth, 1900), 38 & James Hine, 'The Old Buildings of Plymouth', PI, I, 1860–1, 22; page 103 WSL, P. O. Hutchinson, Journals, IV, 56–7; page 104 Charles Vancouver, *General View of the Agriculture of the county of Devon* (1808), 94; page 105 R. T. Shears, *Conservation of Devonshire Cottages* (1968), no page number; page 106 by kind permission of Allhallows Museum; page 107 DEI, no reference number; page 108 Henry Francis Whitfeld, *Plymouth and Devonport: in times of war and peace* (Plymouth, 1900), 372 & 388 & Thomas Mawson & Sons, *Exeter of the Future* (1914); page 113 WSL, SC263; page 115 WSL, p&d05509; page 116 WSL, P. O. Hutchinson, Journals, IV, 6; page 117 WSL, A. W. Searley, *A book about Kingsbridge,* volume 1, viii; page 120 DRO, 118M/E3; page 121 SC1676 & SC1826; page 123 James Fortescue, *Dissertations* (1759); page 125 WSL, p&d007598; page 128 WSL, p&d040341; page 130 WSL, SC2475; page 131 WSL, SC2498; page 132 WSL, P. O. Hutchinson, Journals, I, 16; page 133 WSL, SC230; page 135 WSL, unlisted oversize photograph; page 136 WSL, p&d02407; page 137 WSL, SC212; page 138 *Letters and important documents relative to the Edystone [sic] lighthouse* (1811), frontispiece; page 140 WSL, sxb/mem 001 dav, between 26 and 27; page 143 WSL, SC2984; pages 144–5 DRO, Z19/2/4 & 76/20/4; page 146 WSL, *Transactions of the Exeter Diocesan Architectural Society,* III & WSL, John Smale Short, *Historical Memoirs of the town and parish of Hatherleigh, Devon, collected from the best authorities,* early nineteenth century, 403; page 147 WSL, SC2754; page 148 WSL, SC3333; page 149 WSL, SC1121; page 150 Exeter City Museums, Antiquities Archive; page 153 author's sketch; page 157 Henry Francis Whitfeld, *Plymouth and Devonport: in times of war and peace* (Plymouth, 1900), frontispiece & 106; page 160 by kind permission of Plymouth Council; page 161 *Photographic View Album of the West of England* (c.1910); page 162 WSL, SC397, SC886, SC3142; page 163 WSL, SC1904, SC889, SC1909, SC394; page 164 WSL, p&d44464–8; page 165 by kind permission of Exeter City Council; page 166 WSL, p&d004684; page 169 WSL, sfdev/1949/mur; page 171 Maurice Drake, *A History of English Glass-painting* (1912), plate xiva & Glasgow Art Gallery and Museum.

Notes

1. WSL, Volume 6 'Screens and Screenwork' by A. Searley, page 300.
2. H. J. Whitfeld, *Rambles in Devonshire with tales and poetry* (1854), 141.
3. Peter Beacham, 'Changing Devon', in *Devon's Heritage: Buildings and Landscape* (Exeter, 1982), 9.
4. Andrew Saunders, *Exploring England's Heritage: Devon and Cornwall* (1991, English Heritage).
5. J. Brooking Rowe, Presidential Address, DAT, XIV, 1882, 6.
6. Rowe, Presidential Address, 29.
7. J. B. R., 'Font at Plymstock church', *WA,* June 1883, 53.
8. Andrew J. H. Jackson, 'The Short-lived school of domestic science at Powderham Castle', *DH,* 59, October 1999, 10–14. Interestingly, a previous member of the family had founded in nearby Kenton an Industrial Home for the training of girls for domestic service in 1861: *White's Directory,* 1878–9.
9. J. Manaton, *Hatherleigh History In Brief* (Exeter, 1951), 13.
10. The Rt Hon. the Viscount Amory, 'Our changing heritage', *DAT,* XCVI, 1964, 40, 38.
11. Richard Polwhele, *The History of Devonshire* (Exeter, 1793), II, 303.
12. His account for Devon was edited by R. Pearse Chope for *Devon & Cornwall Notes & Queries* in 1918 as part of a collection of topographical accounts. For Leland and other travellers' accounts see Todd Gray (ed.), *East Devon: the Travellers' Tales* (Exeter, 2001) and *Exeter: the Travellers' Tales* (Exeter, 2000).
13. See Joyce Youings, 'Some Early Topographers of Devon and Cornwall', 50–61, and Malcolm Todd, 'From Romanticism to Archaeology: Richard Colt Hoare, Samuel Lysons and Antiquity' in Mark Brayshay (ed.), *Topographical Writers in South-West England* (Exeter, 1996).
14. Polwhele, *Devon,* II, 165, 299.
15. Robin Stanes, 'Devon Agriculture in the mid-eighteenth century: the evidence of the Milles enquiries', in M. A. Havinden and Celia M. King, *The South West and the Land* (Exeter Studies in Economic History, 2, 1969), 43.
16. E. D. Mackerness, 'Richard Hole of the Exeter Society of Gentlemen, an eighteenth century Shakespearean critic', *DAT,* LXXXVIII, 1956, 130; *Essays by a Society of Gentlemen at Exeter* (1796)
17. Blackwell, 'North Devon Athenaeum', 174.
18. W. G. Hoskins, *Devon* (Newton Abbot, 1954), 255–6; Crispin Gill, *Plymouth, a new history, 1603 to the present day* (Newton Abbot, 1979), 95; J. N. Bennett, 'Historical sketch of the origin and progress of the Plymouth Institution', *PI,* I, 1858–9, 15.
19. Reginald Lane, *Old Sidmouth* (Tiverton, 1990), 61.
20. Robert Newton, *Victorian Exeter, 1837–1914* (Leicester, 1968), 14.
21. G. W. G. Hughes, 'Number Seven, The Close, Exeter', *DAT,* XCIV, 1962, 461.
22. *The Western Miscellany: a journal of literature, science, antiquities and art for the West of England, 1849* (Exeter, 1850), 61–66, 94–8, 127–30, 158–62, 224–6, 288; Joseph Besley Gribble, *Memorials of Barnstaple* (Barnstaple, 1994 edn), 417–418; Jones, *Chudleigh,* 133; Charles John Plumptree, *An address on the celebration of the first anniversary of the Dawlish Literary and General Knowledge Society* (Dawlish, 1851); White's Directory, 1878–9.
23. Eric V. Kingdom, 'Tavistock Library', *DAT,* LXXVIII, 1946, 229.
24. Cecil Torr, *Small Talk at Wreyland* (Cambridge, 1921), II, 72.
25. W. H. K. Wright, *The libraries, public and private of Plymouth* (Library Association, 1901), 1–23.
26. Fred W. Hunt, *Libraries of Devonport: naval, military and civil* (Devonport, 1901); A. J. Southward and E. K. Roberts, 'The Marine Biological Association, 1884–1984', *DAT,* 116, 984, 155–99.
27. John B. Whitton, A history of libraries in Exeter, in particular the Exeter city Library (MA dissertation, University of Sheffield, 1975).
28. Audrey M. Erskine, 'Exeter Cathedral Library and Archives', *DH,* 8, April 1974, 17.
29. D. Wyn Evans, 'Devon's Parochial Libraries at Exeter University', *DH,* 24, April 1982, 18.
30. Anne Welsford, 'Mr Newte's Library in St Peter's Church, Tiverton', *DAT,* 107, 1979, 19.
31. *White's Directory,* 1878–9.
32. Newton, *Victorian Exeter,* 14; Whitton, History, 1.
33. Thomas Greenwood, *Public libraries: a history of the movement and a manual for the organisation and management of rate-supported libraries* (1891), 228.
34. Hunt, *Libraries,* 3–4.
35. Roger Jones, *A Book of Newton Abbot* (Bradford on Avon, 1979), 127–8.
36. Alfred E. Blackwell, 'The North Devon Athenaeum at Barnstaple', *DAT,* XCIII, 1961, 174–83; J. Stevens, 'The Plymouth Athenaeum, 1812–1962', *DAT,* XCIV, 1962, 575–78. Bideford had its free library in 1877: *White's Directory,* 1878–9.
37. J. N. Bennett, 'Historical sketch of the origin and progress of the Plymouth Institution', *PI,* 18.
38. Alison Grant, 'The Athenaeum's predecessors: need and provision', in *The North Devon Athenaeum, 1888–1988* (Barnstaple, 1988), 6–8.
39. *White's Directory,* 1878–9.
40. Todd Gray, *Exeter Unveiled* (Exeter, 2003), 29.
41. Margery Rowe, 'Exeter City Record Office', *DH,* 5, October 1972, 13–15; Brian Carpenter (ed.), *Ten Centuries of Devon's Archives* (Friends of Devon's Archives, Exeter, 2002), 8–13; *A Guide to the Archives Department of the Plymouth City Libraries, part one* (Plymouth, 1962), ix.
42. Hilda H. Walker, 'The Story of the Devonshire Association', *DAT,* XCIV, 1962, 46.
43. *The Regulations of the Barnstaple Literary and Scientific Institution* (Barnstaple, 1845), 5.
44. *Journal of the Torquay Natural History Society,* volume 1, 1909–1914, 3–4.
45. *TEDAS,* volume 1, 1843.
46. *Dock Literary and Philosophical Society* (Plymouth, 1810), 3.
47. J. N. Bennett, 'Historical Sketch of the origin and progress of the Plymouth Institution',*PI,* I, 1858–9, 15.
48. R. A. J. Walling, *The Story of Plymouth* (1950), 228.
49. Walter Minchinton, 'The University of Exeter and Devon history', *DH,* 8, April 1974, 3–12.
50. W. Walmesley, H. G. Hurrell and V. C. Wynne-Edwards, First report of the Devon Birdwatching and Preservation Society, *DAT,* LXI, 1929, 405.
51. *Proceedings of the Devon Exploration Society* (vol. 1, 1929–32), 103; John Bosanko, 'The Archaeological Achievement', PDAS, 38, 1980. The North Devon Archaeological Society was formed in 1958.
52. Walter Minchinton, 'The Devon Historic Buildings Trust', *DH,* 7, 10 1973, 7–9. Its remit was to rescue threatened buildings.
53. F. J. M. Laver, 'Notes on the origins of the Sid Vale Association', *DAT,* 107, 1975, 21.
54. John Caldwell, 'A Provincial Horticultural Society', *DAT,* XCII, 1960, 104–5.
55. John Caldwell, 'Some notes on the first British Beekeeping Society', *DAT,* LXXXVIII, 1956, 65.
56. Tristram Risdon, *The Chorographical Description or Survey of the county of Devon* (Barnstaple, 1970 edn), 269.
57. Risdon, *Devon,* 70–73, 110, 304, 15, 186, 213. The name 'Saxon School' continued in Tavistock through to the end of the seventeenth century: Lady Radford, 'Tavistock Abbey', *TEDAS,* 3rd series, 4, 74.
58. Polwhele, *Devon,* I, 180, 237; II, 86, 58, 8, 2.
59. Hoskins, *Devon.*
60. Andrew Fleming, *The Dartmoor Reaves* (1988), 12–19.
61. W. T. P. Shortt, *Sylva Antiqua Iscana, Numismatica, quinetiam figulian or Roman and other antiquities of Exeter* (Exeter, 1840).
62. James Davidson, *Notes on the Antiquities of Devonshire which date before the Norman Conquest* (Exeter, 1861), 13, 15, 16, 17, 23, 25.
63. Rowe, Presidential Address, *DAT,* XIV, 1882, 30.

64. William Stukeley, *Itinerarium Curiosium* (1776) edited by R. Pearse Chope, *Devon & Cornwall Notes & Queries,* 1918 and by Gray, *Exeter the Travellers' Tales,* 41–5.

65. Polwhele, *Devon,* I, 154–6; DRO, 564M/F1–17. The seventeen surviving volumes of Reverend Swete's travels have been edited by Todd Gray, *Travels in Georgian Devon* (Tiverton, 1997–2000), in four volumes.

66. Todd, 'From Romanticism to Archaeology', 90–91.

67. William Crossing, 'Preservation of Dartmoor Antiquities', *WA,* September 1881, 94.

68. *WA,* October 1881, 115. The same comment was made during a Parliamentary debate on the topic.

69. Simon Timms, '"Deep Breathing to Grimspound": archaeologists discover Dartmoor', *PDAS,* 52, 1994, 6–9.

70. John Allan, 'Ralegh Radford', *PDAS,* 56, 1998, 1–4.

71. First Report of the Ancient Monuments Committee, *DAT,* LIV, 1923, 61–3. See Simon Timms, 'From ancient monuments to historic landscapes: the quest to conserve Devon's archaeological heritage', *PDAS,* 51, 1993, 4–8.

72. Much of the following information has been derived from Michael Ross, *Planning and Heritage* (1991).

73. F. M. Griffith, 'Devon County Sites and Monuments Register', *DH,* 20, April 1980, 23.

74. For example see *An Inventory of the Historical Monuments in Dorset,* I (1952) and II (1970).

75. These comprise work on Denbury hillfort, Oldstone, Bampton motte and bailey, Loddiswell hillfort, motte and bailey, Inner Froward Point battery, Eylesbarrow Tin Mine, Woodbury Hillfort, Grimspound, Holne Chase Hillfort, Tor Royal, Challacombe, Headland Warren, Druid Mine (forthcoming) and Brixham Battery (forthcoming).

76. John Summerson, Introduction, in *50 years of the National Buildings Record, 1911–1991* (RCHME, 1991).

77. Stewart Brown, 'Recent Building recording and excavations at Leigh Barton, Churchstow, Devon', *PDAS,* 56, 1998, 7.

78. Michael Ross, *Planning and the Heritage* (1991); Pamela Cunnington, *Caring for Old Houses* (2002 edn, Yeovil); Wayland Kennet, *Preservation* (1972).

79. 14th report on ancient monuments, *DAT,* 67, 1935.

80. Mellor, *Exeter Architecture,* 83–4, 87–8; *WMN,* 3 11 1934; RAMM, St Katherine's Priory box file; Todd Gray, *The Garden History of Devon* (Exeter, 1995), 193.

81. David Richardson, 'Case Studies of Repair and Restoration', 64–5.

82. It also owns one car park.

83. Percy Russell, *A History of Torquay* (Torquay, 1960), 132, 63; John R. Pike, *Paignton* (Torbay, 1993), 38.

84. Society for the Protection of Ancient Buildings Archives, local files. The local correspondent was G. B. Longstaff, M.D.

85. Jones, *Newton Abbot,* 113.

86. Alan Endacott, *Okehampton Castle,* Devon (English Heritage, 2003), 35.

87. The Association began as Mutual Household in 1955 and Flete is on a 60 year lease.

88. David Richardson, 'Case Studies of Repair and Restoration', in *Devon's Heritage; Buildings and Landscape, 52–3, 76–7; Twenty years of progress, 1973 to 1993* (Devon Historic Buildings Trust, 1993).

89. David Richardson, 'Case Studies', 53, 54–5, 58–9, 66–7, 72–3; Landmark Trust annual reports.

90. Both collections are housed in the Westcountry Studies Library.

91. W. H. H. Rogers, *The Ancient Sepulchral Effigies of Devon* (1877); H. T. Ellacombe, 'The church bells in the towers of all the parish churches of Devon', *EDAS,* 2nd series, 1, 221–410. see also volume two; Kate M. Clarke, 'The Baptismal Fonts of Devon', *DAT,* 1913–1915; Harry Hems, 'Rood and other screens in Devonshire churches, past and present', paper read to Society of Architects, 21 April 1896; Frederick Bligh Bond, 'Devonshire screens and rood lofts', *DAT,* xxxiv, 1902, 549–50; Frederick Bligh Bond and Dom Bede Camm, *Rood Screens and Rood Lofts* (1909), vol. 2.

92. William Lack, H. Martin Stucklefields and Philip Whittemore, *The Monumental Brasses of Devonshire* (Monumental Brasses Society, 2000).

93. *TEDAS,* volume 1, 1843.

94. Chris Brooks, 'The Victorian Restoration of Uffculme Church', in *Uffculme, a Culm Valley Parish* (Uffculme, 1988), 49–50; Bridget Cherry and Nikolaus Pevsner, *Devon* (1989), 97–101.

95. *TEDAS,* vol. 1, 1843, 3.

96. J. Ingle Dredge, 'Frithelstock Priory in the Deanery of Hartland', *TEDAS,* 3rd series, 1, 1893, 6–10.

97. Report of the Frithelstock Committee, *PDAS,* II, 3; 14th report on ancient monuments, *DAT,* 67, 1935.

98. *Report on the records of the city of Exeter* (Historical Manuscripts Commission, 1916), vii–xi.

99. *EPG,* 6 & 13 December 1867. See also the introduction by Stuart A. Moore in his catalogue, 1863–70, at the Devon Record Office.

100. *Report on the records of the city of Exeter,* xi.

101. R. N. Worth, 'The Historical Manuscripts Commission – Plymouth', *WA,* April 1884, 245.

102. *A Guide to the Archives Department of Plymouth City Libraries,* ix.

103. WSL, Devon Pamphlets I, *Inaugural Meeting of the Devon & Cornwall Record Society,* 26 August 1904.

104. Report of the Committee on Devonshire Records, *DAT,* XXI, 1889, 123–31. The President of the Association gave his Presidential Address on the topic at Crediton in 1882.

105. W. Y. Drake, 'Tavistock Records', *WA,* June 1886, 8–10; 'Tavistock Borough Records', *WA,* March, 1886, 232–3.

106. DRO, Z19/18/9.

107. John Pike Jones and J. F. Kingston, *Flora Devoniensis or a descriptive catalogue of plants growing wild in the county of Devon arranged both according to the Linnæan and natural systems* (1829).

108. *Flora Sidostiensis* (Sidmouth, 1849); Hannaford, *Flora Tottensis* (Totnes, 1832); Philip Henry Gosse, *A Naturalist's Rambles on the Devonshire Coast* (1853); Charlene Chanton, *Ferny Combes, a ramble after ferns in the glens and valleys of Devonshire* (1857).

109. Peter W. Hopkins, 'The Amphibeans and reptiles of Devonshire: a review (1584–1957) and survey', *DAT,* 89, 1957, 192–204. The most recent study is *Atlas of the Devon Flora,* edited by R. B. Ivimey-Cock for the Devonshire Association in 1984.

110. Polewhele, *Devon,* I, 101–104.

111. H. G. Hurrell, 'The changing fauna of Devon', *DAT,* XCVIII, 1966, 38; Polwhele, *Devon,* I, 130–1; H. G. Hurrell, Twelfth Report on Mammals, *DAT,* XCIII, 1961, 118–119; H. G. Hurrell, 25th report on mammals, *DAT,* 106, 1974, 28. See also the 30th report in volume 111. A polecat was found at Ivybridge in 1998: L. E. Hurrell, 39th report on mammals, *DAT,* 132, 2000, 371.

112. H. G. Hurrell, 22nd report on Mammals, *DAT,* 103, 1971, 233; H. G. Hurrell, 24th report on Mammals, *DAT,* 105, 1973, 201.

113. H. G. Hurrell, first report on Mammals, *DAT,* LXXXII, 1950, 122 & 8th report on Mammals, *DAT,* LXXXIX, 1957, 287.

114. *WMN,* 23 4 1992; *E&E,* 27 5 1991; *WMN,* 21 10 1989.

115. H. G. Hurrell, 25th report on Mammals, *DAT,* 106, 1974, 281; *E&E* & *WMN,* 18 9 1991; *Nature in Devon,* no. 10, 1989.

116. I am grateful to Margaret Parkinson for this reference.

117. I am grateful to Margaret Reed for this reference.

118. H. G. Hurrell, 27th report on mammals, *DAT,* 108, 1976, 204.

119. DRO, 346M/F325.

120. Jack Simmons (ed.), *A Devon Anthology* (1971), 38, citing Richard Pococke in 1750.

121. Kennet, *Preservation,* 39.

122. DRO, 546M/F9, edited by Todd Gray, *Travels in Georgian Devon,* III, 15.

123. W. Harding Thompson, Devon, *A Survey of its Countryside, Moorland and Rivers with some suggestions for their preservation* (1932), x, 4, 54.

124. Peter Laws, *A Guide to the National Trust in Devon and Cornwall* (Newton Abbot, 1978), 12.

125. Thompson, *Devon,* 127.

126. W. F. Collier, 'Dartmoor and the County Council of Devonshire', *DAT,* XXVII, 1895, 213.

127. *A Short History of the rights of Commoners upon the forest of Dartmoor* (Plymouth, 1890).

128. See Jeremy Butler, *Dartmoor Atlas of Antiquities* (Torquay and Tiverton, 1991–7), 5 vols; Helen Harris, *The Industrial Archaeology of Dartmoor* (Newton Abbot, 1968); *The Archaeology of Dartmoor; perspectives from the 1990s*, DAS, 52, 1994.

129. See Peter Hamilton-Leggett, *The Dartmoor Bibliography, 1534–1991* (Tiverton, 1992).

130. Hugh Peskett, *Guide to the parish and non-parochial registers of Devon and Cornwall, 1538–1837* (DCRS, ES Vol. II, 1979), 171, 56; *Wolford Chapel, Devonshire, England* (undated flyer); *E&E*, 28 9 1966.

131. J. E. B. Gover, A. Mawer and F. M. Stenton (eds), *The Place-names of Devon* (Cambridge, 1931–2), in two volumes.

132. *Bright, bonny and bracing: Seaton, Beer and neighbourhood* (1908 edn), 63.

133. Torr, *Wreyland*, I, 112 & III, 69; WSL, Bishopsteignton cuttings file, Bishopsteignton Ancient Houses and Families by W. D. Cleland.

134. See W. Pengelly, 'The signs of the Hotels, Taverns, Inns, wine and spirit vaults and beer shops in Devonshire', *DAT*, V, 1872, 416–509.

135. J. Gale Pedrick, *The Hotel Nomenclature of Teignmouth* (Teignmouth, 1894).

136. WSL, Belstone parish folder, A2, note of 6 8 1902.

137. Polwhele, *Devon*, I, 212.

138. WSL, S080/dev/dev, *Devonshire its scenery, traditions and antiquities*, c.1836.

139. H. Fulford Williams, 'North Tawton: A Devon market town', *DAT*, LXXXVI, 1954, 130.

140. C. Whybrow, 'The Bratton Death Club', *DCNQ*, XXXII, part III, Winter 1971, 65–71. For another Club Walk see Bart Long and Hamlyn Parsons, 'Colyton Club Day (c.1825)', *DAT*, LXXXV, 1953, 105–113.

141. Geoffrey Wilson, 'Public Hire Chairs in Exeter', *DCNQ*, XXXVI, part VIII, Autumn 1990, 265–9.

142. Francis Young, 'A discursive gossip about Kingsbridge' in Ellen Luscombe, *Myrtles and Aloes; or, Our Salcombe Sketch Book* (Kingsbridge, 1861), 129.

143. Walter Stephens, *Highways and Byeways of Plymouth* (Plymouth, 1943), 17, 15.

144. Sabine Baring Gould, *Songs and Ballads of the West* (1895) & *Songs of the West: Folk Songs of Devon and Cornwall Collected from the Mouths of the People* (1905); Simon Trezise, *The West Country as a Literary Invention* (Exeter, 2000), 199.

145. DRO, DQS OB, 1633–40, Bapt. 1637.

146. Memorial University Main Library, Coll-039 Arch, diaries of William Harding.

147. John Smale Short, *Historical Memoirs of the town and parish of Hatherleigh Devon collected from the best authorities* (c.1821–1840), 395.

148. DRO, 189Madd3/F5/5. Other sayings which are still in use are 'a faint heart never won a fair lady, 'one good turn requires another', 'out of the frying pan, into the fire', 'a burnt child dreads the fire', 'much ado about nothing', 'like father like son', 'one swallow makes no summer, 'to hit the nail on the head', 'to make a mountain of a molehill', 'charity begins at home', 'as mad as a March hare', 'to carry coals at Newcastle', 'to reckon ones chickens before they be hatched' and 'birds of a feather flock together'.

149. John M. Martin, 'Pages from a manuscript history of Hatherleigh', *DAT*, XXXVIII, 1906, 301–302.

150. Polwhele, *Devon*, I, 148.

151. See Todd Gray (ed.), *Devon Household Accounts, 1627–59*, DCRS, 1995–6, vols 38–9.

152. Bruce W. Oliver, 'The Castle of Barnstaple', *DAT*, LX, 1928, 215; Mary Ravenhill and Margery Rowe, *Manuscript Maps*, I, 69–70.

153. PLSL, sale particulars, Seven Trees, 1 May 1928. The house is located near Beaumont Park on Baring Street; Mary Ravenhill, 'Sir William Courten and Mark Pierce's Map of Cullompton of 1633', in Todd Gray (ed.), *Devon Documents* (DCNQ, 1996), between xx and xxi.

154. E. Masson Phillips, 'Supplementary Notes on the Ancient Stone Crosses of Devon', *DAT*, LXXXVI, 1954, 175.

155. Polwhele, *Devon*, I, 94.

156. Risdon, *Devon*, 277.

157. Kearley, 'Old Plymouth Trees', *WA*, October 1881, 113.

158. Arthur J. Chapple, *Walk Beer with Me* (Seaton, 1995), 39.

159. E. Capern, 'Wishing Trees', *WA*, July 1882, 58.

160. J. E. R. W., 'King John's oak, Shute Park', *WA*, August 1885, 61.

161. E. Parfitt, 'Wishing Tree', *WA*, April 1882, 9.

162. G. W. Copeland, '104th Annual Meeting', *DAT*, XCVIII, 1966, 33.

163. Polwhele, *Devon*, I, 94–5, 96.

164. A. H. A. Hamilton, 'The Introduction of the Culture of Silk into Devonshire in the reign of James the first', *DAT*, XLIII, 1911, 234–5.

165. Jane Hayter-Hanes, *A History of Chagford* (Chichester, 1981), 31; Day, *Holsworthy*, 60–1.

166. Charles Edward Long, *Diary of the Marches of the Royalist Army during the Great Civil War kept by Richard Symonds* (Camden Society, OS 74, 1859), 42–3, 78–80, 83–93.

167. Alice J. Bere, *Buckland Monachorum* (Buckland Monachorum, n.d.), 28–9.

168. E. Masson Phillips, 'Stone crosses in Devon, part one', *DAT*, LXIX, 1937, 340.

169. Davidson, *Notes*, 38.

170. Polwhele, *Devon*, II, 218–219.

171. Short, *Hatherleigh*, 412.

172. St Bridget Nurseries took on the firm in 1969 and has kept what remains of the collection of papers. This includes wage books and catalogues mostly from the turn of the twentieth century.

173. Hutchinson wrote in his diary of 7 October 1875 'gave some Roman Penates to Royal Albert Memorial Museum' but there is no collaborative record to show that he did so. I am grateful to John Allan for this reference.

174. John Allan, 'Artifacts at Exeter City Museums from Bligh's Second Voyage to Tahiti', *Pacific Arts*, Numbers 11 & 12, July 1995, 43; *The Western Luminary*, 28 9 1813; *Polynesian Art at Auction, 1965–1980* (Northboro, Massachusetts, 1982), 22.

175. R. Hansford Worth, 'Marchants Cross, Meavy', *DAT*, LXXIV, 1942, 203–4.

176. Beatrix F. Cresswell, 'Churchyard and Wayside Crosses in the Neighbourhood of Exeter', *DAT*, XLVII, 1915, 188.

177. Bob Mann, *The Lost Folly of Totnes: Mayor Taunton and his Monument* (Totnes, 1999).

178. 'An account of the church of Ottery St Mary', *TEDAS*, I, 1843, 48.

179. T. J. Northy, 'Relics of the old church of St Mary Major, Exeter', *WA*, May 1883, 18.

180. Mary R. Ravenhill and Margery M. Rowe, *Early Devon Maps* (Exeter, 2000), 54–5.

181. Gray, *Travels in Georgian Devon*, I, 8; Polwhele, *Devon*, I, 154–6.

182. Gray, *Garden History*, 78–9.

183. Arthur S. Parker, *How to increase the attractions of Exeter* (Exeter, 1893), 19.

184. White, *Torquay*, 164–5, 130.

185. *The Saturday Review*, 14 September 1878, page 335.

186. R. N. Worth, 'The Historical Manuscripts Commission – Plymouth', *WA*, April 1884, 245.

187. 'Old Plymouth Relics', *WA*, November 1882, 127.

188. WSL, William Henry Rogers, Notes on Bideford (no date given), I, 46.

189. J. Brooking Rowe, *The History of the Borough of Plympton Erle* (Exeter, 1906), 268.

190. N. F. Lightfoot, 'A paper on some churches in the deanery of Tavistock', *TEDAS*, II, 1847, 57.

191. N. F. Lightfoot, 'A paper on some churches in the deanery of Tavistock', *TEDAS*, II, 1847, 57.

192. I am grateful to Mrs Rosemary Smith for this information.

193. Report of Visiting Committee, *TEDAS*, II, 1847, 120.

194. Report of Visiting Committee, *TEDAS*, II, 1847, 122.

195. W. J. Coppard, 'An account of the church of Wembury in South Devon', *TEDAS*, IV, 1853, 302, 301.

196. Cherry and Pevsner, *Devon*, 38.

197. J. W., 'Collyton Barton, Chumleigh', *WA*, December 1882, 150.

198. The figures were 21 inches long and were acquired by Mr Farmer of Sun Street: T. J. Northy, 'Relics of the old church of St Mary Major, Exeter', *WA*, May 1883, 18.

199. *E&E,* 3 February 1936. Professor John Caldwell of the Botany Department had written to the embassy in London after a visit to Washington where he saw the cherry trees given by the Japanese.

200. Edwin S. Chalk, 'The manors, parish and churches of Blackborough alias All Hallows', *DAT,* XLII, 1910, 348.

201. Edward Ashworth, 'On certain architectural antiquities of the forest of Dartmoor and its border churches', *TEDAS,* IV, 1853, 165.

202. R. Hansford Worth, 'Notes on some moorland churches', *PI,* XII, 40–1.

203. Clive Ponsford, *Devon Clocks and Clockmakers* (Newton Abbot, 1985), 64; Todd Gray, *Exeter Engraved* (Exeter, 2000), I, 49. The remaining fragments were later taken to the Royal Albert Memorial Museum where they are housed today.

204. Beatrix Cresswell, 'Chained books and libraries in Devonshire parish churches', *TEDAS,* 3rd series, vol. 3, 1911, 96.

205. Jones, *Chudleigh,* 78.

206. Polwhele, *Devon,* II, 232.

207. William Crossing, *A Hundred Years On Dartmoor* (reprint 1987, Exeter), 97–8. The cover has an alternative title – *One Hundred Years On Dartmoor.*

208. 14th report of the Barrow committee, *DAT,* 24, 1892, 47.

209. W. F. Collier, 'Some Sixty years', 89.

210. Hoskins, *Exeter,* 133–5.

211. Daniel and Samuel Lysons, *Magna Britannia: Vol. 6 Devon* (1822), 411.

212. Lysons, *Devon,* 314.

213. Kate M. Clarke, 'The Baptismal Fonts of Devon (i)', *DAT,* XLV, 1913, 317, 320.

214. Kate M. Clarke, 'The Baptismal Fonts of Devon (ii)', *DAT,* XLVI, 1914, 433–4.

215. Kate M. Clarke, 'The Baptismal Fonts of Devon (iii)', *DAT,* XLVII, 1915, 350.

216. Rogers, *Ancient,* 21.

217. Clarke, 'The Baptismal Fonts of Devon (i)', 324–5.

218. W. B. Stephens, *Seventeenth Century Exeter* (Exeter, 1958), 13–14; Gray, 'Devon's Coastal and Overseas Fisheries', 254.

219. Peskett, *Parish Registers,* lii.

220. *E&E* 3 4 1981.

221. Neil Holbrook and Paul T. Bidwell, *Roman finds from Exeter* (Exeter, 1991), 274.

222. Jones, *Chudleigh,* 91–2.

223. Lady Radford, 'Tavistock Abbey', 74.

224. *E&E,* 24 1 1981 & 13 4 1988.

225. Edwin S. Chalk, 'The town, village, manors and church of Kentisbeare', *DAT,* XLII, 1910, 310.

226. Todd Gray, *The Lost Chronicle of Barnstaple, 1586–1611* (Exeter, 1998), 1–12.

227. H. Tapley-Soper, *Notes & Queries,* CLVI, 424.

228. Peskett, *Parish Registers,* 158.

229. Peskett, *Parish Registers,* xxxi.

230. *WA,* May 1883, 20; 'H. Sharrock, 'The gibbet near Stoke Church', *WA,* September 1886, 105.

231. RAMM, file on the Kelland memorial stone.

232. 'The Big Steal', *SPAB* News, 24, No. 1, 2003, 32–40.

233. *WMN,* 17 2 2003; *Culm Valley Gazette,* 2 9 2003.

234. Chris Brooks, Secretary's Report, Devon Buildings Group, Newsletter Number 4, October 1987, 6.

235. Margaret C. S. Cruwys, *A Cruwys Morchard Notebook, 1066–1874* (Exeter, 1939), 31–2.

236. *Bright, bonny and bracing: Seaton, Beer, and neighbourhood* (1908 edn), 49.

237. Jones, *Chudleigh,* 75. 124.

238. Polwhele, *Devon,* II, 308.

239. *WMN,* 8 7 1994 & *E&E,* 11 7 1994.

240. Polwhele, *Devon,* II, 319.

241. Risdon, *Devon,* 127.

242. DRO, parsonage rebuilding bundles, box 1.

243. Todd Gray, *Dartmoor Engraved* (Exeter, 2001), 4–5.

244. E. H. Young, 'A short account of Okehampton Market', *DAT,* LVII, 1925, 212.

245. Hems, Roods and other screens, 9–10.

246. *EPG,* 18 2 1854.

247. Lysons, *Devon,* 549; Thomas Westcote, *A view of Devonshire* (Exeter, 1845), 199.

248. WSL, William Henry Rogers, Notes on Bideford, I, 113.

249. Jones, *Newton Abbot,* 31–2.

250. Helen Harris, 'The Sourton Tors Iceworks, North-west Dartmoor, 1874–86', *DAT,* 120, 1988, 177–94.

251. Christopher J. Schmitz, 'The development and decline of the Devon barites industry, 1875–1958', *DAT,* 109, 1977, 117–33.

252. Robin Stanes, 'Leases for Whestone Pits in Broadhembury', *DCNQ,* xxxviii, part viii, autumn 2000, 252–3.

253. G. W. Copeland, '104th Annual Meeting', *DAT,* XCVIII, 1966, 33.

254. Stewart Brown, *Berry Pomeroy Castle, PDAS,* 54, 1996; Gray, *Garden History,* 41–2.

255. Lysons, *Devon,* 529.

256. Freddy Woodward, *Forts or Follies? The Story of Plymouth's Palmerstone's forts* (Tiverton, 1998).

257. Lane, *Old Sidmouth,* 62–3.

258. Gray, *Garden History,* 95–8.

259. Bridget Cherry, 'The Devon Country House in the Late Seventeenth and Early Eighteenth Centuries', *PDAS,* 46, 1988, 93; Lysons, *Devon,* 602; Michael Trinick, *Dunsland House, Devon* (National Trust, 1969), 20; John Allan, 'Great Potheridge', *Archaeological Journal,* 157 (2000), 460–6.

260. Gray, *Garden History,* 93–5.

261. Rosemary Lauder, *Vanished Houses of North Devon* (Callington, 1981), 67.

262. Gray, *Garden History,* 116–118; Rosemary Lauder, *Vanished Houses of South Devon* (Bideford, 1997), 48–66.

263. DRO, 152M/Estate/A/Devon/Box 76, correspondence, 1844–7, Box 39 includes an inventory of the house in 1844 & Box 68, contract, 31 May 1845; E. M. G. Belfield, *The Annals of the Addington Family* (Winchester, 1959), 160–1.

264. Gray, *Garden History,* 226–7; Hoskins, Devon, 510; WSL, px333.33upo/tre.

265. Cherry and Pevsner, *Devon,* 187; WSL, Silverton parish folder including newspaper cuttings for unidentified newspapers of 14 11 1901, 13 4 1901 and 13 11 1901; Lauder, *South Devon,* 93–112.

266. Gray, *Garden History,* 109; Hoskins, Devon, 509; Lauder, *South Devon,* 115–127.

267. Gray, *Garden History,* 209–210.

268. Gray, *Exeter Engraved* (Exeter, 2000), I, 98.

269. Jeanette Lee, 'Devon County Pauper Lunatic Asylum, Exminster: the early years', *DH,* 55, October 1997, 21; Cherry and Pevsner, Devon, 442; Frances Griffith, *Devon's Past, an aerial view* (Exeter, 1988), 115; C. Brooks and J. Cox, 'Charles Fowler and the Devon County Asylum, Exminster', *Devon Buildings Group Newsletter,* I, April 1986, 11–14.

270. Janice Wallace, 'The Devon House of Mercy, Bovey Tracey, 1863–1940', *DAT,* 33, 2001, 213; Torr, *Wreyland,* III, 105.

271. Gill, *Plymouth,* 152; WEH, 31 7 1978. The building was converted to housing for the elderly in 1982: *WEH,* 14 5 1978.

272. Harry Hems & P. T. Leonard, 'Revelstoke Church', *WA,* March 1882; Cherry and Pevsner, *Devon,* 700; Phillips, 'Supplementary Notes on the Ancient Stone Crosses of Devon', 85.

273. Stabb, *Some Old Devon Churches,* I, 45–6.

274. WSL, Davidson's notes, Broad Nymet; Cherry and Pevsner, *Devon,* 194.

275. DRO, 1726A Add2/PV1, meeting 19 May 1870; WSL, Beatrix F. Cresswell, Notes on Devon Churches: Deanery of Woodleigh (1923), 201–206; Cherry and Pevsner, *Devon,* 746.

276. Nicholas Orme and Margaret Webster, *The English Hospital, 1070–1570* (New Haven, 1995), 260.

277. Lysons, *Devon,* 536.

278. Percy Russell, *The Good Town of Totnes* (Torquay, 1963, 27; Lysons, Devon, 536, 610.

279. Harding, 'Ecclesiastical', 266–88; Orme and Webster, *Hospitals,* 230–1.

280. Lysons, *Devon,* 601.

281. J. Brooking Rowe, 'The Plympton Maudlyn House', *WA*, September 1886, 92–3.
282. Short, *Hatherleigh,* 44–5.
283. Kathryn Morrison, *The Workhouse* (English Heritage, 1999), 3, 10–12, 203; Gray, *Exeter the travellers' tales,* 40.
284. Jones, *Newton Abbot,* 124.
285. Gray, *Exeter Engraved,* I, 92; Todd Gray, *The Victorian Under Class of Exeter* (Exeter, 2000), 72–96; Morrison, *The Workhouse,* 11–12.
286. Arthur Charles Ellis, *An Historical Survey of Torquay* (Torquay, 1930), 289.
287. May Oliver, 'Newton Tracey and a forgotten Quaker burial ground', *DAT,* LXXXVI, 1954, 165.
288. Torr, *Wreyland,* II, 120.
289. Short, *Hatherleigh,* 17.
290. Peter Orlando Hutchinson, 'A history of the town, parish and manor of Sidmouth in the county of Devon, III', *The Sid Vale Monthly,* January 1939, no. 67, vol. 6, 5–7; Thomas, *Religion and the Decline of Magic,* 711.
291. DRO, Blackawton glebe terrier, 1613.
292. Torr, *Wreyland,* II, 5.
293. Russell, *Totnes,* 79.
294. I am grateful to Bob Letcher for this information.
295. George Pulman, *The Book of the Axe* (1875), 690.
296. Fox, *Kingsbridge,* 30.
297. See Chris Brooks, Secretary's Report, Devon Buildings Group, Newsletter Number 5, April 1988, 1.
298. Hugh Fowler, 'Biographical notice of the late Mr Thomas Fowler of Torrington with some account of his inventions', *DAT,* VII, 1875, 171–8.
299. F. J. M. Laver, 'Science and the Devonshire Association', *DAT,* 122, 1990, 4–5.
300. Lysons, *Devon,* 568–9.
301. William Webb, *Memorials of Exmouth* (Exmouth, 1872), 82.
302. Risdon, *Survey,* 52; Polwhele, *Devon,* II, 220–221.
303. Richard B. Prosser, *A List of Patents granted under the old law, 1617 to 1872, to persons resident in Devonshire* (London, no date given).
304. Fox, *Kingsbridge,* 26–7.
305. Edward Windeatt, 'Wooden water and sewage pipes', *WA,* April 1882, 9; E. Parfitt, 'Wooden water and sewage pipes', *WA,* May 1882, 22; Edward Capern, 'Wooden Water Pipes', *WA,* July 1882, 58.
306. Todd Gray, *Lost Exeter: Five Centuries of Change* (Exeter, 2002), 10–13; A. Kneel and Ramson Pickard, 'The Modern Water Supply of Exeter', *DAT,* LXV, 1933, 334–51.
307. David Hawkings, 'The Early Water Supply of Plymouth: An Introduction', *DH,* 24, April 1982, 9–14; David J. Hawkings, *Water from the Moor* (Exeter, 1987); Eric Hemery, *Walking the Dartmoor Waterways* (Newton Abbot, 1991).
308. Gray, *Garden History,* 135–7; *A Guide to Knowle Cottage the villa of T. L. Fish Esquire Sidmouth* (Sidmouth, no date given), 27–8; Simmons, *Anthology,* 53; Butcher, *Sidmouth,* no page number; *Western Luminary,* 22 11 1853; *North Devon Journal,* 24 11 1853.
309. W. E. Buckley, 'Drake's ship', *WA,* July 1886, 45–6; Harry Kelsey, *Sir Francis Drake: The Queen's Pirate* (New Haven, 1998), 218; John Sugden, *Sir Francis Drake* (1990), 150.
310. Philip Carter, *Newton Abbot,* forthcoming; Eric Dudley, Gustav Milne and Scott Appleton, 'The Boat found at Kingsteignton, Devon, in 1898', *The International Journal of Nautical Archaeology* (2001), 30:2, 266–72.
311. Harry Hems, 'The Last of a Toll Gate', *WA,* December 1881, 133.
312. James Coulter, *Tawstock and the Lords of Barnstaple* (Bideford, 1996), 166–7. The remaining trees are thought to have died from disease.
313. Hawker, 'Changes in Travelling', *DAT,* XVII, 1885, 456.
314. Edwin S. Chalk, 'The Church of St Andrew, Cullompton', *DAT,* XLII, 1910, 185.
315. Gray, *Exeter Unveiled,* 35; George M. Doe, *Old Torrington Landmarks* (Bideford, 1931), 17; R. N. Worth, *History of Plymouth* (Plymouth, 1890), 339; Llewellynn Jewitt, *The Plymouth, Devonport and Stonehouse Guide* (Plymouth, 1863), 51–2.
316. John Tindall, 'Sidmouth Foreshore', *DAT,* LXI, 1929, 341.
317. Hoskins, *Devon,* 158–65; Richard Oliver, 'Canals and railways in the nineteenth century', in Kain and Ravenhill, *Historical Atlas,* 366; David St John Thomas, *A Regional History of the Railways of Great Britain: The West Country* (Newton Abbot, 1981 edn).
318. Thomas, *A Regional History,* 91.
319. Worth, 'Early Western Railroads', 81, 83; Helen Harris, *The Industrial Archaeology of Dartmoor* (Newton Abbot, 1992 edn), 77–80; Thomas, *A Regional History,* 86–7; Griffith, *Devon's Past,* 106.
320. Harris, *Industrial Archaeology,* 105–115, 92–7; William Crossing, *Amid Devonia's Alps; or Wanderings & Adventures on Dartmoor* (Plymouth, 1888), 43.
321. R. Hansford Worth, 'Early Western Railroads', *PI,* X, 1887–90, 83–9.
322. Gill, *Plymouth,* 117–118.
323. Worth, 'Early Western Railroads', 79.
324. Harris, *Industrial Archaeology,* 115.
325. Harris, *Industrial Archaeology,* 94–5; Andrew Swift, *Devon Railway Stations (Southern Railway) on old picture postcards* (Nottingham, 2001).
326. Thomas, *Regional History,* 73–6.
327. Hunt, *Then and Now,* 54, 52.
328. Martin Langley and Edwina Small, *The Trams of Plymouth: a 73 years story* (Bradford on Avon, 1990), 89–104.
329. John J. Beckerlegge, 'Plymouth Transport in Recent Years', *DAT,* LXXX, 1948, 182–3; Gill, *Plymouth,* 156–7, 175.
330. Hoskins, *Exeter,* 130; Newton, *Victorian Exeter,* 209, 301–302. The railings are on Hele Road. I owe this reference to Roger Brien.
331. Langley and Small, *Trams,* 103.
332. E. A. G. Clark, *The Ports of the Exe Estuary, 1660–1860* (Exeter, 1968 edn), 28–9, 32–4, 41–3; Hoskins, *Devon,* 156–8. A fuller list of the canals is provided by Charles Hadfield in *The Canals of South West England* (Newton Abbot, 2nd edn 1985), 190–193.
333. Edwin Welch, 'Cann quarry canal and railway', *DAT,* 100, 1968, 119–121.
334. Joan Rendell, *The Story of the Bude Canal* (Callington, 1987), 33; Hoskins, *Devon,* 158, 504.
335. Fraser Halle, *Letters, historical and botanical; relating chiefly to places in the vale of Teign* (1851), 33.
336. W. H. Wilkin, 'Notes on Membury, part III', *DAT,* LX, 1928, 181.
337. Tindall, 'Sidmouth Foreshore', 341.
338. Gray, *Garden History,* 128–9; DRO, tithe map for Exminster, c.1842.
339. *E&E,* 3 4 1981.
340. Griffiths, 'A field to the spoiler', 273.
341. Gray, *Lost Exeter,* 2–9.
342. Polwhele, *Devon,* II, 235; Lane, *Old Sidmouth,* 40–1.
343. Keith S. Perkins, 'Lord Morley's Flying Bridge', *DH,* 41, October 1990, 19.
344. Keith S. Perkins, 'The Puffing Giant: origins of the Dartmouth Floating Bridge', *DH,* 30, April 1985, 4–8.
345. Christian Michell and Margaret Common, 'Staunton, a deserted South Hams village', *DH,* 16, Spring 1978, 21.
346. *EFP,* 25 1 1844, 17 12 1829, 8 6 1848, 5 9 1839, 27 1 1853, 27 11 1867, 15 7 1863, 23 1 1834, 12 11 1840, 29 3 1832, 16 10 1845, 13 1 1848.
347. See Gray, *Garden History,* appendix two, list of garden allotment records in the Devon Record Office.
348. Todd Gray, 'Walled gardens and the cultivation of orchard fruit in the south-west of England', 114–28 in C. Anne Wilson (ed.), *The Country House Kitchen Garden, 1600–1950* (Stroud, 1998); Todd Gray, 'Their idols of worship: fruit trees and the walled garden in early modern Devon', in Stephen Pugsley (ed.), *Devon Gardens: an historical survey* (Stroud, 1994), 28–41.
349. Michael Havinden and Robin Stanes, 'Agriculture and Rural Settlement, 1500–1800', in Roger Kain and William Ravenhill (eds), *Historical Atlas of South-West England* (Exeter, 1999), 288; Lysons, *Devon,* 455.
350. *Changing Face of Devon* (Exeter, 1979); *Orchards, a practical guide for management* (Exeter, 1999).
351. Gray, 'Idols', 34–5.

352. David J. Hawkings, 'John Tradescant and the Plymouth Strawberry', *DH,* 37, October 1988, 28; Colin Rogers, 'The Historical Background', 17 in *The Magic Tree* (Tiverton, 1989).

353. Gray, *Lost Chronicle,* 67; Gray, 'Idols', 38, 31, 32; *The Magic Tree,* 69.

354. Margaret Parkinson, 'A parish wildlife centenary, 1894–1994', *DAT,* 126, 1994, 127.

355. John Grant, *A few remarks on the large hedges and small enclosures of Devonshire, and the adjoining counties* (Exeter, 1844).

356. *EFP,* 9 1 1845.

357. DRO, Chanter 850, 339. There was an accusation of plucking up a hedge on the commons; John Roberts, 'Enclosure and Riot from 1575', *DCNQ,* XXXVIII, part IV, autumn 1998, 110–116.

358. DRO, 1092addA/pz3, edited by Robin Stanes, 'The Devonshire Hedgebank', *DCNQ,* XXXVI, part IX, spring 1991, 301–305; Richard Bass, 'The Devonshire Hedgebank', *DCNQ,* XXXVIII, part x, autumn, 2001, 311–314.

359. Risdon, *Devon,* 348; DRO, 48969–74, leases for 1613 to 1659; DRO, Combe Martin glebe terrier, 1613.

360. Lysons, *Devon,* 501; Gray, *Dartmoor Engraved,* 4–5.

361. John Hall and Ann Hamlin, 'Deserted Medieval Settlements in Devon', *DH,* 13, October 1976, 5–6.

362. John Robert Chanter, *Archaeology of North Devon* (n.d.), 53.

363. R. N. Worth, 'Hallsands and Start Bay', *DAT,* 36, 1904, 302–46, 41, 1909, 301–308 & 55, 1923, 131–47; Steve Melis, *Hallsands, a village betrayed* (Newton Abbot, 2002).

364. Polwhele, *Devon,* I, 38; Harold Fox, *The Evolution of the Fishing Village: Landscape and Society along the South Devon Coast, 1086–1550* (Leicester, 2001), 33–4; DRO, CR20048. The survey shows 19 dwellings, houses and cottages as well as several cellars and a garden for sixteen named individuals.

365. Todd Gray (ed.), *Early-Stuart Mariners and Shipping* (Devon & Cornwall Record Society, NS 33, 1990), 52.

366. Walter Minchington and John Perkins, *Tidemills of Devon and Cornwall* (Exeter, 1971); Walter Minchington, *Windmills of Devon* (Exeter, 1977). For confusion over one folly see Reg Carter, 'Folly or Tower', *North Devon Heritage,* No. 9, 1997, 29.

367. *WMN,* 16 February 1993.

368. For the reminiscences of one man, who worked at Lundy, see David Mapp, 'Another Life', *North Devon Heritage,* 15, 2003, 13–15,

369. Jason Semmens, *Eddystone – 300 years* (Fowey, 1998), 127–36, 140.

370. Hoskins, *Devon,* 495.

371. Daniel Radford, 'Working men's dwellings' (*DAT,* 1890, XXII), 138–42.

372. W. J. Odgers, *Report on the sanitary condition of Plymouth* (Plymouth, 1847).

373. G. W. Copeland, 'Widey Court', *DAT,* LXXXVII, 1955, 230–1; PLSL, sale particulars, Widey Court, 4 August 1921.

374. G. W. Copeland, 'Radford', *DAT,* LXXVII, 1945, 149–53; Brian D. R. Steele, *A History of Radford* (Plymouth, 1990), 4.

375. Chalkley *et al,* *Plymouth,* 77.

376. Ernest J. Pearn, *Whiteigh – the troublesome formative years* (Kingsbridge, 1989), 6, 9, 11–12, 14.

377. Todd Gray, *Devon Country Houses and Gardens Engraved* (Exeter, 2001), I, 47–52.

378. Gray, *Garden History,* 138.

379. Polwhele, *Devon,* II, 213–214; Cherry and Pevsner, *Devon,* 915.

380. Chris Brooks, Secretary's Report, Devon Buildings Group Newsletter, Number 4, October 1987, 9.

381. DRO, 1508M/London/SS/Harbours and Rivers/2/1; Jack Simmons, *A Devon Anthology* (1971), 132–3.

382. Lane, *Old Sidmouth,* 59–61, 25–7.

383. Kevin Lee, *The Golfer's Guide to the Westcountry* (Aldermaston, 2001), 54; Robert H. K. Browning, *Golf in Devon* (no date given), 6.

384. *WMN,* 12 5 1977. The course had opened in 1884; the race course at Shute can be seen on an estate map: Cornwall Record Office, Buller papers held at Antony, FX/23.

385. F. J. Laver, 'Note on the origins of the Sid Vale Association', *DAT,* 107, 1975, 22.

386. Polwhele, *Devon,* II, 339.

387. F. J. Snell, *The Chronicle of Twyford* (Tiverton, 1892), 274.

388. Hamlyn Parsons, 'The Court Entries of the borough of Ashburton, 1747–1805', *DAT,* LXXXVII, 1955, 242, 249.

389. George M. Doe, 'An Unofficial Municipal Diary, 1751–1797', *DAT,* LXIX, 1937, 345; Doe, 'Ancient', 55; J. J. Alexander and W. R. Hooper, *The History of Great Torrington in the county of Devon* (Sutton, 1948),140.

390. Russell, *Totnes,* 79–80; T. W. Stainthorpe, 'Ye Ancient Bull Ring at Totnes', *DAT,* XXXII, 1900, 106–107.

391. J. H. Porter, 'Beastly Baiting', *DCNQ,* autumn 1987, xxxvi, part ii, 54–8.

392. W. F. Collier, 'Some sixty years of reminiscences of Plymouth', *DAT,* XXIV, 1892, 88; Whitfeld, *Plymouth and Devonport,* 340.

393. J. H. Porter, 'Beastly Baiting', *DCNQ,* xxxvi, part ii, 54–8; Murray T. Foster, 'A Short History of Cullompton', *DAT,* XLII, 1910, 167.

394. Snell, *Chronicle,* 274–5. I am grateful to John Allan for information on the location of Exeter's cockpit.

395. Andrew Brice, *The Mobiad* (Exeter, 1770), 169; Jones, *Chudleigh,* 25; J. H. Porter, 'Cockfighting in the Eighteenth and Nineteenth Centuries: from Popularity to Suppression', *DAT,* 118, 1986, 63–70; Murray T. Foster, 'A Short History of Cullompton', *DAT,* XLII, 1910, 167.

396. Torr, *Wreyland,* I, 24; Philipps, 'The Ancient Stone Crosses of Devon', 333.

397. Report of the Committee reporting the state of S. Mary Major church, Exeter, *TEDAS,* VI, 1861, 142–5; David Francis, *Lost Churches* (Exeter Civic Society, 1995), 8–9; Gray, *Exeter Engraved,* II, 25–8; Gray, *Lost Exeter,* 44–5.

398. W. E. Tate, 'A hand list of English Enclosure Acts and Awards, part 9(c), Devonshire Enclosure Acts and Awards', *DCNQ,* XXII, 81–7.

399. Chapple, *Walk Beer with Me,* 16.

400. Thomas Shapter, *The History of the Cholera in Exeter in 1832* (1849); Gray, *Lost Exeter,* xxvi–xxviii; Gray, *The Victorian Under Class of Exeter.*

401. W. J. Odgers, *Report on the sanitary condition of Plymouth* (Plymouth, 1847).

402. Odgers, *Report,* v, vi, 14, 15, 18.

403. Worth, *History of Plymouth,* 224; Whitfeld, *Plymouth and Devonport,* 400–411, appendix page 6; Brice, *The Mobiad,* 50.

404. W. H. K. Wright, 'Some further peeps at old Plymouth', *PI,* XIV, 1905, 239.

405. Whitfeld, *Plymouth and Devonport,* 407.

406. PLSL, Henry Whitfeld, 'A letter to the lady of the manor' listed under *The Curse of Devonport.*

407. Gray, *Lost Exeter,* xxix–xxx.

408. Gill, *Plymouth,* 152–3.

409. DRO, 152M/Box 49/Estate 6 (Upottery), letter of 13 January 1820 from J. G. Coplestone.

410. Cherry and Pevsner, *Devon,* 786; Charles Vancouver, *General View of the Agriculture of the County of Devon* (New York, 1969 edn), 94–7.

411. R. T. Shears, *Conservation of Devonshire Cottages* (Exeter, 1968).

412. Shears, *Conservation of Devonshire Cottages,* unnumbered.

413. White, *Torquay,* 262–6.

414. Gray, *Lost Exeter,* 10–19.

415. Aileen Fox, 'The Underground conduits in Exeter, exposed during reconstruction in 1950', *DAT,* LXXXIII, 1951, 175.

416. Lysons, *Devon,* 302.

417. Snell, *Chronicle,* 133.

418. Gray, *Lost Exeter,* xxv–xxvi.

419. Trixie M.Lamb, *The Ancient Tower of St Leonard's: a history* (Newton Abbot, 1973); Jones, *Newton Abbot,* 113.

420. Gray, *Lost Exeter,* 36–9, 31, 54–9.

421. *EFP,* 7 8 1823; Gray, *Lost Exeter,* xxiii–xxv.

422. Whitfeld, *Plymouth and Devonport,* 166, 372, 97, 404; Worth, *Plymouth,* 417; Gill, *Plymouth,* 108.

423. Gray, *Lost Exeter,* 10–13.

424. Roy Strong, *Lost Treasures of Britain* (1990), 9.

425. Robert Burnard, 'The Disappearing Stone Monuments of Dartmoor', *DAT,* XXXIV, 1902, 167.

426. W. F. Collier, First report of Committee on Dartmoor, *DAT*, IX, 1877, 120–1.
427. Griffiths, 'A field to the spoiler', 273.
428. Phillips, 'Stone Crosses', 313, 323, 338.
429. Thomas Sharp, *Exeter Phœnix, a plan for rebuilding* (1946); *A Plan for Plymouth, the report prepared for the city council* (Plymouth, 1943).
430. *A Plan for Plymouth*, vii, 1–6; Brian Chalkley and John Goodridge, 'The 1943 Plan for Plymouth' in Brian Chalkley, David Dunkerley and Peter Gripaios (eds), *Plymouth, maritime city in transition* (Newton Abbot, 1991).
431. Hugh Meller, *Exeter Architecture* (Chichester, 1989), 44.
432. *The Opening of the Exeter Street Viaduct and Roadway, Friday 7th February 1958* (Plymouth, 1958).
433. *A Plan for Plymouth*, 6.
434. Meller, *Exeter Architecture*, 69.
435. Eric. V. Kingdon, 'Tavistock Library', *DAT*, LXXVIII, 1946, 251–2; Joy Beer, 'The Tavistock Subscription Library', *DH*, 40, April 1990, 21. It was also claimed that the recent building stood in the way of traffic improvements.
436. DRO, L1258M/SSC/DL/91.
437. Gray, *Garden History*, 95.
438. Philip Chilwell De La Garde, 'High Street, Exeter', *TEDS*, VI, 1862, 254.
439. James Hine, 'The Old Buildings of Plymouth', *PI*, I, 1860–1, 22.
440. James Hine, 'A plea for the picturesque in Devonshire towns', *DAT*, IX, 1877, 156–63.
441. J. Brooking Rowe, *The ecclesiastical history of old Plymouth* (Plymouth, 1873), 56, 51.
442. Stanhope Nourse, 'Modern Enormities', *TEDAS*, 3rd series, 3, 1905, 54.
443. Cecil Torr, *Small Talk at Wreyland* (Bath, 1970 edn), I, 19.
444. WSL, A. W. Searley, Screens & Screenwork, Vol. 6, Dr. Trelawny-Ross, 'War Memorials', 299.
445. Thompson, *Devon*, 13.
446. Gray, *Lost Exeter*, 42–5; Audrey Erskine, Vyvian Hope and John Lloyd, *Exeter Cathedral, a short history and description* (Exeter, 1988), 71–86.
447. Gray, *Exeter Unveiled*, 55.
448. Todd Gray, 'The Travels of Mrs Parry Price through Devon in 1805', *DAT*, 128, 1996, 65–89.
449. Gray, *Devon Country Houses and Gardens*, I, 142–5; Gray, *Lost Exeter*, xxx.
450. Edward Ashworth, 'Account of the church of St John the Baptist, Broadclist, Devonshire', *TEDAS*, III, 1849, 55.
451. Edward Ashworth, 'On certain architectural antiquities of the forest of Dartmoor and its border churches', *TEDAS*, IV, 1853, 166.
452. Rogers, *Ancient*, 3.
453. Parry, *Teignmouth*, 56–7.
454. G. W. G. Hughes, 'Moreton Hampstead', *DAT*, LXXXVI, 1954, 79.
455. W. J. Coppard, 'On the church of S. Mary, Plympton', *TEDAS*, V, 1856, 36.
456. Jones, *Chudleigh*, 78.
457. H. T. Ellacombe, 'The parish church of S. George, Devon', *TEDAS*, 2nd series, 1867, I, 99–100.
458. R. Hansford Worth, 'Notes on some moorland churches, II', *PI*, 1895, XII, 138–9.
459. Torr, *Wreyland*, I, 103–104.
460. Polwhele, *Devon*, II, 377.
461. Rogers, *Ancient*, 21.
462. Clarke, 'The Baptismal Fonts of Devon', ii, 22–3, and iii, 28–9.
463. Bere, *Buckland Monachorum*, 22, 30; Bond, screens and roods, 550.
464. Hems, Rood and other screens, 3–4.
465. Hems, Rood and other screens, 1–12; Cherry and Pevsner, *Devon*, 767.
466. Bond, Screens and Rood Lofts, 549–50.
467. Hems, Roods and other screens, 10.
468. Polwhele, *Devon*, II, 1793.
469. Bond, Screens and Rood Lofts, 549–50; Harry Hems, 'Ashburton Church', *WA*, IV, 117.
470. Polwhele, *Devon*, II, 211.
471. P Russell, 'Gallants Bowers', *DAT*, XCV, 1963, 69–70.
472. DRO, tithe maps Exminster and Hennock; WSL, ordnance survey maps, 1905, 1954 for Exminster, 1955 for Hennock; W. I. Leeson Day, *Holsworthy* (Devonshire Association Parochial History of Devon, No. 2, 1934), 50. The tithe map at the Devon Record Office shows that the maze was 1 rood and 34 perches; An estate map of Pitt House does not show the maze in 1904: DRO, DD59598.
473. Torr, *Wreyland*, I, 34–5.
474. *The Gardens at Bicton Park* (presumably Bicton, no date given), 9.
475. Gray, *Garden History*, 68–71.
476. Gray, *Garden History*, 174; Robert Waterhouse, 'Garden Archaeology in South Devon', in Robert Wilson-North, *The Lie of the Land* (Exeter, 2003), 73.
477. Polwhele, *Devon*, II, 31.
478. DRO, 346M, F (garden correspondence).
479. Waterhouse, South Devon, 66–9; Gray, *Garden History*, 23, 115–116, 92.
480. Gray, *Garden History*, 211–213.
481. Polwhele, *Devon*, II, 156; Gray, *Garden History*, 145–8.
482. Robert Iles, 'The Medieval, Tudor and Stuart Parks of Devon', in Pugsley, *Devon Gardens, an historical survey*, 21–7; Lysons, *Devon*, 101; Robert Waterhouse, 'Garden Archaeology in South Devon', 77.
483. H. G. Hurrell, first report on Devonshire mammals, *DAT*, 1950, LXXXII, 117.
484. Charles Worthy, *Devonshire Parishes, or the antiquities, heraldry and family history of 28 parishes in the archdeaconry of Totnes* (Exeter and London, 1887), I, 287–8.
485. Peter Orlando Hutchinson, *The Sidmouth Guide* (no date given), no page number.
486. Cherry and Pevsner, *Devon*, 916–917; David Mawson, 'Thomas Mawson at Wood and the Early Twentieth-Century Garden', 106–22, in Pugsley, *Devon Gardens*.
487. Gray, *Travels in Georgian Devon*, II, 159.
488. Gray, *Garden History*, 203–207.
489. Richard Stone, The Creation of Endsleigh, 76–90; DRO, T1258M/E18 (map of 1770). Ingesley is shown as a single building with two parts.
490. Gray, *Garden History*, 115–116.
491. DRO, tithe maps of Combeinteignhead and Haccombe.
492. Lysons, *Devon*, 10; Cherry, *Devon*, 127.
493. Robin Fausett, 'Castle Hill: The Formal and Transitional Garden', in Pugsley, *Devon Gardens*, 44–9; DRO, 1262M/E1/96.
494. Gray, *Travels in Georgian Devon*, I, xvi–xvii.
495. Edward Parfitt, 'On Earthquakes in Devonshire', *DAT*, XVII, 1885, 281–4.
496. Polwhele, *Devon*, I, 80–1.
497. Edmund Butcher, *A new guide descriptive of the beauties of Sidmouth* (Exeter, n.d.), no page numbers.
498. Parry, *Notes on old Teignmouth*, 50.
499. Chapple, *Walk Beer*, 15–16.
500. See accompanying illustration.
501. *WMN*, 1 7 1972.
502. *WMN*, 21 7 1971 & 27 9 1971; James Coulter, *Tawstock and the Lords of Barnstaple* (Bideford, 1996), 166–7.
503. Polwhele, *Devon*, II, 204–205.
504. DRO, 1392M/19/42/1–2.
505. Day, *Holsworthy*, 1, 44, 50.
506. H, 'Old Plymouth Trees', *WA*, September 1886, 105; Hugh Smallacombe, 'Old Tree in Tavistock Road, Plymouth', *WA*, 1886, 238.
507. C. Spense Bate, 'The inscribed stones and ancient crosses of Devon, III', *PI*, VIII, 152; Phillips, The Ancient Stone Crosses of Devon, Part One', 330.
508. A plaque was placed on the stone support in 1953.
509. Phillips, 'The ancient stone crosses of Devon: part 1', 307.
510. E. Masson Phillips, 'The ancient stone crosses of Devon: part II', *DAT*, LXIX, 1938, 324; Stabb, *Some old Devon churches*, I, 59.
511. Parry, *Notes on old Teignmouth*, 45.

512. Polwhele, *Devon,* II, 77, 117.
513. Lysons, *Devon,* 9.
514. Gray, *Exeter the Travellers' Tales,* 60.
515. Peskett, *Parish Registers,* 135.
516. Grace Johnstone, 'An Old Parish Chest', *DAT,* XXI, 1889, 78.
517. Davidson, *Notes,* 33.
518. Gray, *Lost Chronicle,* 94–5.
519. 'Great flood in Somersetshire AD 1607', *WA,* IV, 63–7; J. F. Chanter, *A history of the parishes of Lynton and Countisbury* (Exeter, 1907), 25–6, 183.
520. Isacke, *Exeter,* 63.
521. Polwhele, *Devon,* II, 101.
522. Lysons, *Devon,* 509.
523. Crossing, *A hundred years on Dartmoor,* 103–104.
524. Webb, *Exmouth,* 46.
525. Webb, *Exmouth,* 54, 61, 62–3.
526. Webb, *Exmouth,* 75.
527. Parry, *Notes on old Teignmouth,* 50.
528. Hunt, *Then and Now,* 52–5.
529. Hoskins, *Devon,* 430.
530. Griffith, *Devon's Past,* 124–7; Deborah Griffiths, 'A Field to the Spoiler: a Review of Archaeological Conservation on Dartmoor', PDAS, 52, 1994, 277; Brian Blakeway, 'The Roadford Operation', Devon Buildings Group Newsletter, Number 10, May 1991, 5–9.
531. Walter Minchinton, *Windmills of Devon* (Exeter, 1977), 19, 39–40.
532. H. Hugh Breton, *The Great Blizzard of Christmas, 1927* (Plymouth, 1928), 49.
533. D. Warrell Bowring, *Ilfracombe throughout the ages* (Exeter, 1931), 77.
534. Clive Carter, *The Blizzard of '91* (Newton Abbot, 1971).
535. Ellis, *Torquay,* 310.
536. Lysons, *Devon,* 589.
537. Polwhele, *Devon,* II, 151.
538. Risdon, *Devon,* 144; WMN, 22 1 2003; Torr, *Wreyland,* III, 28.
539. Lane, *Old Sidmouth,* 52.
540. Simmons, *Anthology,* 95.
541. Peter Orlando Hutchinson, 'A history of the town, parish and manor of Sidmouth in the county of Devon, III', *The Sid Vale Monthly,* August 1939, no. 74, vol. 7, 7–9.
542. Bernard Myers, 'Raising the Dust over Pennington Point', *Devon Conservation Forum Focus,* November 2001, 21.
543. WSL, Peter Orlando Hutchinson, Diaries, I, 16 and V, 30.
544. Tindall, 'Sidmouth Foreshore', 327; Eric Shanes, *Turner's Rivers, Harbours and Coasts* (1981), 37; Philip Ziegler, *Addington* (1965), 105; E. M. G. Belfield, *The Annals of the Addington Family* (Winchester, 1959), 116.
545. Peter Christie, 'A Short History of the Theatre in Bideford', *DAT,* 127, 1995, 24–5.
546. Cruwys, *Cruwys Morchard Notebook,* 33–6; Polwhele, Devon, I, 11. John Stabb wrote that this happened in 1688: Stabb, *Some Old Devon Churches,* I, 40–1.
547. Worthy, *Devonshire,* I, 185.
548. Polwhele, *Devon,* I, 11.
549. Polwhele, *Devon,* I, 13.
550. Lysons, *Devon,* 355, 329; Polwhele, *Devon,* I, 14.
551. Polwhele, *Devon,* I, 15. Polwhele noted that Parkham was hit 'about this time',
552. Alexander and Hooper, *Great Torrington,* 57.
553. Worthy, *Devonshire,* I, 155.
554. Fox, *Kingsbridge,* 16.
555. N. F. Lightfoot, 'A paper on some churches in the deanery of Tavistock', *TEDAS,* II, 1847, 57.
556. Worthy, *Devonshire,* II, 187.
557. Day, *Holsworthy,* 59.
558. Stabb, *Some Devon Historic Churches,* 52.
559. R. Hansford Worth, 'Notes on some moorland churches, II', *PI,* XII, 1895, 139.
560. WSL, S080/dev/dev.

561. Polwhele, *Devon,* I, 11.
562. J. B. R., *The Two Widecombe Tracts, 1838, giving a contemporary account of the great storm, reprinted with an introduction* (Exeter, 1905).
563. K. A. Westcottt, 'The Spire and Roofs of Hatherleigh Church: Investigations following the storm damage of 1990', *DAS,* 50, 1992, 61.
564. Polwhele, *Devon,* I, 11.
565. Polwhele, *Devon,* I, 13.
566. Gray, *East Devon the Travellers' Tales,* 4–5.
567. Ellis, *Torquay,* 311.
568. Derek Lean, *Storm Force: the West Country's wild winter of 1989/90* (Plymouth, 1990).
569. Snell, *Chronicle,* 169; Polwhele, *Devon,* I, 7.
570. Brice, *The Mobiad,* 20.
571. Alexander & Hooper, *Great Torrington,* 146.
572. Robert Harcourt Weston, *Letters and Important Documents relative to the Edystone lighthouses* (1811), 4–6.
573. Polwhele, *Devon,* I, 8, 14.
574. *The Blizzard in the West* (Kent, 1891), 87, 96, 95, 103, 124, 128, 140; WMN, 15 7 1891.
575. Lysons, *Devon,* 75.
576. Bere, *Buckland Monachorum,* 18.
577. *Torquay Directory,* 21 March 1926; WMN, 12 9 1903, Baring Gould, *A Book of the West,* 227–8; Torr, *Wreyland,* I, 24.
578. S. Baring-Gould, 'Dancing Trees', *Plymouth and Exeter Gazette,* 7 November 1907; Torr, *Wreyland,* I, 24.
579. Chalk, 'The town, village, manors and church of Kentisbeare', 312.
580. Ellis, *Torquay,* 475.
581. Gill, *Plymouth,* 122.
582. Henry Francis Whitfeld, *Plymouth and Devonport: in times of war and peace* (Plymouth, 1900), 421–2; M. M. Oppenheim, *The Maritime History of Devon* (Exeter, 1968), 88; Wasley, *Blitz,* 11–12.
583. A. R. Pye and R. Robinson, *An archaeological survey of the gunpowder factory at Powder Mills Farm, Postbridge, Devon* (Exeter Museums and Archeological Field Unit, 1990), 4–5.
584. E. L. Jones, 'Fire Disasters: The Special Case of East Devon', *DH,* 20, April 1980, 11.
585. Jones, *Chudleigh,* 83.
586. *Inaugural Meeting,* 2.
587. *The Saturday Review,* 14 September 1878.
588. G. M. Doe, 'An ancient North Devon borough; its surroundings and associations in the past', *DAT,* LXXI, 1939, 46.
589. Alexander and Hooper, *Great Torrington,* 123.
590. DRO, 2346M/E44; Polwhele, *Devon,* I, 277; Mary R. Ravenhill and Margery M. Rowe (eds), *Early Devon Maps* (Exeter, 2000), 16–17. See DRO, 1660/A add4/E1.
591. R. N. Worth, 'The Historical Manuscripts Commission – Plymouth', *WA,* April 1884, 245.
592. Torr, *Wreyland,* II, 72.
593. Todd Gray (ed.), *Devon Household Accounts, 1627–59; part II, Henry, fifth Earl of Bath, and Rachel, Countess of Bath, 1637–1655* (DCRS, 1996), xii.
594. Murray T. Foster, 'A Short History of Cullompton', *DAT,* XLII, 1910, 170.
595. Ellis, *Torquay,* 468; Robert Harcourt Weston, *Eddystone,* 8–10.
596. Gray, *East Devon The Travellers' Tales,* xii–xvi.
597. Pulman, *Book of the Axe,* 689–90; Bertram Jacobs, *Axminster carpets (hand-made), 1755–1957* (Leigh on Sea, 1970), 59.
598. Polwhele, *Devon,* II, 226, 235.
599. DRO, parsonage rebuilding papers, box 1, East Anstey, 4 June 1831.
600. William Harding, 'A paper on the church and chantry on the Ancient Exe Bridge', *TEDAS,* III, 1849, 171.
601. William Harding, 'An account of some of the ancient ecclesiastical edifices of Exeter', *TEDAS,* IV, 1853, 114.
602. N. F. Lightfoot, 'A paper on some churches in the deanery of Tavistock', *TEDAS,* II, 1847, 57; Worthy, *Devonshire,* I, 223.
603. WMN, 27 7 1992.

604. Peskett, *Parish Registers*, 62, 68, 80, 84, 92, 93, 101, 106, 111, 114, 138, 163.
605. Anthony J. Lambert, *Devon from Old Photographs* (National Trust, no date given), 15.
606. Lysons, *Devon*, 168; Polwhele, *Devon*, III, 399.
607. DRO, 1324A/PR5.
608. Lysons, *Devon*, 469.
609. Lysons, *Devon*, 387.
610. Lane, *Old Sidmouth*, 18–19.
611. Gray, *Garden History*, 83.
612. Gray, *Devon Country Houses and Gardens*, I, 63.
613. Gray, *Garden History*,, 218–219.
614. Gray, *Garden History*, 153.
615. Angela Ruthven, *Clovelly, a Guide Book* (Bideford, 1976 edn), 58–9.
616. G. W. Copeland, 'Notes on Devon Dovecotes', *DAT*, LXXXVIII, 1956, 198.
617. Paul Pattison, 'Oldstone: A mansion and its gardens in south Devon: a survey by the Royal Commission on the Historical Monuments of England', *PDAS*, 50, 1992, 125–6. The southern walled garden, bridge, hermitage, boathouse and gate piers are also listed.
618. Gray, Garden History, 68.
619. *WMN*, 31 10 1963, 21 1 1993.
620. Michael Trinick, *Dunsland House, Devon* (National Trust, 1969); Gray, *Garden History*, 92–3; Cherry, 'Devon Country Houses', 102; Lauder, *North Devon*, 33–44.
621. DRO, 961Madd/E12.
622. DRO, 961Madd5/F40; Cherry and Pevsner, *Devon*, 90, 172, 401, 694, 356.
623. Gray, *Devon Country Houses and Gardens*, I, 118–123.
624. John Cock, *Records of the ancient borough of South Molton in ye county of Devon* (Exeter, 1893), 153–8.
625. W. H. Jones, *Occasional Papers chiefly upon the antiquities and folklore of Dartmoor* (Exeter, 1893), XII; F. D. Gentry, *'Take care of your fire and candle'* (Exeter, 1985); Hoskins, Devon, 379, 496; Gray, *Lost Chronicle*, 81–2 Rose-Troup, The Great Fire at Ottery St Mary, 1866 (Exeter, 1936), 7; Micaiah Towgood, *Afflictions Implored: a sermon preached at Crediton in Devon, August 21 1743* (Exeter, 1743); Lysons, *Devon*, 391, 438, 603; Webb, Exmouth, 75; Murray T. Foster, 'A Short History of Cullompton', *DAT*, XLII, 1910, 170; DRO, 181M/E1 (Halberton); DRO, 906M/Z9 (Sidbury).
626. Lt Colonel Harding, *The History of Tiverton in the county of Devon* (1845), I, 37–40, 44–5, 79, 100, 101–105, 141, 142, 150–1, 154, 158, 193.
627. Snell, *Chronicle*, 49–50.
628. Stanley D. Chapman (ed.), *The Devon Cloth Industry in the Eighteenth Century* (DCRS, NS 23, 1978), viii.
629. Gentry, *Fire*, 5; Lysons, *Devon*, 108.
630. Lysons, *Devon*, 105; Mary Jones, *The History of Chudleigh* (1875 edition revised by William W. Snell), 75, 94.
631. Rose-Troup, *Great Fire*, 7.
632. Towgood, *Afflictions*, 3.
633. Lysons, *Devon*, 105; Jones, *Chudleigh*, 75, 94.
634. Short, *Hatherleigh*, 211.
635. Snell, *Chronicle*, 133.
636. Cruwys, *Cruwys Morchard Notebook*, 56.
637. EFP, 21 1 1860; Dick Passmore, *The Story of the Theatre Royal, Exeter* (Exeter, 2002), 5, 7, 10–22.
638. DRO, 123M/L340-1; DRO, 942B/T40.
639. James Cossins, *Reminiscences of Exeter fifty years since* (Exeter, 1877), 66.
640. Symonds, *Diary*, 39.
641. Brice, *The Mobiad*, 121.
642. Polwhele, *Devon*, II, 241, 278; Stebbing Shaw, *A Tour to the West of England in 1788* (1789). Reprinted in Todd Gray (ed.), *East Devon The Travellers' Tales* (Exeter, 2000), 42–3.
643. Harry Hems, 'The last thatched house in Exeter', *WA*, May 1882, 29; Zephyrus, 'Thatched houses in Exeter', *WA*, August 1882, 81; Censor, 'Thatched Houses, Exeter', *WA*, September 1882, 90; Harry Hems, 'Thatched Houses, Exeter', *WA*, September 1882, 90.

644. William Crossing, *A Hundred Years On Dartmoor* (reprint 1987, Exeter), 97. The cover has an alternative title – One Hundred Years On Dartmoor.
645. DRO, 55/6/7/4–9.
646. Pulman, *Book of the Axe*, 588.
647. Charles Worthy, *Ashburton and its neighbourhood* (Ashburton, 1885), 48.
648. *WMN*, 30 3 1998.
649. Polwhele, *Devon*, II, 83.
650. Manaton, *Hatherleigh*, 8.
651. Worthy, *Devonshire*, I, 182–3.
652. Hoskins, *Two thousand years in Exeter*, 137; Gray, *Garden History*, 39; Gray, *Lost Exeter*, 66–7.
653. Gray, *Devon Country Houses & Gardens*, I, 47–52.
654. C. Gaskell Brown et al, 'Buckland Abbey', *DAS*, 53, 1995, 25–82.
655. Abby Hunt, 'An Earthwork Survey of Dunkeswell Abbey', *DAS*, 2000, 58, 215–21.
656. Hoskins, *Devon*, 405; *Hartland Abbey* (Hartland, no date); Cherry and Pevsner, *Devon*, 473–4.
657. Edward Ashworth, 'Notes on some churches in the deanery of Honiton', *TEDAS*, III, 2nd series, 1878, 21; J. P. Allan and R. J. Silvester, 'Newenham Abbey, Axminster', *PDAS*, 39, 1981, 159; Gray, *Garden History*, 162–3; Cherry and Pevsner, *Devon*, 144.
658. H. P. R. Finberg, *Tavistock Abbey, a study in the social and economic history of Devon* (Newton Abbot, 1969), 265–9, 285–8.
659. Lysons, *Devon*, 524; M. Rhodes and L. Retallick, *Torre Abbey Souvenir Guide* (Torbay, 2000); J. T. White, *The History of Torquay* (1878), 80.
660. Edward Windeatt and Hugh R. Watkin, *The Priory for nuns of St Mary, Cornworthy, Devon*, 30.
661. Griffith, *Devon's Past*, 80.
662. John Allan, *St Nicholas Priory, Exeter* (Exeter, 1999).
663. Polwhele, *Devon*, II, 368.
664. Polwhele, *Devon*, II, 369; Jones, *Chudleigh*, 63.
665. Cherry and Pevsner, *Devon*, 629–30; Hoskins, *Devon*, 507.
666. Gribble, *Barnstaple*, 17–25.
667. Cherry and Pevsner, *Devon*, 517–518.
668. 14th report on ancient monuments, *DAT*, 67, 1935.
669. Hoskins, *Devon*, 448; Cherry and Pevsner, *Devon*, 615.
670. Polwhele, *Devon*, II, 150.
671. Polwhele, *Devon*, II, 361.
672. Polwhele, *Devon*, II, 73.
673. Polwhele, *Devon*, II, 103.
674. Butcher, *Sidmouth*, no page number; Polwhele, *Devon*, II, 235.
675. Polwhele, *Devon*, II, 237, 59–60.
676. *E&E*, 8 June 1920.
677. Polwhele, *Devon*, II, 367.
678. Polwhele, *Devon*, II, 75.
679. Polwhele, *Devon*, II, 331.
680. Cherry & Pevsner, *Devon*, 285; Polwhele, *Devon*, II, 330.
681. William Harding, 'The Church of Colebrooke', *TEDAS*, V, 1856, 17.
682. Polwhele, *Devon*, II, 357.
683. Lysons, *Devon*, 571.
684. Minchinton, *Windmills*, 54–5.
685. Robert Whiting, *The Blind Devotion of the People: Popular religion and the English Reformation* (Cambridge, 1989), 66–7.
686. 'An account of the church of Ottery St Mary', 34.
687. Erskine, Hope and Lloyd, *Exeter Cathedral*, 53–5.
688. Whiting, *Blind Devotion*, 77.
689. William Harding, 'An account of some of the ancient ecclesiastical edifices of Exeter', *TEDAS*, 1853, IV, 113.
690. Whiting, *Blind Devotion*, 78–82, 77; Jones, *Chudleigh*, 97.
691. Whiting, *Blind Devotion*, 77–8.
692. Frances Rose Troup, *Bishop Grandisson student and art-lover* (Plymouth, 1929), 18.
693. Whiting, *Blind Devotion*, 77; E. Masson Phillips, 'Supplementary notes on the ancient stone crosses of Devon (third paper)', *DAT*, 1943, LXXV, 263.
694. *EFP*, 8 February 1849.

695. See E. Masson Phillips' surveys of stone crosses in *DAT*, 1937–9, 43, 54. It has been suggested that the font at Spreyton also used parts of a cross as the supports. A broken shaft of a churchyard cross was found in the wall of the church of Clyst St George in the late nineteenth century: Ellacombe, 'Clyst St George', *TEDAS*, 117.
696. See Theo Brown's articles on holy wells in *Transactions of the Devonshire Association* for 1957 to 1960, 1963, 1966 and 1975.
697. Doe, 'An Ancient North Devon Borough; it's surroundings and associations in the past', 49–50.
698. Phyllis Hembry, *The English Spa, 1560–1815* (1990), 4–20.
699. Theo Brown, 'Holy and notable wells of Devon', *DAT*, LXXXIX, 1957, 213; Boggis, *Diocese of Exeter*, 584.
700. Rogers, *Ancient*, 21.
701. 'An account of the church of Ottery St Mary', *TEDAS*, I, 1843, 40, 35; Stoyle, *Loyalty and Locality*, 213.
702. Thomas George Norris, 'Observations on Church Dilapidation', *TEDAS*, I, 1843, 25; J. Simmons, 'A Frenchman's impressions of Devon & Cornwall in 1706', *PI*, XXII, 173.
703. William Harding, 'An Account', 114.
704. Margaret Westcott, in Gray, Rowe and Erskine, *Tudor & Stuart Devon*.
705. Lysons, *Devon*, 511; Risdon, *Devon*, 72.
706. 'The Plymouth Hoe in the olden times', *WA*, April 1882, 4–5; John M. Wasson (ed.), *Records of Early English Drama: Devon* (Toronto, 1986), lxi, lxvii, 244; Paul Newman, *Lost Gods of Albion* (Stroud, 1987), 103.
707. Symonds, *Diary*, 41.
708. *Collections towards a description of the county of Devon by Sir William Pole* (1791), xi; Gray, *Devon Country Houses and Gardens Engraved*, I, 76.
709. DRO, DD4534. See also DD4548.
710. G. W. Copeland wrote a series of articles on Devon church-houses in the *Transactions of the Devonshire Association* from 1961 to 1967. For Blackborough see Chalk, 'The town, village, manors and church of Kentisbeare', 316.
711. Whiting, *Blind Devotion*, 77, 68–9.
712. John Allan, 'An Angel from Pinhoe and Other Medieval English Alabasters in Devon', *PDAS*, 59, 2001, 161, 164–7.
713. Eamon Duffy, *The Voices of Morebath: Reformation and Rebellion in an English Village* (New Haven and London, 2001), 143–4, 162–4, 171–2, 178; DRO, Chanter 855A, 310. This is a copy of his will.
714. In his book of 1793 he referred it as 'an old Manuscript' and in one instance suggested it was nearly 90 years old: Polwhele, *Devon*, II, 357.
715. Keith Thomas, *Religion and the Decline of Magic* (1971), 112–121.
716. Polwhele, *Devon*, II, 83.
717. Polwhele, *Devon*, II, 44.
718. Polwhele, *Devon*, II, 191.
719. Polwhele, *Devon*, II, 197.
720. Polwhele, *Devon*, II, 204.
721. Polwhele, *Devon*, II, 74.
722. Polwhele, *Devon*, II, 153.
723. Polwhele, *Devon*, II, 103.
724. Sabine Baring-Gould, *A Book of the West* (1900), 39.
725. Whiting, *Blind Devotion*, 79.
726. Gray, *Lost Exeter*, 56–7.
727. Christopher Stell, *An inventory of non-conformist chapels and meeting-houses in South-West England* (HMSO, 1991), 62–102.
728. Chris Brooks, 'Sudden Death in Dartmouth: an Obituary for the Methodist Church', Devon Buildings Group Newsletter, Number 10, May 1991, 14–17.
729. Griffiths, 'A field to the spoiler', 275–6.
730. Lysons, *Devon*, 179. See Derek Gore, *The Vikings and Devon* (Exeter, 2001).
731. Lysons, *Devon*, 155; Oppenheim, *Maritime History of Devon*, 18.
732. Gray, *Devon Household Accounts*, II, xxix.
733. Lysons, *Devon*, 121, 144; Hooker, *Exeter*, 53.
734. R. N. Worth, 'The Historical Manuscripts Commission – Plymouth', *WA*, April 1884, 245; Walling, *Plymouth*, 33; John J. Beckerlegge (ed.), *Plymouth Memoirs* (Plymouth, 1951), 17–18.

735. Todd Gray, 'Turkish Piracy and Early Stuart Devon', *DAT*, 121, 1989, 159–71; Todd Gray, 'Turks, Moors and the Cornish Fishermen: Piracy in the Early Seventeenth Century', *Journal of the Royal Institution of Cornwall*, NS X, 1990, 468.
736. Minchinton, *Windmills*, 44.
737. Gill, *Plymouth*, 23–32; M. Stoyle, *A list of civil war fortifications at Plymouth* (Exeter Museums Archaeological Field Unit, report 93.82, December 1993), 6, 9.
738. Mark Stoyle, *From Deliverance to destruction: Rebellion and Civil War in an English City* (Exeter, 1996), 72, 187–8, 82–5, 87, 104, 108, 1009, 125, 128, 136–7; DRO, 76/44add2/1–2.
739. Kent Archives Office, U269 O261/4; Stoyle, Loyalty and Locality, 66, 104; *A History of Modbury* (Modbury, 1971), 14; R. W. Cotton, *Barnstaple and the northern part of Devonshire during the Great Civil War* (Exeter, 1877), 420–1, 432–5, 140–1; Eugene A. Andriette, *Devon and Exeter in the Civil War* (Newton Abbot, 1971), 162–3; John S. Wardman, *The Forgotten Battle: Torrington 1646* (Torrington, 1996), 136–141.
740. Alexander and Hooper, *Great Torrington*, 57.
741. Oppenheim, *Maritime History of Devon*, 73–4; Trump, *Westcountry Harbour*, 29–30.
742. *Plan for Plymouth*, 16; H. P. Twyford, *It came to our door: the story of Plymouth throughout the second world war* (Plymouth, 1975 edn); Gerald Wasley, *Blitz, an account of Hitler's aerial war over Plymouth in March, 1941, and the events that followed* (Exeter, 1991), 120, 123–4, 160, 182; Gill, *Plymouth*, 195–7.
743. *Mount Edgcumbe* (Mount Edgcumbe House and Park, 1993), 18–19.
744. Brian Moseley, *Plymouth through the lens, No. 3* (Plymouth, 1987), 35, 39.
745. J. Allan Young, 'The Plymouth Athenaeum, a short history of its growth', *DH*, 14, May 1977, 13.
746. James Orchard Halliwell, *A brief description of the ancient and modern manuscripts in the public library, Plymouth* (1853), 10. This was the catalogue for the Plymouth Proprietary Library; *A Guide to the Archives Department of Plymouth City Libraries*, xiii.
747. *WMN*, 26 March 1942; C. W. Bracken, 'An early Plymouth Deed (1329)', *DCNQ*, XVIII, 171. Fortunately Bracken had listed and made transcripts of many of the documents.
748. *WMN*, 10 May 1941; W. H. K. Wright, W. Leonard Emery and Sydney Smith, *Index catalogue of the reference department including the Devon & Cornwall Library and the Library of the Plymouth Medical Society* (Plymouth, 1892), 305–536.
749. Peksett, *Parish Registers*, 103, lii.
750. Gerald Wasley, *Devon at War, 1939–1945* (Tiverton, 1994), 81.
751. G. W. Copeland, 'Charles Church, Plymouth', *DAT*, LXXXI, 1949, 271–3.
752. *Plan for Plymouth*, 16; *The Blitz then and now* (1988), II, 492–6.
753. Andre Savignon, *With Plymouth Through Fire: a documentary narrative of 1940–1941* (Hayle, 1968), 49.
754. Thomas Sharp, *Exeter Phœnix* (1946), 35; Hoskins, *Exeter*, 131–2; Wasley, *Devon at War*, 95–9.
755. Personal communication with Mrs Margery Rowe.
756. DRO Newsletter, May 1992; Joan Sinar in Brian Carpenter (ed.), *10 Centuries of Devon's Archives* (Friends of Devon's Archives, 2002), 21; A. R. Wallace, *Exeter Cathedral* (Exeter, no date given).
757. Hugh Peskett (ed.), *Guide to the parish and non-parochial registers of Devon and Cornwall, 1538–1837* (DCRS, ES, II, 1979), 142–7, 152; Communication with Mrs Margery Rowe.
758. Cresswell, 'Churches', 190.
759. Fifth Report of the Committee of Works of Art in Devonshire, *DAT*, XVI, 1884, 139–42; Gray, *Victorian Under Class of Exeter*, 94–5.
760. Gray, *Lost Exeter*, 24–5; *WA*, August 1881, 81 & October 1881, 105.
761. Sharp, *Phoenix*, 42.
762. Russell, *Torquay*, 134, 174.
763. Polwhele, *Devon*, II, 206.
764. Ken Doughty, *Aveton Gifford, brief notes on the church and village* (Aveton Gifford, 1998); Cherry and Pevsner, *Devon*, 140.
765. Harry Hems, 'The old parclose screen at Aveton Giffard church', *WA*, March 1886, 239–40.

766. *The Church of St Nicholas, Dunkeswell* (parish flyer).
767. Wasley, *Devon at War*, 186–8.
768. Grace Bradbeer, 'The evacuation of the South Hams', *DAT*, 100, 1968, 231–45.
769. Gray, *Travels in Georgian Devon*, I, xviii.
770. Wasley, *Devon at War*, 90, 167.
771. Keith A. Saunders, *Devon Aerodromes in Old Photographs* (Stroud, 1994), 7, 37.
772. Wasley, *Devon at War*, 43–5.
773. Smale, *Hatherleigh*, 434; J. Manaton, *Hatherleigh History in brief* (Exeter, 1951), 9.
774. Harold Murray, *Kaleidoscope: an old journalist's snapshots* (1946), 96; Alieen Fox, *Aileen: a pioneering archaeologist* (Leominster, 2000), 102–106.
775. Chris Brooks, 'Bare Ruined Choirs? Coming problems and Devon's historic churches', Devon Buildings Group Newsletter, Number 12, March 1994, 6.
776. Lady Radford, 'Tavistock Abbey', *TEDAS*, 3rd series, 4, 72–3.
777. Charles E. Eldred & W. H. K. Wright, *Streets of Old Plymouth* (Plymouth, 1901).
778. Jones, *Chudleigh*, 86–7.
779. DRO, DQS, Bundle Box Easter 1625, 15 & OB, 1633–40, Easter 1634.
780. Anthony Greenstreet, 'The Armada Service', *DH*, 56, April 1998, 13–16.
781. Todd Gray (ed.), *Devon Household Accounts, 1627–59, part one* (DCRS, 1995, NS 38), 239–41.
782. Mervyn Madge, *Tamerton Treacle Mines and other tales of Cornwall and the West Country* (Plymouth, 1984), 7.
783. Lysons, *Devon*, 536.
784. Lysons, *Devon*, cclxxii.
785. Worthy, *Devonshire*, I, 155.
786. WSL, William Henry Rogers, Notes on Bideford, I, 110.
787. Joyce Youings, 'Tudor Barnstaple: New life for an ancient borough', *DAT*, 121, 1989, 5.
788. PLSL, ts by Neill Mitchell, 'The Radford Estate, Plymstock, South Devon', 2.
789. *Plymouth Evening Herald*, 19 April 2003, page 4.
790. Boringdon Hall Hotel History (information sheet printed by the hotel).
791. The tale may have originated with a report in *The Western Morning News* of 19 July 1839 which stated that a craftsmen connected with Philip of Spain had worked on the wood carving in the house.
792. Gray, *Exeter Unveiled*, 65–7.
793. W. H. H. Rogers, 'Whitford near Shute', *WA*, 2 1886, 301–302.
794. Edward Jeboult, 'Ancient portrait of the pope from an old Devonshire church', *WA*, 2 1886, 206.
795. Hems, Roods and other screens, 9; H. H. R, 'A noteworthy font cover', *WA*, 3 1884, 240; Shaugh Prior church, information sheet; Cherry, *Devon*, 723–4; J. B. Stother, 'Shaugh Prior Font Cover', *WA*, 12 1885, 139–40.
796. Kent Archives Office, U269/P11/6.
797. Personal communication with Peggie Upham.
798. Gray, *Garden History*, 23.
799. Ravenhill and Rowe, *Manuscript Maps*, II, 262 & I, 162–3, 66.
800. *WMN*, 13 1 1937; Cresswell, *Exeter Churches*, 69.
801. *The Gentleman's Magazine*, May 1791. I am grateful to John Allan for this reference.
802. Cresswell, *Exeter Churches*, 147.
803. The Rt Hon. the Viscount Amory, 'Our changing heritage', *DAT*, XCVI, 1964, 40.

Index